Teaching and Counseling Gifted and Talented Adolescents

TEACHING and COUNSELING GIFTED and TALENTED ADOLESCENTS

An International Learning Style Perspective

Edited by ROBERTA M. MILGRAM,
RITA DUNN,
and GARY E. PRICE

PRAEGER

Westport, Connecticut
London

This research was partially funded by St. John's University Center for the Study of Learning and Teaching Styles, New York; Price Systems, Inc., Lawrence, Kans.; and Tel Aviv University, Ramit Aviv, Israel. The editors wish to acknowledge the generosity of the Center's governing Board and the expertise and gracious contribution of Ms. Madeline Larsen, its Executive Secretary.

Library of Congress Cataloging-in-Publication Data

Teaching and counseling gifted and talented adolescents :
   an international learning style perspective / edited by Roberta M. Milgram,
Rita Dunn, and Gary E. Price.
      p. cm.
   Includes bibliographical references (p.) and index.
   ISBN 0–275–93640–6 (alk. paper)
     1. Gifted children—Education—Cross-cultural studies.
   2. Cognitive styles in children.   3. Learning, Psychology of.
   4. Gifted children—Identification.   I. Milgram, Roberta M.
   II. Dunn, Rita Stafford.   III. Price, Gary E.
   LC3993.22.T43   1993
   371.95—dc20   92–35348

British Library Cataloguing in Publication Data is available.

Library of Congress Catalog Card Number: 92–35348
ISBN: 0–275–93640–6

First published in 1993

Praeger Publishers, 88 Post Road West, Westport, CT 06881
An imprint of Greenwood Publishing Group, Inc.

Printed in the United States of America

The paper used in this book complies with the
Permanent Paper Standard issued by the National
Information Standards Organization (Z39.48–1984).

10 9 8 7 6 5 4 3 2

This book is dedicated to the adolescents of Brazil, Canada, Egypt, Greece, Guatemala, Israel, Korea, the Philippines, and the United States, in the hope that the knowledge it contributes will ultimately help them and students like them throughout the world to realize their abilities more fully.

Contents

Preface

This decade has seen the emergence of two powerful concepts that influence curriculum and instruction: (1) learning style—the understanding that individuals master difficult information or skills in different ways and (2) multidimensional giftedness—the recognition that individuals may express their giftedness in different ways and at different levels. In addition, we are becoming increasingly aware of the unique impact of culture on intellectual and personal-social development, in general, and on giftedness and learning style, in particular. This book is designed to give teachers, counselors, gifted education specialists, and parents in each country an understanding of the specific learning style components that characterize gifted adolescents in their culture. It has particular value for teachers in the United States in their efforts to individualize instruction for culturally diverse school populations.

The book provides teachers with the theoretical and practical information needed to meet the daily challenge of individualizing instruction for gifted and talented children of different learning styles. It consists of sixteen chapters, divided into two major parts. Part One consists of six chapters that present the broad theoretical background of the concepts of giftedness and learning style. It provides a general overview and focuses on conceptual clarification, that is, on the definition and explanation of giftedness and learning style. In addition, the instruments used to assess learning style and giftedness and the subjects studied in each country are described in detail. The chapters provide an overall rationale for considering individual learning style when teaching and counseling gifted and talented learners. The authors present specific instructional principles and teaching strategies that were derived from the general literature and from resources on giftedness, talent, and learning style.

In Part Two, data on the learning styles of gifted and talented learners in seven countries are presented in detail. In addition, pilot data on the learning styles of adolescents representing a wide range of abilities in Egypt and in Greece are presented. The part ends with an overview and integrative summary of the findings on the learning styles of gifted and talented learners in the countries studied. Cross-cultural differences and similarities are compared and contrasted.

The book contributes to the literature of both learning styles and giftedness. The book reflects an advanced concept of giftedness that goes beyond IQ and emphasizes the many realms in which gifted behavior can be manifested. By the same token, in applying learning style theory to youngsters gifted and talented in a wide variety of domains, the book expands the literature on learning style as well.

It has been a difficult task to coordinate a research project that took place in such widely diverse settings around the world. We would like to thank each author for her/his extraordinary efforts in bringing this project to fruition. Finally, we thank the students, teachers, and administrators of the schools whose co-operation made this study possible.

Part I

Learning Style and the Realization of Giftedness

Chapter 1

Learning Styles of Gifted Students in Diverse Cultures

Rita Dunn and Roberta M. Milgram

Many theoreticians and practitioners in education place high priority on the realization of giftedness. They value the benefits to be derived from such fulfillment to the individual learner and to the society in which he or she lives. Gifted adults are those whose attainments in a specific socially valuable domain are extraordinary. The life achievements of these individuals frequently bring them society's recognition and rewards.

Gifted adults can be divided into four groups. First are gifted adults whose abilities were identified at an early age, who benefited from stimulation in their homes and enrichment in their schools, and who have realized their abilities to a large extent. By contrast, a second group consists of adults who also were identified as gifted as children and who also benefited from opportunities at home and at school, but did not demonstrate gifted achievements as adults.

A third group of gifted adults includes those whose school accomplishments in their youth were totally unremarkable. The eminent scientist Albert Einstein, according to the frequently repeated story, failed mathematics in elementary school. Steve Wozniak, the developer of the first Apple home computer, was a high school dropout. Bill Gates, the president of Microsoft, the largest producer of computer software in the world, dropped out of Harvard. The list of adults not identified as gifted when they were children but who grew up to become highly gifted and creative adults is long indeed. The fourth group, which some authorities claim is the largest of all (National Commission 1983) is of high-ability youngsters, similar to those in group three, except that they fail to actualize their potential.

The children in groups three and four were not identified as gifted because their abilities and talents were different from those generally considered indicative of giftedness in classrooms. Few efforts are made to differentiate what is being taught to learners of this kind in terms of special interests and abilities and to individualize how they are taught in terms of their unconventional learning styles. We usually focus attention on the exceptional attainments of gifted people—that is, we focus on their products, the things they do. It is important to realize, however, that gifted people are not only different in their output but also at the input stage. They first perceive the world differently and then proceed to process the information differently. Schools have a major role to play during both phases. They must strive to identify individual differences among learners in the way they register and process experience and to provide educational experiences in terms of those individual differences.

Schools in democratic societies are committed to providing equal opportunity for all children to realize their potential abilities. It is erroneous to believe that equal opportunity means that all children receive the same curriculum in school or that they are taught in the same way. Children differ greatly in their cognitive abilities and personality characteristics. Teaching all children the same thing in the same way results in unequal, rather than equal, opportunity. Some educators use the equal opportunity argument to justify separating gifted youngsters from their nongifted age peers and teaching them in seemingly homogeneous settings, claiming that they require this arrangement to guarantee them equal opportunity. This approach is based upon the notion that gifted children as a group are highly similar in their interests and abilities. Convincing evidence exists, however, that such is not the case. There are wide differences in the pattern and level of abilities. A child may be highly gifted in one academic domain and average or below in another. In landmark decisions the Supreme Court of the United States decided that, when it came to black and white children, there is no such thing as separate but equal but, rather, that separate is inherently unequal. We suggest that this principle applies to the segregated versus integrated gifted education as well. Part- or full-time special schools may serve the needs of some gifted children, but such administrative arrangements, in effect, deny equal educational opportunity for many other gifted learners. Most proponents of special education for gifted learners would hardly agree with this seemingly preposterous statement. In the section that follows, we will define giftedness in a manner that makes it clear that one could not possibly offer each of the different kinds of gifted learners a special school designed to enhance each particular ability. The most promising setting for meeting the diverse needs of gifted learners is the regular heterogeneous classroom. The challenge, however, is formidable. Teachers will require much help in understanding the special needs of gifted learners and support with methods and materials required to do the job.

The rationale for recommending teaching of gifted learners in regular class-rooms as the preferred administrative arrangement for providing for the special needs of this group is based upon our understanding of two basic concepts: learning style and giftedness. There have been many studies of learning style and of giftedness. The literature of giftedness, however, has given scant attention to learning style. By the same token, research on the learning styles of gifted learners has hitherto been limited to investigation of high-IQ children. The current volume is the first effort to integrate the broad but distinct separate knowledge bases that have accumulated on these two topics.

This chapter is divided into three parts: (1) What is giftedness? (2) What is learning style, or what is known about the learning styles of gifted and talented learners? (3) What is the rationale for considering learning style in gifted learners from an international perspective, and what were the overall guidelines that directed the investigation?

WHAT IS MEANT BY GIFTED AND TALENTED?

Giftedness is now widely recognized as a multidimensional phenomenon that goes beyond definition in simple terms of IQ scores. The Terman (1925) and Terman and Oden (1947, 1959) definition of IQ as children who score 140 or higher on standardized measures of IQ such as the Stanford Binet reigned from the early part of the century until the 1950s. At that point, the theoretical formulations of Guilford (1956, 1967), Mednick (1962), Wallach and Kogan (1965), and others led to intensive research efforts focusing on the process of creative thinking that resulted in a broadened view of the phenomenon of giftedness to include creativity (Wallach 1970, 1971). For more than twenty years, research focused on the distinction between intelligence and creativity, with creativity defined in terms of cognitive process as reflected in a wide variety of measures of divergent thinking.

In the 1970s, Marland (1972), then U.S. Commissioner of Education, proposed a multifaceted definition of giftedness that was adopted by the U.S. Office of Education and enacted into law by the Congress of the United States as the Gifted and Talented Children's Act of 1978. The broad definition not only included creativity but spoke of leadership ability, or abilities in the performing and visual arts.

Since the early period of interest in giftedness, emphasis in the field has been on the process of identification and on meeting the pressing needs of the special programs servicing learners identified as gifted. Most of these efforts were not based upon theory or guided by it. It was not until the 1970s and 1980s that theories of giftedness, some with clearly spelled-out practical implications for gifted education, appeared in the literature (Renzulli 1986a, 1986b; Sternberg 1988; Sternberg & Davidson 1986). As part of the accelerated theoretical development, Milgram postulated a comprehensive and integrative model, the Structure of Giftedness (1989, 1990a, 1991a).

The 4 x 4 model of the Structure of Giftedness, presented in Figure 1.1, was designed: (1) to contribute to the conceptual clarification of the diverse abilities that characterize gifted and creative individuals; (2) to highlight the important role of personal-social, sociological, and cultural as well as cognitive dimensions in the conceptualization of giftedness; and (3) to be amenable to empirical

Figure 1.1
Milgram 4 x 4 Structure of Giftedness

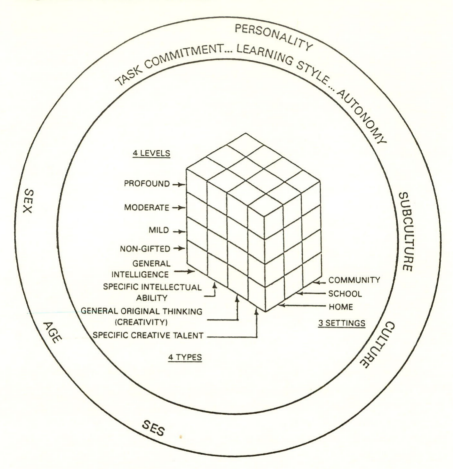

investigations of construct and predictive validity with currently available psychometric instruments.

In the 4 x 4 model, giftedness is depicted in terms of four categories, four ability levels, and three learning environments embedded in a framework of individual differences.

Four Categories of Giftedness

The first category, *general intellectual ability* or *overall general intelligence*, refers to the ability to think abstractly and to solve problems logically and systematically. This ability is measured by IQ tests and most frequently reported as IQ scores.

The second category, *specific intellectual ability*, refers to a clear and distinct intellectual ability in a given area, such as mathematics or foreign languages, music or science. These abilities are manifested in performance that is competent but not original. Specific intellectual abilities in children and adolescents are often, but not invariably, expressed in superior academic performance in school subjects as reflected in specific school grades and standardized achievement tests.

The third category, *general original or creative thinking*, is the process of generating ideas that are imaginative and clever (Guilford 1967). Original-thinking people are different from others in that they perceive and define problems differently, notice things that others ignore, and produce a large number of ideas or solutions to problems, some of which are unique and imaginative. This ability is measured by tests of divergent thinking, and has been referred to by Barron and Harrington (1981) ''as raw creative ability,'' as distinguished from ''effective creative ability,'' the fourth category of giftedness discussed next.

The fourth category, *specific creative talent*, refers to clear and distinct domain-specific creative ability. It is original or creative thinking applied to a real-world performance area. An example of ability in this category is the generation of highly original ideas or products in science, mathematics, art, music, social leadership, business, politics, or any other human endeavor.

The realization of potential talent often requires time to incubate and develop as a result of life experience. Specific creative talent is measured in children and adolescents by means of questionnaires tapping leisure-time, out-of-school activities of children.

Levels of Giftedness

Gifted behavior may be found in children and adults at mild, moderate, and profound levels. These levels are hierarchical in organization and become increasingly infrequent in occurrence as one moves from nongifted to profoundly gifted. For example, eminent performance—that is, creative or original attainment so high that comparison is hardly possible—is the profound level of the fourth category, specific creative talent.

Three Settings

The realization of potential abilities is dependent on the complex interaction of cognitive abilities with environmental opportunities. The 4 x 4 model reflects this understanding by citing three settings (school, home, and community) that affect giftedness.

School experiences can make a major contribution to the realization of giftedness in adults. Unfortunately, few eminent adults mention their schools and teachers as important influences in the development of their giftedness (Bloom 1985). The behavior and attitudes of parents of gifted children are frequently among the critical influences on the development of giftedness. Many gifted adults cite the efforts of their parents in stimulating and directing their developing talents (Bloom 1985). These findings are particularly interesting in view of the widespread view of the parents of gifted learners as over-involved and meddling. Albert and Runco (1987) emphasized that the concept of family is changing. In the modern world it is important to specify the individuals included when discussing family processes. For example, the differential influences of single parent or blended families on the developing child have to be considered.

Communities influence the specific opportunities of special education available to gifted learners through policy decisions that determine budgets. In addition, some communities create opportunities for gifted learners to broaden the scope and depth of their educational experiences by supporting mentorships and internships and by providing access to community institutions such as universities and museums.

The Circle of Individual Differences

The circle of individual differences includes age, sex, socioeconomic status, subculture, culture, and especially personality characteristics. Interactions among these variables and those in the 4 x 4 design inside the circle are critical in their influence on the realization of potential abilities.

A number of authoritative and integrative summaries of research on individual differences in giftedness have appeared in recent years (e.g., Barron & Harrington 1981; Glover, Ronning, & Reynolds 1989; Janos & Robinson 1985; Tannenbaum 1983; Milgram 1990). In the 4 x 4 model, Milgram (1989, 1991a) specifically highlighted learning style as a major variable influencing the realization of all categories and levels of giftedness.

WHAT IS LEARNING STYLE AND WHY IS IT IMPORTANT?

Learning style is defined as the conditions under which each person begins to concentrate on, process, internalize, and retain new and difficult information and skills (Dunn, Dunn, & Treffinger 1992). According to the Dunn and Dunn (1972, 1975, 1978, 1992, 1993) model, which has evolved over the past quarter-century, learning style comprises a unique combination of elements that permit receiving, storing, and then retrieving for use the knowledge and skills to which individuals have been exposed and that they find relevant or interesting.

Learning style characteristics make the identical instruction effective for some students and ineffective for others. What facilitates learning for one person actually impedes it for others. The Dunn and Dunn model is based on the theory that:

1. Most individuals can learn;
2. Everyone has strengths, but people have strengths that are very different from each other's;

3. Individual instructional preferences exist and can be measured reliably;

4. Many students can learn to capitalize on their learning style strengths when concentrating on new and/or difficult academic material;

5. Instructional environments, resources, and approaches can be tailored to respond to different learning style strengths; and

6. Students attain significantly higher achievement and attitude test scores when instructional environments, resources, and approaches match their individual learning styles than when they do not.

Although conceived of as an outgrowth of practitioner observations combined with scholarly research conducted at more than 85 institutions of higher education (Annotated Bibliography 1993), the Dunn and Dunn learning styles model traces its roots to two distinct learning theories: cognitive style theory and brain lateralization theory.

Cognitive style theory suggests that individuals process information differently based on either inherent or learned traits. Many previous researchers investigated the variables of field dependence/independence, global/analytic, simultaneous/successive, and/or right/left-preferenced processing. As the Dunns and their associates conducted studies to determine whether relationships existed among these cognitive dimensions and students' environmental, emotional, sociological, and physiological characteristics, they found that certain variables often clustered together. Relationships appeared to exist between learning persistently (with few or no intermissions), in quiet and bright light, in a formal seating design, and with little or no intake and being an analytic/left processor (Dunn, Bruno, Sklar, & Beaudry 1990; Dunn, Cavanaugh, Eberle, & Zenhausern 1982). Similarly, students who often requested breaks while learning and who learned more easily in a softly illuminated, music-filled environment, while seated informally and snacking, often revealed high scores as global/right processors. Field dependence correlated in many ways with a global versus an analytic cognitive style and elicited similar clusterings as left and right preferences.

In some cases, more characteristics allied themselves with global- and right-preferenced tendencies than with those of their processing counterparts. Thus, although global/rights often enjoyed studying with their peers and using tactual strengths, analytic/lefts did not reveal the reverse, nor did their sociological or perceptual traits evidence consistent similarities (Dunn, Cavanaugh, Eberle, & Zenhausern 1982).

As the relationships among various cognitive styles were evidenced, brain lateralization theory emerged based, to a large extent, on the writing of French neurologist Paul Braco, whose research led him to propose that the two hemispheres of the human brain have different functions. Subsequent investigations demonstrated that the left hemisphere appears to be associated with verbal and sequential abilities, whereas the right hemisphere appears to be associated with emotions and spatial, holistic processing (Kirby & Das 1977; Luria 1973).

Those conclusions, however, continue to be challenged. Nevertheless, people clearly begin to concentrate, process, and remember new and difficult information under very different conditions.

THE IMPORTANCE OF LEARNING STYLE

The research on learning styles explains why, in the same family, certain children perform well in school and others do not. It exposes the differences in style among siblings, between parents and their offspring, and among members of the same community, career or professional group, and culture. The research also explains how boys' and girls' styles differ and why some learn to read early and well—and others do not. During the past twenty-five years, research conducted at St. John's University in New York City has provided clear directions for either teaching students through their individual learning styles *or* teaching them to teach themselves by capitalizing on their personal style strengths (Dunn, Beaudry, & Klavas 1989; Dunn & Dunn 1992, 1993).

Everybody has a learning style, but mothers' and fathers' styles tend to differ from each other and children's styles do not necessarily reflect those of their parents. Thus, spouses often learn differently from each other *and* from their children. This is important to remember because parents frequently try to teach their offspring in the same way that *they* learned when they were young, and that is likely to produce frustration and failure for both! This is particularly true because, in the same family, siblings are unlikely to have similar learning styles.

Restak (1979) and Thies (1979) both believe that at least three-fifths of learning style is derived biologically. Thus, whether a person learns best in bright light or in low light, in quiet or with music, at a conventional desk or on a sofa, easy chair, or the floor, depends to a greater extent than we heretofore believed on the biological makeup of that individual. However, learning style is more than the environment in which learning occurs; it includes each human's emotional, sociological, physiological, and psychological characteristics (see Figure 1.2).

THE COMPONENTS OF INDIVIDUAL LEARNING STYLE

The Environmental Characteristics of Learning Style

Learning in Quiet or Sound-Filled Environments. In the same family, one sibling needs comparative quiet while concentrating on difficult information; the other often accomplishes more when surrounded by music, conversation, or some kind of sound. One child pleads, "Ssssh!" and the other hums to himself while concentrating. Without an understanding of learning styles, it is difficult to understand that both—wanting quiet *and* wanting sound while learning—are normal and appropriate, but for opposite styles. Researchers have demonstrated that, when children are permitted to learn in ways that complement ("match") their styles, they achieve statistically higher test scores than when they concen-

Figure 1.2
Learning Styles Model

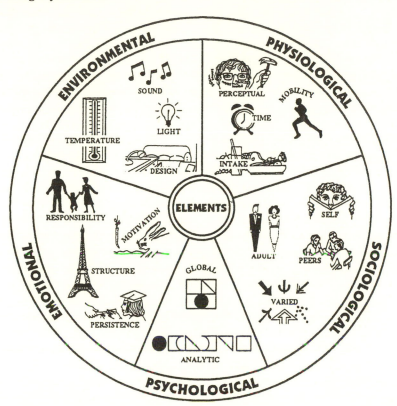

trate in environments that are opposite to their preferred way of learning (Pizzo 1981, 1982; Pizzo, Dunn, & Dunn 1990). What teachers must remember is that, when a young person needs sound while concentrating on difficult material, the music that is permitted should contain no lyrics (DeGregoris 1986). When the rendition being heard includes only the melody, but the child is familiar with the words to that song, the child's mind is likely to begin "singing" the lyrics, which then causes distraction. For youngsters who need sound, music blocks out all the extraneous noises in their environment. The child who *needs* sound hears things that others do not, and those things prevent the youngster from concentrating.

Learning in Well or Softly Illuminated Environments. Most educators believe that there is a minimum level of illumination necessary for all students. To the contrary, what is adequate for some is insufficient for others and the *cause* of hyperactivity to many. Some children need a great deal of light to concentrate or they become drowsy and literally cannot think. Others become "nervous" or hyperactive because of what seems to many as "normal" lighting. What is amazing is that the amount and kind of illumination present literally can either increase or decrease achievement test scores for many learners (Dunn, Krimsky, Murray, & Quinn 1985; Krimsky 1982).

Learning in Warm versus Cool Environments. Almost everyone understands that certain people find it impossible to concentrate on difficult material when they are *hot*, and others have that identical problem when they are *cold*. People react differently to the same temperature based on their biological preferences. How differently? Students who need warmth achieve less when they are cool and need to take tests than when they are warm, while people who need cool temperatures do not perform as well on tests when they are warm (Murrain 1983).

Learning in Formal versus Informal Seating Designs. Ergonomics—the study of the efficiency of people working with machines and technology in various physical environments—recognizes that people who sit for any length of time in seats without appropriate back support find it extremely difficult to concentrate. Research conducted at St. John's University's Center for the Study of Learning and Teaching Styles, New York, indicated that some people enjoy sitting in a wooden, steel, or plastic chair and can work that way for long periods of time (Hodges 1985; Shea 1983); generally speaking, those are the ones who tend to become high achievers in school. When the relationships between academic achievement and being able to sit at conventional desks were examined, it was found that students who could sit could also concentrate for long periods of time; those who could not sit in formal furniture could not "think," and thus could not maintain attention or remember the information to which they had been exposed (Dunn, Cavanaugh, Eberle, & Zenhausern 1982).

We experimented with permitting students who could not sit for more than ten to twelve minutes in conventional school desks to do their work in easy chairs, couches, on bean bags, or on the floor; and we were surprised to find that those youngsters could achieve as well in the informal seating as the formal preferred students did in their traditional places (Shea 1983). We then provided furniture that both matched and mismatched each student's seating preferences on an alternate daily basis over an entire school semester. The same results occurred (Hodges 1985). Formally preferred and informally preferred students achieved equally well when sitting in furniture that matched their design preferences and equally poorly when in mismatched designs! Similar research was conducted in South Africa with identical results (Nganwa-Bagumah 1986).

During the past two decades, many schools throughout the United States have experimented with providing both formal and informal seating in classrooms to permit youngsters of all ages to determine for themselves which design helps them to learn quickly, easily, and comfortably (Dunn & Griggs 1988b; Klavas 1991). Often, students who think better with sound than in quiet, who need soft rather than bright light, and who concentrate better in an informal than in a formal seating tend to be global learners—children who learn very differently from their counterparts, analytic learners. The latter students' preferences also tend to cluster, but this group usually learns best in the opposite environments—in a quiet, brightly illuminated, traditional chair and desk. The two groups are equally intelligent and perform equally well, but only when the environment complements their learning style.

This section introduced the four environmental elements of learning style—sound, light, temperature, and design—and reported the effects of matches and mismatches on student achievement and attitude test scores.

The Emotional Characteristics of Learning Style

Learning When Emotionally Motivated or Unmotivated. Most young children are motivated toward learning, producing, experimenting, and experiencing—activities that develop insight into one's abilities. Children become and remain motivated when they enjoy the activities in which they engage. When they feel good about their improvement, they continue to the exclusion of other opportunities and begin to develop sustained interests. A recent doctoral study of secondary school students corroborated that motivated young people achieve higher test scores than their unmotivated peers (Garrett 1991).

There are children who are so parent motivated that they devote themselves entirely to developing talents in areas of interest to their parents. When that is the child's choice, it is fine; many talented children became that way because of parental role modeling or encouragement. But in cases of excellence in a specific domain, it usually is the child's decision to exert commitment to that domain. Teacher-motivated students often aspire toward career or personal goals that reflect those of teachers who serve well as their role models. Other young people become involved in fields related to the interests of their friends, and still others determine their directions based on self-explored interests. Whatever the young person chooses is correct if that choice was made independently. Even if minds change and choices that once appeared exciting no longer remain attractive, the person is always free to redirect attention, focus, and explore newer—we hope better—choices!

Learning with or without Interruptions. Teachers always have admonished certain children for "not paying attention" and rewarded others because they completed assigned tasks as soon as they could. Teachers may not understand the nature of persistence; it is a quality that is evident at an early age among some and rare among others. Analytic students usually are persistent because they are "sequential" learners: they move from the beginning of a task to the end in a series of small, discrete stages (Dunn, Bruno, Sklar, & Beaudry 1990; Dunn, Cavanaugh, Eberle, & Zenhausern 1982).

Global children do not learn that way; they consider a whole concept, idea, assignment, or endeavor. They often think a long time about what they will do before they begin doing it. In addition, globals dislike working on only one thing at a time; they enjoy multiple activities simultaneously. Thus, globals consider a task, begin it, work for a relatively short amount of time, and then take a break. They begin again and then take another break. They engage in varied and diversified activities in between completing a single task and often report it as boring to remain with the same content or task without change. Thus, being a global learner appears to be directly related to a lack of persistence, but that is *not* a negative quality. Globals complete tasks; they merely complete them in their own way, time, and manner.

Learning via Self-Decision Making versus Following Others' Directives. Many teachers verbalize that children must do as they are told. When it is a question of safety, that is indisputable. However, schools impose regimentation on virtually every aspect of a child's day. When adults constantly restrict and structure decision-making powers, youngsters cannot learn to make wise choices without direct supervision. In addition, many children may become nonconforming, a state in which following someone else's directives becomes insufferable and the individual yearns to do the opposite of what he or she is required to do (White 1981).

Of course, it is necessary for a child to follow safety and health directives, but children who have opportunities to do things their way often become young adults who function independently—a quality that may enable them to resist negative peer- or authority-oriented activities. When they become adults, they tend to find careers in which following others' directives is not a requirement. Instead, they utilize their creativity and innovativeness. Most children learn the difference between what is appropriate and what is not by experience.

Highly conforming people follow others' directives; they feel comfortable and secure when doing so. Teachers do not consciously wish to create highly conforming children, or to "break the will" or spirit of those who challenge them, but in effect that is what happens repeatedly in school. Children have a need for opportunities in which to "flex muscle," "sow seeds," "find their way"— whichever phrase best explains young people's requirements for trying things on their own. Schools need to provide opportunities for decision making where it seems important to the children. We may need to require conformity in certain instances, but should do so only when we consider it vital, either to us or to the children's well-being. We also need to provide options, alternatives, and decision-making opportunities if we are to rear citizens capable of determining right from wrong and acting on their beliefs.

Learning via Internal versus External Structure. Some children ask for explicit information for almost everything they do; such youngsters tend to be externally structured. They derive a sense of security from knowing what and how to do it. Others are self-structured; they enjoy experimenting with multiple strategies that they identify and, eventually, accomplish what must be done in their way. Both types are fine; both are equally capable. They just are different from each other and profit from opposite types of instruction (Dunn, White, & Zenhausern 1982).

The Sociological Characteristics of Learning Style

Learning Alone and Independently. The brightest children are self-motivated and spend hours by themselves enjoyably involved in whatever it is they find interesting. Sometimes the youngsters need no other children; toys, books, games, music, dance, art, sculpting, their own imagination, or other leisure activities are sufficient to maintain their mental and spiritual health. Indeed, many gifted children learn better alone than with peers (Perrin 1984). We need to respect such youngsters' need for solitary time, privacy, and undirected thinking.

During certain educational cycles, teachers alternately require that all their students either work alone or work cooperatively with others. When required to master difficult academic studies, children should be encouraged to complete them in their own sociological preference. "Learning alone" children find concentrating on work with others suffocating. Just as they are about to solve a problem, others begin questioning what the problem is. In addition, bright minds often skip steps; they take quantum leaps while learning. Average children take longer and process the identical information differently. Those differences cause consternation and frustration among gifted children.

Learning with Classmates. Certain children play and learn well with just one other child; they cannot cope with more than one, and a group causes anxiety or distress. All children should have their sociological preferences respected; opportunities in school should be provided for completing every assignment individually, in pairs, and through small-group interactions. Should social problems arise, the teacher needs to see that, in the future, the number in the group should be restricted to each child's comfort level. They also should pay equal attention to the type of youngster with which each gets along well.

Learning with a Group. Some children function well in a small group, on a team or as part of a committee; many more do not (DeBello 1985; Dunn, Giannitti, Murray, Geisert, Rossi, & Quinn 1990; Miles 1987; Perrin 1984). There is nothing either good or bad about the number of others with whom a youngster can concentrate; all children need to feel comfortable in order to perform well. The ability to concentrate fully with others in attendance develops among some, but not among others. Many people are uncomfortable in crowds. What constitutes "too many" differs among individuals. There is no specific advantage or disadvantage to working either alone, as a pair, in a group, or in a variety of sociological groupings. There is, however, an advantage to having students understand themselves and what works for each personally. Opportunities for interaction are one thing; mandates are another.

Learning with Peers. Some children only enjoy interacting with others like themselves. They like people with similar interests, talents, or abilities—and those people do not have to be children. When art-interested, peer-oriented, youngsters meet someone with talent in any phase of art, they hover around the person, interact for long periods of time, and become absorbed in talking, observing, experimenting, and emulating what such a person does. For peer-oriented children, this is an excellent way of expanding interests and talents, and eventually developing giftedness in this special focus. Such interests need to be supplemented with visits to exhibits, lessons, experiments, reading, and further interactions, but all are stimulating to children excited by an activity when they are with others equally positive about it.

Peer orientation becomes apparent among children who share interests in stamp collecting, model or kite building, music, singing, dancing, sports, and so forth. They begin to live, breathe, and derive nurture from others who feel as they do. This is a positive reaction and should be supported and encouraged when the child chooses the involvement. Teachers acknowledge that such interactions are positive in nonacademic areas; they need to be shown that it is equally positive for students to voluntarily study and complete assignments together with classmates of their choice.

Learning with an Authoritative versus a Collegial Adult. Some adolescents respond best to an authoritative adult—someone who directs and provides specific guidelines and levels of expectation. Others respond best to a collegial adult—a person who acts like a friend rather than a teacher, is less directive and more option-providing, and interacts with the student on a personal basis. Both types of adults are fine, but only for the right match in style. Young people who need a collegial teacher feel alienated from an authority. Conversely, students who require authoritative grownups feel insecure with ones who assume the role of a chum; they need a directive, supportive adult in their lives.

Too often, teachers behave as they feel most comfortable, with little understanding of what individual students need. A teacher who is aware of his or her students' sociological preferences can be both collegial and authoritative to different youngsters at the same time. For example, it is easy to say: "Relax for one minute Suzy, and then begin your homework" and a moment later to tell Samantha "Stop daydreaming, Sammy. Get your work done now." If Samantha were to ask why Suzy could relax for a moment whereas she must stay on task without interruption, it would be perfectly alright to respond (with a warm smile), "Sue needs a collegial teacher; you need an authoritative teacher, and that is what I am—for you!"

Learning in Patterns versus Needing a Variety of Interactions. In every classroom, some youngsters feel most comfortable with patterns and routines, whereas others love variety and change. One wants to do the same favored activities repeatedly; the other invariably tries new and different approaches—for example, rarely follows the identical sequence or does the same activity in the same way twice! This quality often reveals itself early in childhood and becomes apparent when one youngster begs to hear the same story reread frequently and another asks for new stories each time.

Neither preferring variety nor routines is more or less valuable; young people merely differ from each other. Be aware of each student's inclinations and either respond to them or, periodically, alternate the procedures you follow so that each has a turn learning his or her way.

The Perceptual Characteristics of Learning Style

Learning by Listening, Reading, Seeing, Manipulating, and/or Experiencing. Educators seem unaware that learning by listening is the least preferred and most difficult way for most students to remember complex or comprehensive information (Bauer 1991; Carbo 1980; Crino 1984; LeClair 1986; Ingham 1989, 1991; Garrett 1991; Gardiner 1986; Kroon 1985; Martini 1986; Weinberg 1983; Wheeler 1980, 1983). Auditory learners can remember approximately 75 percent of what they hear, but *less than 30 percent of the school-age population is auditory* (Urbschat 1977; Crino 1984; LeClair 1986). Thus, when students either do not do the things they have been told to do *or* cannot remember what they were told, it usually is because they find it difficult to absorb and remember spoken directives, particularly if a series of commands have been given (Lemmon 1985).

Girls are more auditory than boys (Pizzo 1981). As a result, girls begin to talk earlier and more distinctly than boys. Girls begin to read earlier and more fluently than most boys, particularly when parents or teachers begin the reading process by teaching them to decode, an emphasis on what alphabetical letters sound like. Because of their built-in auditory proficiency, most girls are better able to hear and remember sounds than most boys (Pizzo 1981; Pizzo, Dunn, & Dunn 1990).

Grown women tend to be more verbal than grown men; grown men tend to lose their hearing years before grown women. Women have stronger auditory memory than men; men tend to be visually and tactually stronger than women. Women often remember best the things they hear, whereas men tend to remember best the things they see (if they are visual preferents) and handle (Dunn, Deckinger, Withers, & Katzenstein 1990; Ingham 1989).

At most, only 40 percent of the school-age population is visual—able to remember approximately two-fifths of what is read or seen. And it is more complicated than that, for visual analytics tend to remember words and numbers; visual globals tend to remember pictures, illustrations, graphs, and symbols (Brennan 1982; Jarsonbeck 1984).

If preschool and elementary children don't remember a great deal of what they hear or see, what do they remember? They remember what they touch, handle, feel, and/or manipulate. We call such learners tactual. Tactual learners constitute our largest group of children. Another large group comprises kinesthetics—those who need to experience what they learn. For example, such young people learn most effectively when they do something—take a trip, bake, build, visit, meet, and interact with others. Thus, tactual students learn most easily through their hands; kinesthetic students learn most easily through whole-body activities. Even the gifted and talented adolescents in this international study proved to be highly tactual and kinesthetic in their learning style preferences (see Chapter 16).

Some children have multiple perceptual strengths; in the United States they almost always become our academically gifted students (Dunn, Dunn, & Treffinger 1992). Others have only a single perceptual strength; when introduced to new and difficult material through that one modality, they achieve well academically (Bauer 1991; Carbo 1980; Ingham 1989, 1991; Martini 1986; Wheeler 1983). Others have no perceptual strengths; they can learn, but they must be taught through a multisensory approach that begins with their single best modality (Bauer 1990; Gardiner 1986; Jarsonbeck 1984; Kroon 1985; Wheeler 1980). Research documents that people learn most easily and efficiently when *introduced* to new and difficult information through their preferred modality, whether auditory, visual, tactual, or kinesthetic (Carbo 1980; Ingham 1989, 1991; Martini 1986) and are then *reinforced* through their secondary or tertiary modality (Bauer 1991; Kroon 1985; Wheeler 1980).

Perceptual strengths are housed in the brain stem. They develop at their own rate in each human. Children first begin learning and remembering difficult things by experiencing them. The second modality to develop is the tactual. Thus, young children need to touch everything that excites their imagination, and they learn through that interaction with objects and people. Some time about third grade, some children begin being visual, and at about sixth grade, many begin becoming auditory (Price 1980a).

However, we should not extrapolate from generalizations. The majority of school-age children remain kinesthetic and tactual throughout elementary school. Among ''average'' high school students in the United States, most are not strongly auditory. Fewer students than teachers ever imagined are neither auditory nor strongly visual (Review of Research 1991).

The Physiological Characteristics of Learning Style

Learning with—or Without—Intake. The need for snacking, chewing, drinking, or biting while concentrating is very real among some young children and many adolescents. It appears to explode at the onset of puberty and gradually is reduced as young adults become grownups (Price 1980a). However, even during the pre-school years, certain little ones need to constantly engage in intake whenever involved in tasks that are mentally challenging to them. Teachers should be aware of this characteristic. When students' Learning Style Inventory printouts indicate a strong need for intake (60 or above), teachers might be willing to experiment with permitting raw vegetables while the youngsters are concentrating on difficult or challenging tasks in school. Avoid permitting other than low-calorie, nutritious snacks. Youngsters who require intake earned statistically higher test scores when permitted to snack while test-taking than when not permitted to do so (MacMurren 1985).

Learning at the Best Time of Day. Learning and task efficiency is related to each person's temperature cycle, thus it is related to when during each day each is likely to be most alert, learn most easily, and behave best. For example, junior high school underachievers became better in math and behaved better when they were reassigned to math classes that matched their chronobiological time preferences (Carruthers & Young 1980). One year later, Lynch (1981) reported that time preference was a crucial factor in the reversal of truancy patterns among high school students.

Virostko (1983) won an international research award when the matching of elementary students' time preferences and their reading and math instructional schedules resulted in significant achievement gains in both those subjects (Dunn, Dunn, Primavera, Sinatra, & Virostko 1987). In addition, when teachers were provided in-service training during their time preferences, they learned more and used what they learned significantly more often than when they received training at their wrong time of day. Lemmon (1985), an elementary school principal in Hutchinson, Kansas, administered the Iowa Basic Skills Tests to students at their best time of day. She reported significantly higher test gains in both subjects compared to each youngster's previous three years' growth as measured by that same standardized test.

Only about 28 percent of school-age students are alert early in the morning; high energy between 7 and 9 A.M. is an adult pattern. In the United States, elementary school students experience their strongest energy highs between 10 A.M. and 2 P.M. Approximately one-third of junior high schoolers are wide awake in early morning when academics are accented; again, the majority come alive after 10 A.M. Almost 40 percent of high school students are early birds, but the majority are late-morning or afternoon preferents. Thirteen percent of these young adults tend to be night people—they think best in the evening. There are exceptions to these data, of course, but this research documented the varied chronobiological factors between and within multicultural groups (Dunn, Gemake, Jalali, Zenhausern, Quinn, & Spiridakis 1990; Dunn & Griggs 1990; Dunn, Griggs, & Price, in press).

Learning Through a Global versus an Analytic Processing Style. For children to learn new and difficult information, they need to be able to concentrate on, absorb, process, and retain it. How they process is one part of their learning style. Most children learn in at least one of three different processing styles—analytic, global, or nonpreferenced—meaning that they can learn regardless of their style *when the information is interesting to them.*

Analytics learn most easily when information is introduced to them in a step-by-step, sequential pattern—one fact after another that gradually builds toward their understanding. Analytics do not mind concentrating on unrelated details as long as they feel that they are moving toward a gradual understanding. For example:

The word *cat* has three alphabetical letters. It is spelled: c a t. The c is a "hard c," which sounds like "K." The a is a "short a"; it sounds like "a." The "t" sounds like "*tuh.*" If you put the three sounds together, they form the word *cat*—*c a t*. A cat is an animal. *C A T* spells *cat*—a certain kind of animal.

Global children do not learn easily that way. Instead, globals learn through short stories called *anecdotes*. When globals hear an anecdote, they pay attention. They listen "all ears," particularly if it relates to their experiences and/or is interesting to them. Globals also learn through humor, illustrations, symbols, and graphics. They understand better when they are introduced to something new and difficult through an anecdote that explains the idea or basic concept of what they need to learn and why they need to learn it. Once globals understand *what* they need to learn and *why* they need to learn it, they can concentrate on the details.

Thus, if you were teaching the word *cat* to a global child, you would describe how you felt something scratching at your neck while still asleep one morning. You might explain the fear you felt as you opened one eye and looked around to see what was waking you. You might laugh and say, "There was my *c a t*, and do you know what my *c a t* was doing? It was purring! What do you think my *c a t* is?" Once you say "purring," most children will know.

Both analytics and globals reason, but by different strategies (Levy 1979; Zenhausern 1980); each strategy makes the most of the neural space that exists (Levy 1982). Analytics and globals are both capable of mastering identical information or skills *if they are taught through instructional methods or resources that complement their styles*. That conclusion was well documented in mathematics (Brennan 1984; Dunn, Bruno, Sklar, & Beaudry 1990; Jarsonbeck 1984), science (Douglas 1979), nutrition (Tanenbaum 1982), and social studies (Trautmnan 1979). Processing style appears to change; the majority of elementary school children are global. However, the older children grow and the longer they remain in school, the more analytic many become.

Neither processing style is better or worse than the other; they merely are different. Globals often prefer learning with other children rather than either alone or directly with an adult (Dunn, Cavanaugh, Eberle, & Zenhausern 1982). They also often prefer to structure tasks in their own way rather than follow someone else's directive. Many underachievers are global, but Cody (1983) found that eight of ten children with an IQ of 135 were global high achievers; with an IQ of 145 or above, nine of ten were global high achievers. The difference between high-IQ and underachieving global students tends to be their motivation and relatively late development of auditory and visual perceptual preferences, through which most conventional instruction occurs.

It is understandable why the motivation of underachievers is lower than that of achievers, but the cause of the differentiation between the two groups may be the biological development of auditory, visual, tactual, and kinesthetic modalities. Although schools cannot intervene in students' biological development, researchers (Bauer 1991; Carbo 1980; Gardiner 1986; Garrett 1991; Ingham 1989; Jarsonbeck 1984; Kroon 1985; Martini 1986; Urbschat 1977; Weinberg

1983; Wheeler 1980, 1983) and schools (Andrews 1990, 1991; Brunner & Majewski 1990; Della Valle 1990; Dunn 1990; Dunn & Griggs 1988a; Harp & Orsak 1990; Orsak 1990; Perrin 1990; Sinatra 1990; Sykes, Jones, & Phillips 1990) have successfully taught students through their existing perceptual preferences.

Learning and Hyperactivity versus Passivity. Some children referred to psychologists are not clinically hyperactive; instead, they often are normal youngsters in need of mobility (Fadley & Hosler 1979). In addition, the less interested they are in what they are doing or being taught, the more mobility they need. A disquieting point is that such youngsters are "almost always boys" (p. 219).

More than 95 percent of hyperactives are males (Restak 1979) and the very same characteristic, when observed in girls, is correlated with academic *achievement*. Boys, however, are required to be passive in school and are rejected for aggressive behaviors there, but are encouraged to engage in typical male aggressions in the world at large—a situation which Restak suggested might lead to role conflict. He added that conventional classroom environments do not provide male students with sufficient outlet for their normal movement needs. He also warned that schools actually *cause* conflict with societal expectations that boys not be timid, passive, or conforming.

Other researchers corroborated Restak's warnings and affirmed that boys labeled hyperactive in school often were fidgety because their teachers provided experiences for them "to think about something"; instead, those young people needed "to do something" (Tingley-Michaelis 1983, p. 26). They also chastised educators for believing that activities prevented rather than enhanced learning!

When researchers began equating hyperactivity with students' normal need for mobility, they experimented with providing many opportunities for learning while engaged in movement kinesthetically. Reports then began to document that, when previously restless youngsters were reassigned to classes that did not require passivity, their behaviors were rarely even noticed (Fadley & Hosler 1979; Koester & Farley 1977). Eventually teachers began indicating that, although certain students thrived in an activity-oriented environment which permitted mobility, others remained almost exclusively in the same area of the room, despite frequent attempts to coax them to move (Hodges 1985; Miller 1985). That led to Fitt's (1975) conclusions that no amount of persuasion increased selected students' interest in movement, whereas others found it impossible to remain seated passively for extended periods. "These are cases of a child's style . . . governing his interactions with and within the environment" (p. 94).

Add to all that the knowledge that almost 40 percent of U.S. secondary school youngsters require formal seating while concentrating, and it is not difficult to understand why so many—particularly boys—squirm, sit on their ankles and calves, squirrel down into their seats, extend their legs out into the aisle, and occasionally fall off their chairs!

Dunn, Della Valle, Dunn, Geisert, Sinatra, & Zenhausern (1986) documented that almost 50 percent of a large, urban junior high school's students could not sit still for any appreciable amount of time. Twenty-five percent could remain immobile if interested in the lesson, and the remaining 25 percent preferred being passive. However, when student preferences for mobility were matched with a treatment that permitted them to change positions and places on demand, they achieved higher test scores than when they were mismatched. Students who required mobility moved from one part of the room to another to master all the information in the lesson, and performed better than when they were required to sit for an entire period. On the other hand, students who disliked moving performed worse when required to move while learning and significantly better when permitted to sit quietly and read.

SUMMARY

In this chapter we have reviewed the Dunn and Dunn theory of learning style and Milgram's conceptualization of giftedness. Individuals have unique learning styles and achieve better on standardized tests when they are taught through their learning style strengths. They also enjoy learning better when provided instructional approaches that complement their learning style strengths. Gifted students have highly individual learning styles, but often are treated as a group with no regard for the uniqueness among them. Thus, gifted students often are taught incorrectly and become disadvantaged, sometimes at risk, for they too achieve best when permitted to learn through their learning style strengths.

Chapters 7 through 13 provide data on the learning styles of gifted adolescents in nine nations. In Chapter 16, Price and Milgram summarize that information to permit comparisons among various cultures and populations. It is critical to bear in mind that all people in the same group—whether academic, talent, school, nation, or culture—do *not* have the same style. Indeed, there are more differences *within* groups than *between* groups (Dunn & Griggs 1990). Nevertheless, the data to be reported on adolescents in may different countries documents the uniqueness and similarities in learning styles among these citizens that may be useful to teachers and counselors in helping them realize their potential more fully.

We conclude this chapter by returning to the grave problem cited at the beginning: the less than maximum realization of potential abilities. Despite the wide variety of models of special education offered to gifted children (Fox & Washington 1985; Milgram & Goldring 1991), it seems that the question of how to provide for the unique needs of these learners remains a challenge (Cox, Daniel, & Boston 1985). We have suggested in this chapter and elsewhere (Milgram 1989; Dunn 1989; Dunn & Dunn 1978, 1992, 1993; Dunn, Dunn, & Treffinger 1992) that the educational process be tailored to complement the unique needs of each learner. This is a formidable task but one that is neither impractical nor impossible. Extensive knowledge about each learner is necessary to customize the educational experience. A comprehensive conceptualization of giftedness, with an emphasis on learning style and the individualization of instructional strategies, provides the knowledge base for prescribing complementary approaches and resources for each youngster. That goal is within reach for gifted children, for they are capable of creating their own materials once they have been shown how to do so (Dunn & Dunn 1992, 1993). Thus, this book provides information concerning the profiles of gifted adolescents in seven countries, demonstrates the similarities and differences among them and within groups, describes how to teach students with widely diversified learning style strengths, and explains how to teach these potentially world-saving humans to teach themselves.

Chapter 2

Identifying Learning Styles and Creativity in Gifted Learners: Subjects, Instrumentation, Administration, Reliability, Validity

Roberta M. Milgram and Rita Dunn

In Chapter 1, the theoretical model of learning style developed by Dunn and Dunn (1972) and the formulation of the 4 x 4 structure of giftedness proposed by Milgram (1989, 1990a, 1991a) were explained. These researchers developed psychometric tools designed to be used in research aimed at establishing the construct validity of each model and in practice by teachers and counselors as they strive to differentiate curricula and individualize instruction.

The Learning Style Inventory, or LSI (Dunn, Dunn, & Price 1989), was administered to adolescent learners in all nine countries in the current international study. The Tel Aviv Activities Inventory (Milgram 1987, 1990b) was administered in seven countries: Brazil, Canada, Guatemala, Israel, Korea, and Philippines, and the United States. The 1987 Activities Inventory was used in all countries except Israel, where the 1990 version was used. In order to avoid needless repetition in each chapter, the Learning Style Inventory and the Tel Aviv Activities Inventory are described in this chapter. Creative or divergent thinking was measured in Brazil with the Torrance Tests of Creative Thinking, or TTCT (Torrance 1974) and in Israel with the Tel Aviv Creativity Test (Milgram & Milgram 1976a). These instruments are discussed later in this chapter. The Milta Measure of General Intelligence (Ortar 1980) was administered only in Israel, and it is described in detail in Chapter 8.

We examined the learning styles of 5,469 adolescents. The subjects in these countries cannot be considered comparable random samples. There were differences in age, sex, and socioeconomic background that indicate the need for caution in comparing these data. The procedure of the study as conducted in each country is presented in the respective chapters. Despite differences among the samples, however, it was a rare opportunity to study the learning styles of gifted youngsters in a large number of cultures. We used a data base that was

Table 2.1
Subjects by Country, Grade, and Sex*

GR	Sex	ISR	PHI	KOR	USA	CAN	GUA	BRA	Total
7	M	116			152		153	171	592
	F	104			180		117	175	576
8	M	60			113	21	58	72	324
	F	63			101	41	73	109	387
9	M	73	102		93	13	115	5	401
	F	90			106	34	73	6	309
10	M	69	98		46	7	15	18	253
	F	85			71	14	5	37	212
11	M	71	95	45	41	3	22		277
	F	74			56	9	13		152
12	M	74	84	47	20	3			228
	F	103			23	12			138
Missing**		3			56	9	20	12	100
Total		985	379	92	1058	166	664	605	3949

*   There were also 113 boys and girls in the 11th and 12th grades from Greece, 36 in the 10th, 11th, and 12th grades from Egypt, and 1371 in grades 9 - 12 from the Philippines for whom only Learning Style scores were available. When these subjects are added the total number of subjects is 5469.

**   Missing data on grade and/or sex.

as inclusive and as comparable as possible for an integrative analysis that is presented in Chapter 16. The distribution of subjects by country, grade, and sex, as presented in Table 2.1, provides a comprehensive framework within which to view the data. The following three-letter abbreviations are used in Table 2.1 and in all other tables in this volume to designate the ten cultures:

BRA	Brazil
CAN	Canada
EGY	Egypt
GRE	Greece
GUA	Guatemala
ISR	Israel

KOR   Korea

MAY   Mayan

PHI   Philippines

USA   United States

Personal data including sex and grade point average were provided by the school administrators in each country.

IDENTIFYING LEARNING STYLE

As Chapter 1 indicated, learning style encompasses individuals' environmental, emotional, sociological, physiological, and global or analytical processing preferences. Knowledge of students' learning style strengths helps teachers help young people master difficult information through complementary instructional resources and approaches (Andrews 1990; Brunner & Majewski 1990, Harp & Orsak 1990; Orsak 1990a,b; Perrin 1993; Sinatra 1990). The self-knowledge that ultimately develops also helps students to teach themselves and to bypass their teacher's style when a mismatch has occurred (Clark-Thayer 1987, 1988; Dunn 1989a; Dunn, Deckinger, Withers, & Katzenstein 1990; Mickler & Zipert 1987). It is important to use a reliable and valid diagnostic instrument to identify learning style, for an unreliable or invalid instrument can only yield unreliable and invalid results.

Instruments for Identifying Learning Style

Several instruments have been developed to identify individual student (K–12) learning styles (Canfield & Lafferty 1976; Dunn & Dunn 1972, 1974, 1977; Dunn, Dunn, & Price 1975; Gregorc 1985; Hill 1964; Hunt 1979; Keefe, Monk, Languis, Letteri, & Dunn 1986; Letteri 1980; Perrin 1983; Ramirez & Casteneda 1974; Schmeck, Ribich, & Ramanaiah 1977). Most of those measure one or two elements on a bipolar continuum. Three instruments—the Learning Style Profile (Keefe, Monk, Languis, Letteri, & Dunn 1986), Cognitive Style Mapping (Hill 1964), the Learning Style Inventory (Dunn, Dunn, & Price 1972, 1975, 1979, 1981, 1984, 1989), and the Learning Style Inventory: Primary Version (Perrin 1983)—are considered comprehensive in nature; that is, they assess multiple elements in combination with each other. The LSI (Dunn, Dunn, & Price 1989) is comprehensive and the most "widely used assessment instrument in elementary and secondary schools" (Keefe 1982, p. 52).

Dunn, Dunn, and Price (1989) defined learning style in terms of each person's (1) immediate environment (sound level, temperature, light, and seating design; (2) emotionality (motivation, persistence, responsibility, and structure); (3) social preferences (learning alone, learning with peers, learning with adults present, learning in varied ways, being motivated by a teacher, and being motivated by a parent); (4) physiological inclinations (perceptual preferences, intake, energy highs and lows, and mobility); and (5) psychological preferences (global/analytic). Research has demonstrated that teachers are able to identify only a few elements of their students' learning styles through observation; other elements appear to be identifiable only through administration of reliable and valid tests (Beaty 1986; Dunn, Dunn, & Price 1977; Marcus 1977). The Learning Style Inventory (Dunn, Dunn, & Price 1989), was the instrument selected to identify the learning styles of the gifted and nongifted adolescents in this international investigation.

The Learning Style Inventory

Developed through content and factor analysis, the Learning Style Inventory (LSI) is a comprehensive approach to the identification of an individual's learning style. The instrument allows analysis of the conditions under which students in grades 3–12 prefer to learn. The Learning Style Inventory assesses twenty-two elements of individual learning style. Presentation of the Dunn and Dunn theoretical formulation of learning style, as presented in Chapter 1 and elsewhere, varies as to the number of learning style elements cited. Nevertheless, the LSI always yields twenty-two scores. Additional indices of individual learning style preference such as impulsive≠reflexive or global≠analytic are measured by other instruments.

The LSI is a self-report instrument on which each subject is asked to rate 104 items (e.g., "When I really have a lot of studying to do, I like to work alone" and "I enjoy being with friends when I study") on a five-point Likert scale from strongly agree (1) to strongly disagree (5). The twenty-two scores yielded by the Learning Style Inventory and a brief description of each are summarized in Table 2.2. For sixteen elements, high scores indicate high preference. Six elements are scored on a bipolar continuum from low to high, with high scores indicating preference for the second pole cited (e.g., silence/sound).

The LSI directions direct students to "answer the questions as if you are describing how you concentrate when you are studying difficult academic material." The LSI can be completed in approximately thirty to forty minutes. After answering all the questions on the LSI answer form (the test itself), each student's answer sheet is optically read and processed individually. Each student then receives his or her own LSI Individual Printout, a graphic representation of the conditions under which each learns most efficiently.

In a two-year study of various learning style models and instrumentation conducted by Ohio State University's National Center for Research in Vocational Education, Kirby (1979) reported that the LSI had established "impressive reliability and face and construct validity" (p. 72). Predictive validity of the LSI was evidenced by many experimental investigations conducted under the auspices of St. John's University's Center for the Study of Learning and Teaching Styles

Table 2.2
The Elements of the Learning Style Inventory

	Element	Description
1.	Noise	Quiet - Sound
2.	Light	Dim - Bright Light
3.	Temperature	Cool - Warm Temperature
4.	Design	Informal -- Formal Design
5.	Motivation	Motivation
6.	Persistence	Persistence
7.	Responsibility	Responsibility
8.	Structure	Structure
9.	Alone/Peer	Learning alone - Peer Oriented Learner
10.	Authority Figures	Authority Figures Absent - Present
11.	Several Ways	Prefers Learning Through Several Ways
12.	Auditory	Auditory Preferences
13.	Visual	Visual Preferences
14.	Tactile	Tactile Preferences
15.	Kinesthetic	Kinesthetic Preferences
16.	Intake	Learns Best While Eating/Drinking
17.	Evening - Morning	Evening - Morning
18.	Late Morning	Functions Best in Late Morning
19.	Afternoon	Functions Best in Afternoon
20.	Mobility	Needs Mobility
21.	Parent Motivated	Parent Motivated
22.	Teacher Motivated	Teacher Motivated

(DeBello 1985; Dunn, Della Valle, Dunn, Geisert, Sinatra, & Zenhausern 1986; Dunn, Dunn, Primavera, Sinatra, & Virostko 1987; Dunn, Gemake, Jalali, Zenhausern, Quinn, & Spiridakis 1990; Dunn, Giannitti, Murray, Geisert, Rossi, & Quinn 1990; Dunn, Krimsky, Murray, & Quinn 1985; Dunn, White, & Zenhausern 1982; Hodges 1985; Kroon 1985; Lynch 1981; MacMurren 1985; Martini 1986; Miles 1987; Pizzo, Dunn, & Dunn 1990; Shea 1983) and by significantly higher achievement on standardized tests when students were taught in ways that were complementary to, rather than dissonant from, their learning styles in school instructional programs (Brunner & Majewski, 1990; Dunn & Griggs 1988; Harp & Orsak 1990; Orsak 1990a,b; Perrin 1990; Sinatra 1990).

In a comparative analysis of the conceptualizations of learning style and the psychometric standards of nine different instruments that purportedly measure learning style preference, only the LSI was rated as having good or better reliability and validity (Curry 1987). In a comparison of the major learning style models and their instrumentation, DeBello (1990) reported the comparatively high reliability and validity of the LSI in contrast to other assessments. The LSI is easy to administer and interpret and has been employed in doctoral research at more than 85 institutions of higher education in the United States and abroad (Annotated Bibliography 1993; Dunn 1990a,b,c,d; Dunn, Beaudry, & Klavas 1989).

Preparing Students for Taking the LSI

Students need to be made aware of the importance of learning style so that they think carefully before answering questions about how they concentrate when trying to master new and difficult information. To help them understand the need to be thoughtful and honest about their style strengths, there are several story books available to explain the concept of learning style. Each describes either animals or friends who like each other and often play together but, invariably, it is difficult for the two to study together because they really do learn differently from each other. Through this global conceptual approach, the various elements of learning style are explained. It is strongly recommended that the appropriate book be read to, by, or with students; and each person's need to learn differently is discussed so that a clear understanding of learning style is developed before any assessment is administered.

In cases where youngsters do not read fluently, or where they have experienced learning difficulties, it is valuable to administer the instrument through a personal interview. The one-on-one relationship that develops as the teacher questions the youngster about his or her preferences often provides new insights into the individual's thinking that may not be afforded otherwise.

In many countries included in this investigation, one of two booklets was read by or with the students in their classes. *Two-Of-A-Kind Learning Styles* by Rosa Pena is a storybook that explains learning style to middle school students. In a high-interest account, Global Myrna and Analytic Victor are close friends who respect their differences, and thus study difficult material through their unique learning styles (Klavas 1990). *Viva la Difference: A Guide Explaining Learning Style to High School Students* by Connie Bouman was the booklet provided for high school participants in this study. Both booklets are available through Professor Rita Dunn, Director, Center for the Study of Learning and Teaching Styles, St. John's University.

LSI answer sheets designed for optical scoring were used in seven countries— Canada, Guatemala, Greece, Israel, Korea, Philippines, and the United States— and the data were analyzed and processed by Price Systems, Inc., Lawrence, Kansas. In Brazil and Egypt, the scoring and analyses of the LSI were done by the investigators with guidance from Professor Gary Price and Professor Rita Dunn.

Discriminant analyses were used to investigate learning style differences among cultural groups and subgroups. Discriminant analysis is designed to compare two or more groups on a set of variables. It is, therefore, especially appropriate for comparisons of the learning styles of different cultural groups, and for the investigation of similarities and differences in learning style between gifted and nongifted groups within a specific culture. In a stepwise analysis, the learning style variable that accounts for the most significant difference between the groups enters into the discriminant equation first. The next variable that accounts for unique additional variance then enters into the discriminant equation. Variables continue to enter the discriminant equation until no additional variables are found that significantly discriminate between the groups. This approach was used to examine learning style differences between learners in each culture and a matched sample of learners in the United States, and also to compare the learning styles of youngsters who are gifted versus nongifted academically and in the specific domains of creativity.

IDENTIFYING CREATIVITY

Creative Thinking

For many years, researchers followed the Terman model of research in giftedness (Terman 1925; Terman & Oden 1947, 1959). Accepting the unidimensional definition of giftedness as 140 IQ or above, they concentrated on delineating the cognitive and personal-social characteristics of such individuals and on trying to sort out the predictors of adult giftedness. By the same token, teachers and principals charged with identifying high-ability youngsters and providing special education for them were quite content to utilize the available standardized instruments to measure intelligence and to use these scores to meet their urgent need for ways to identify gifted learners. Accordingly, from the 1920s to the 1950s, there was little theoretical development and negligible progress was made in the development of additional psychometric tools useful in identifying able learners.

Since the 1950s, we have witnessed accelerated theoretical and empirical development in the field of giftedness. What many people would cite as a major advance was the expansion of the term giftedness to include creativity. The broadening of the definition of giftedness was more than a semantic change. It represented an extended understanding, in that new abilities were now postulated to be included in giftedness, especially creativity. Since the 1950s, there has been rapid growth both in formulations of creativity and in its measurement. Readers interested in comprehensive and authoritative information on the theoretical and empirical advances are referred to Dunn, Dunn, and Treffinger (1992); Glover, Ronning, and Reynolds (1989); Isaksen (1987); Runco (1991); Runco and Albert (1990); and Sternberg and Davidson (1986).

The most popular approach to studying creativity focuses on original thinking. Numerous tests of divergent thinking were developed and used widely in selecting students for special education programs (Runco 1991; Torrance 1987). In the current international study, creative thinking was measured in two countries, Brazil and Israel. In Brazil the most widely used measure of divergent thinking was utilized—the Torrance Test of Creative Thinking or TTCT (Torrance 1974; Torrance & Ball 1978). The TTCT was administered and scored according to the directions provided by the test author. Detailed information on the TTCT as it was used in the current study may be found in Chapter 13. Recent data on the test were supplied by Torrance (1987). In Israel, two verbal items were selected from the Tel Aviv Creativity Test or TACT (Milgram & Milgram 1976a), and an abbreviated and revised form of the Wallach and Kogan (1965) instrument, was used. Each item was scored for the number of discrete responses according to the standardized instructions for scoring provided by the test authors. Scores of the two items were combined for a total score.

Both measures are similar to other widely used measures based upon ideational fluency as the operational definition of creative thinking in which subjects are asked to generate as many responses as they could to a variety of verbal and figural stimuli. The Tel Aviv test is psychometrically advanced in a number of ways. It is shorter and more easily administered and scored than many other similar tests. It yields scores distinct from IQ in group administration for children at the average IQ level and higher (Milgram & Milgram 1976a). The development of the Tel Aviv Creativity Test, including detailed psychometric data, may be found in research reports (Milgram 1980; Milgram & Milgram 1976a, 1976b; Milgram, Milgram, Rosenbloom, & Rabkin 1978) and in studies designed to establish the reliability and validity of the test (Hong, Whiston, & Milgram, in press; Milgram 1983; Milgram & Arad 1981; Milgram & Milgram 1976b). Wallach and Wing (1969) and Wing and Wallach (1971) investigated divergent thinking as a predictor of creative, intrinsically motivated activities in college students. On the basis of their findings, they urged that creative thinking be used in college student selection, claiming that the recommended procedure would succeed in selecting students who would later make outstanding contributions in the real world. Not all of the evidence supports the validity of ideational fluency-based measures of creative thinking as predictors of creative performance in the real world (Barron & Harrington 1981). On the other hand, the severe criticism of these measures and the call for abandoning them entirely in the measurement of creativity also are unjustified. For a recent and authoritative discussion and evaluation of the most recent research on divergent thinking, the reader is referred to the work of Runco (1991).

Performance of Creative Leisure Activities

Another, perhaps more promising, approach to the measurement of creativity in young people focuses on creative activity. Probably the most important reason for the frequent failure to recognize in children and youth the abilities that later emerge as remarkable life accomplishment in adults is the difference between what we call remarkable achievement in children and in adults. In children a high GPA (grade point average)—that is, attaining high grades in a variety of school subjects—is the generally accepted standard for being identified as a gifted learner. High scholastic achievement in children is assumed to be an early indication of remarkable accomplishments to come. Unfortunately, neither the practical experience of educators nor research findings support this assumption. Giftedness in adults is not general intellectual ability but rather a specific ability that reflects original thinking in a particular life domain.

Gifted behavior in adults is often preceded by highly focused interest, ability, and activity in a specific sphere of life over a period of many years. The intense domain-specific activities that often characterize the childhood and adolescent years of those destined to be gifted adults are intrinsically motivated and frequently done in their leisure time rather than in school. The hobbies and activities that young people do for their own enjoyment and by their own choice, and not in order to fulfill school requirements or to earn grades or credits, may be highly intellectual endeavors (e.g., computer programming, working out mathematical solutions, conducting scientific experiments, composing music). Numerous investigators have stressed the importance of expanding our view of giftedness, but have not considered the role of out-of-school activities in the development of talent.

If our goal is to improve the procedures utilized in the identification of children with extraordinary abilities, it would seem appropriate to concentrate on understanding the role of freely chosen, out-of-school leisure activities. They may be better predictors of significant adult accomplishments than the most widely used current predictors—that is, overall intellectual ability and school grades (Milgram 1989, 1990a, 1991a). One reason why these activities may indeed predict adult accomplishment is that their performance requires not only intellectual abilities but also task commitment, persistence, and other cognitive and personal-social attributes that strongly determine life outcomes.

A series of innovative studies of intrinsically motivated, creative activities and accomplishments in adolescence was conducted by Holland and his associates

(Holland 1961; Holland & Austin 1962; Holland & Nichols 1964; Richards, Holland, & Lutz 1967). They examined thousands of retrospective self-reports of college-age students and found creative attainments in high school to be associated with continuing creative activity in college.

Building upon the work of Holland and his associates and that of Wallach and Wing (1969) cited above, Milgram developed the Tel Aviv Activities Inventory and investigated out-of-school activities in children and adolescents. A major innovation of the new scale was to replace the general undifferentiated list of items tapping creative accomplishment with the following eight specific domains of creative activity: science, music, fine arts, social leadership, writing, community service, drama, sports, and dance. The instrument has been used in studies of individual differences in creative performance in children ranging in age from age 7 through high school (Milgram & Milgram 1976b; Milgram et al. 1978; Milgram, Yitzhak, & Milgram 1977; Kfir 1989; Gorsky 1990).

These studies provided evidence for the short-term predictive validity of out-of-school activities with reference to adult accomplishment. In addition, in a recent follow-up study that spanned eighteen years, Hong, Milgram, and Whiston (in press) reported evidence for the predictive validity of self-reports of out-of-school attainments of adolescents as a predictor of vocational choice and accomplishment in young adults.

The enormous investment of time and effort over an extended period of time that frequently characterizes the development of talent (Bloom 1985) makes it clear that the actualization of talent is not only a gift but an achievement. Terman (1925), the pioneer investigator of giftedness, reported a large number and wide variety of out-of-school activities for the intellectually gifted children whom he subsequently followed throughout their lives. Others, unfortunately, did not follow his lead on this topic nor did he examine the relative efficacy of leisure activities as predictors of future eminent achievements. McClelland (1973) called for testing for competence rather than for intelligence and suggested that the best testing is criterion sampling. One reason why his recommendation has not been implemented in the identification of gifted and talented learners is the lack of appropriate psychometric instruments. Our data suggest that self-reports of out-of-school activities may serve as an instrument for criterion sampling testing in children with reference to gifted behavior in adults.

Tel Aviv Activities Inventory (Milgram 1987). The instrument is a self-report biographical questionnaire designed to measure the extracurricular interests, activities, and accomplishments of adolescents. It consists of two distinct parts. Part A provides the data for the international study. It consists of fifty-four items that assess nonacademic talented accomplishment in eight domains of creativity. The areas and the number of questions in each subscale (in parentheses) are as follows: Science (8), Social Leadership Activities (11), Dance (2), Music (9), Fine Arts (8), Literature/Writing (6), Drama (4), and Sports (6).

The subject responds to items 1–54 in two ways. First he or she indicates a simple yes or no to indicate participation in that activity. This is scored 1 or 2 and allows us to computerize the results and do our analyses immediately. Scores are computed by counting the number of yes responses to items and assigning one point for each one. Points were added to yield scores for each activity area and a total score.

In addition, each page contains a column that subjects are requested to use to give details on their answer. These open-ended responses cannot be immediately scored by computer. They are, however, very important. They help guarantee veridicality of response on the one hand and provide valuable clinical data for counseling purposes on the other. The following are examples of the items of the instrument:

Did you ever build a scientific model (not as part of a course)? Which?

Did you work out original solutions to mathematical problems? (Proofs for theorems or propositions not given by the teacher or textbook.)

Have you ever won an individual prize in music? Which?

Has any of your artistic work ever been exhibited publicly? Elaborate.

Have you ever directed a play, film, videotape, ballet, or dance performance? Where?

Part B also was administered. It consists of nine items in which subjects indicate activities in which they participate for enjoyment and entertainment. These include questions on time spent reading; listening to music; attending films, concerts, and plays; and watching television. These data were not reported in the current international study.

The Tel Aviv Activities Inventory (Milgram 1990b). The inventory is a revision of the 1987 instrument described above. It is also a two-part, self-report biographical questionnaire. One item was dropped from Sports, three items were added to Literature/Writing, a few items were changed, and two domains of creative activity were added—Computer and Foreign Language. In addition, an administration procedure utilizing an answer sheet for scoring by means of optical scanning was introduced. Part A of the 1990 Tel Aviv Activities Inventory consists of sixty-two items that tap out-of-school activities and yields scores in eleven areas. The areas and the number of questions in each subscale (in parentheses) are as follows: Science (7), Mathematics (1), Computer (4), Social Leadership Activities (11), Foreign Language (2), Dance (2), Music (9), Fine Arts (8), Literature/Writing (9), Drama (4), and Sports (5). Subjects indicate their out-of-school activities by marking yes or no to each of the items on an answer sheet. Examples of such achievements include receiving an award for a science project, publishing an article or poem in a magazine or newspaper outside of school, being chosen for a leadership position in a youth group, or giving a solo dance performance. Part A also includes nine items tapping non-domain-specific leisure activities that children do mainly for enjoyment, such as reading, watching television, listening to music, and belonging to clubs. In Part B, subjects are asked to elaborate on the activities they reported in Part A and to report activities that did not appear in Part A.

The Tel Aviv Activities Inventory (Milgram 1987, 1990b) was scored and tabulated under the supervision of the investigators. In all countries except Brazil, the data were submitted to Price Systems, Inc., for analyses.

The construct validity of the 1990 Tel Aviv Activities Inventory was investigated by means of factor analysis in 934 junior and senior high school students (Hong, Whiston, & Milgram, in press). The findings provide evidence of moderate to good construct validity for the Tel Aviv Activities Inventory. The factorial structure of the questionnaire is similar to the theoretical intent of Milgram (1989, 1990a, 1991a). Of the ten independent factors identified in the current edition of the Tel Aviv Activities Inventory, seven conform to the postulated subscales.

In Chapter 1, a 4 x 4 theoretical model of the Structure of Giftedness was presented in which each of the creative abilities cited above was postulated to obtain at four levels—nongifted, mild, moderate, and profound. Empirical support for the construct validity of the Milgram 4 x 4 model of the Structure of Giftedness has been reported (Hong & Milgram, in review). The current investigation of learning style in gifted learners in nine countries is a challenge of unprecedented magnitude. Despite concerted efforts to coordinate all aspects of the research project, understandably there were differences in samples, instruments, and procedures. Accordingly, to maximize comparability of the data, we simplified the analysis of the data on creative activity. In the analyses presented in the chapters that follow, we examine the learning style preferences of learners characterized by high versus low abilities in each of the specific domains. For example, we report on the learning style of children with high versus low creative accomplishments in science, foreign languages, or original thinking. This provides an excellent base for future studies that include the full 4 x 4 analyses.

The Tel Aviv Activities Inventory may be useful for career counseling with gifted and talented children. Instruments that focus on out-of-school activities may contribute to identifying hidden talent in youngsters. Many of these strengths currently are excluded from serious consideration in identification procedures that focus, for the most part, on intelligence test scores and school grades. The Tel Aviv Activities Inventory may provide an early indication of career interests and specific abilities. It provides counselors and teachers with an additional tool in their efforts to recognize extraordinary abilities among students and to help guide adolescents to greater realization of their talents. Identifying career interests in adolescents is a pressing problem to counselors and constitutes a major ongoing challenge (Milgram 1991b). The leisure-activities approach is a promising way of meeting this challenge and is worthy of serious consideration.

Chapter 3

Teaching Gifted Adolescents Through Their Learning Style Strengths

Rita Dunn

Education of the gifted, at least in the United States, moves in cycles. In alternate decades, we recognize the enormous contributions that gifted children are likely to make to the societies in which they live when they become adults, and we endeavor to maximize their potential by grouping them for instruction. However, although gifted children may be clustered together in classes for the exceptionally able, their teachers teach them as if they all learn identically—a system unsupported by this research. Indeed, the data from this international research demonstrate that gifted adolescents with different talents learn very differently from each other.

In most schools, the identification of gifted learners and the recommendation for participation in special classes is determined mainly by high performance on either IQ or achievement tests—measures we now recognize as biased in favor of analytic processors. These tests emphasize recall of details and unrelated facts rather than a student's ability to conceptualize and engage in holistic understanding. IQ and achievement tests do simplify the recognition of some abilities, but "the complex potential of a child's talents, sustained interests, and special aptitudes cannot be represented by performance on a limited number of questions in a fixed period of time" (Dunn, Dunn, & Treffinger 1992, p. 2). IQ and achievement tests do not begin to tap the wide range of abilities included in giftedness as it exists among many young people. By some estimates, a typical IQ test measures only 10 to 15 percent of the many kinds of intelligence that have been identified and can be described with some degree of accuracy. Such tests may be a good measure of short-term memory, vocabulary, and spatial reasoning, but they miss creative imagination; leadership charisma; social sensitivities; interpersonal intuition; artistic, musical, dramatic, athletic, or mechanical talents; and practical abilities ("street smarts"). Identifying giftedness solely in terms of an IQ score requires "disregarding a number of talents that most of us would consider *gifts*" (Dunn, Dunn, & Treffinger 1992, p. 4).

Cyclically, after schools engage in several years of separating the gifted from their nongifted classmates, socially sensitive educators become concerned about the isolation that may occur when extremely able children have few experiences interacting with the "real world." Some advocate teaching gifted learners in regular classrooms (Milgram 1989) and others suggest teaching them to teach themselves to avoid the frequent repetition and concomitant boredom that many of these rapid learners experience when required to adjust their pace to that of their academically "average" and "slow" classmates (Dunn, Dunn, & Treffinger 1992).

Periodically, these cycles repeat themselves, but usually with only a limited research base—one which rarely examines gifted students from the perspective of unique individuals within one or more groups, dependent upon their special types of talent. This study was designed to do exactly that. It is the first extensive examination of the learning styles of gifted and talented adolescents in a number of culturally, religiously, and racially diverse nations, and how they prefer to learn new and difficult academic material. The data from this investigation demonstrated cross-cultural differences in learning style and in specific types of creativity. Moreover, within each culture, students with different talents—different manifestation of giftedness—learned significantly differently from each other (see Chapter 16) and from their nongifted counterparts. Especially important was the finding that within classifications of giftedness some essential similarities in learning style were revealed. Thus, the gifted in science and mathematics appeared to have similar clusters of learning style traits, but they learned in patterns that were different from the gifted in art, music, dance, or language. Across cultures, there was some evidence that each of the talent groups revealed similar learning style patterns within their unique area of giftedness, but learned significantly differently from other talent groups.

What certain researchers had been reporting prior to this international study has now been confirmed: gifted students learn differently from each other (Coleman 1988; Dunn, Dunn, & Treffinger 1992; Mein 1986) and from other types of students (Dunn & Price 1980a; Dunn, Price, Dunn, & Griggs 1981; Griggs & Price 1980a,b, 1982). For example, many differences in learning style have been revealed:

1. Among average, gifted, and highly gifted students in grades five through twelve (Cody 1983);

2. Between gifted and nongifted elementary (Perrin 1984; Ricca 1983) and secondary students (Vignia 1983);

3. Between low- and high-reading achievers in the seventh and eighth grades (Murray 1980);

4. Between the learning disabled and the gifted (Pederson 1984);

5. Among gifted minority students; and

6. Between students high or low on divergent thinking and feeling variables (Wittig 1985).

However, because most schools classify as gifted those students who perform well on achievement and IQ tests and tend to ignore students' giftedness within various talent areas, whenever the learning styles of identified gifted students were examined in the past, the majority of the sample revealed strong preferences for quiet, bright light, and a formal seating design. Few needed intake and many were persistent; once they actually began working, they tended to continue their tasks with very few breaks or self-imposed interruptions. Preferring quiet, bright light, a formal design, and little intake and completing assignments in extended study or concentration intervals are characteristic of analytic processors (Bruno 1988; Dunn, Bruno, Sklar, & Beaudry 1990; Dunn, Cavanaugh, Eberle, & Zenhausern 1982). In addition, because conventional instruction occurs essentially through class lectures or discussions, those who achieved well in school usually were auditory learners. Thus, previous reports of the learning style characteristics of gifted students often included high-auditory memory—an uncommon trait among the nongifted.

Invariably, however, academically gifted youngsters often revealed two or more perceptual strengths. In addition to being highly auditory, they often also were highly visual and/or tactual, and/or kinesthetic (Dunn & Price 1980a; Griggs & Price 1980a,b; Kreitner 1981; Ricca 1983). Because traditional teaching rarely incorporated tactual or kinesthetic instruction for achieving students, those characteristics often remained unused or unnoticed, although both Stewart (1981) and Wasson (1980) revealed that academically gifted students strongly favored learning through a variety of activities, games, projects, independent studies, and programmed learning sequences rather than through lectures, drill, recitations, or discussions. In this multinational examination of the learning styles of gifted and talented adolescents in various domains, researchers reported auditory, visual, tactual, and/or kinesthetic Learning Style Inventory test scores of 60 or above—occasionally two or three strong perceptual memory channels (most youngsters have only one). However, despite the ability of the gifted students in this international study to utilize two or more sensory modalities, they often preferred tactual and/or kinesthetic learning. The difference between these extremely talented adolescents and underachievers is that the latter group can only learn easily and efficiently through those modalities; the gifted have choices but often prefer a hands-on or experiential (direct, active involvement) approach. Thus, effective teaching designed to respond to gifted adolescents should provide instruction through all senses to allow for preferences, interests, and variety needs. Effective instruction designed to respond to nongifted adolescents *must* introduce new and difficult material tactually and kinesthetically.

Previous studies in the United States indicated that many high-IQ gifted youngsters were persistent (Dunn & Price 1980a; Griggs & Price 1980a; Price, Dunn, Dunn, & Griggs 1981; Ricca 1983). High-IQ gifted students tend to be highly motivated (Cody 1983; Cross 1982; Dunn & Price 1980a; Griggs & Price 1980a; Price, Dunn, Dunn, & Griggs 1981); that also was true of many of the talented and gifted in this international study. Thus, gifted youngsters need to be able to progress academically as quickly as they wish, and should be permitted to succeed at their own pace without either unnecessary interruptions or having to delay their progress until their classmates complete their work.

In previous studies, high-IQ gifted students also were highly independent and preferred to learn by themselves rather than with others (Cross 1982; Griggs & Price 1980a; Kreitner 1981; Price, Dunn, Dunn, & Griggs 1981; Ricca 1983), unless the "others" were similarly achieving peers (Perrin 1984). In this research concerned with the learning styles of gifted and nongifted adolescents in multiple nations, with only a few exceptions gifted or talented students also reported wanting to learn alone; they tended to be either self motivated, teacher motivated, or desirous of obtaining feedback from those they viewed as being authorities in the same talent area. Only a small group of Israeli scientifically gifted and those Koreans with exceptional talent in music and art preferred learning with peers. Thus small-group instructional strategies such as Team Learning, Circle of Knowledge, Group Analysis, Brainstorming (Dunn & Dunn 1992a, 1992b), or cooperative learning, generally speaking, would not be the most effective instructional approaches for teaching most gifted students—unless specific individuals were either peer-oriented or required Learning in Several Ways (Learning Style Inventory scores of 60 or above). A high score on that item would be an indication that such learners either wish to learn with others or require diverse strategies to maintain interest in academic content. Certainly, a program designed for gifted and talented youngsters should capitalize on their personal sociological preferences and not be determined by persons who advocate a single approach for all students.

Previous studies of high-IQ gifted students often identified them as being formal-design (Cody 1983) and bright light (Griggs & Price 1980a) preferents. However, we now understand that those characteristics reflect the analytic inclinations of students who perform well on school tests. We also know that when global learners are permitted to work in an environment responsive to how they learn, they achieve better than they have previously (Andrews 1990). When taught with instructional resources that complement their processing style, globals achieve as well as analytics taught with complementary instructional resources (Brennan 1984; Bruno 1988; Dunn, Bruno, Sklar, & Beaudry 1990; Douglas 1979; Trautman 1979).

"The preference for high versus low structure is another element that consistently discriminates between the gifted and nongifted" (Dunn 1989a, p. 92). Dunn and Price (1980a) found that high-IQ gifted youngsters often preferred low structure and flexibility when learning. Lyne (1979) studied adults and college students and found a relationship between cognitive development and structure. Adults at the lower stages of cognitive development preferred a highly structured format, whereas those at the higher stages preferred more flexibility and diversity in learning. On the other hand, these data address high-IQ "majority" inclinations; within the total group, there were many individuals with different traits, and certainly this study has shown that many differences exist within the various talent areas. Thus, wide variations exist in the amount of structure individual gifted and talented students prefer.

INDIVIDUALIZING INSTRUCTION FOR GIFTED AND TALENTED ADOLESCENTS

Given the differences in how gifted and talented adolescents learn, and the general characteristics of gifted students across the board, any system of instruction designed for these learners will need to provide:

1. Resources responsive to each individual's strongest perceptual preference;
2. Varying levels of independence, with an accent for most on either self-pacing or teaching one's self;
3. Alternative environments responsive to personal needs for sound versus quiet, low versus bright illumination, warmth versus cool, informal versus formal seating arrangement, food and liquids, and mobility needs;
4. Options for learning alone, with a friend or two, with the teacher, and/or in varied treatments as the occasion requires; and
5. Opportunities to experiment with energy highs and lows at different times of the day.

In addition, because many gifted students score low on Responsibility, (suggesting that they are nonconformists [White 1981]), they often need to be told why what they are being required to do is important to who ever is doing the asking; to be spoken to collegially rather than authoritatively; and to be given options and choices rather than mandates.

The following instructional systems are intended as model teaching strategies. They are all appropriate for certain gifted students and not for others. Matches must be determined by consideration of the individual's intellectual, personal, and social interests, attitudes, and values. Individualized instruction can be effectively implemented on the basis of scores on the Learning Style Inventory and descriptions provided herein of responsiveness to specific approaches to selected style traits.

Instructional Strategy 1: Contract Activity Packages (CAPs)

Contract Activity Packages are self-contained units of study that teach a specific topic or theme (Dunn & Dunn 1972, 1974, 1978, 1992, 1993). They simultaneously permit self-motivated students to teach themselves and adult-motivated students to follow the teacher's outline. CAPs normally consist of six parts, each of which serves a special purpose.

1. Clearly stated *objectives* tell the student exactly what must be learned.

Sample:

• Explain at least three (3) ways in which folktales are valuable to continuing a culture.

• Name at least three (3) characteristics of most folktales.

• Name and describe at least two (2) American folktales.

• Choose a culture other than American and name and describe at least two (2) of its folktales.

• Write an original folktale.

• *Tell* a historical folktale and explain its background.

Because gifted students and those interested in a particular CAP topic understand exactly what they must learn, they are able to progress as quickly and independently as their ability and motivation permit.

2. *Resource Alternatives* are choices of materials through which students may learn the information required by the CAP's objectives. Those materials permit youngsters to learn through their strongest perceptual senses.

Sample:

• Books:

Adams, Dennis. (1992). *Tales Told by the Nomads*.

Brunner, Ron. (1991). *How to Write a Folktale: Introduction*.

Garden, Grace. (1991). *Folktales the World Over*.

Hill, David. (1988). *Japan: Through Its Folktale History*.

Johnson, James. (1982). *The Talking Animal World*.

Marschak, Maya. (1989). *Old World Spoken History*.

Nolan, William. (1987). *The Book of Irish Folklore*.

Weiss, Sarah. *Russian Folk Tales for a Long Winter Night*.

Williams, Diana. (1992). *Spanish Songs: Stories From the Past*.

• Tactual Resources:

Pic-A-Hole with Folktale Cards

Electroboard 1, 2: Folktales

Flip Chute Cards: All About Folktales

Task Cards: 1 Folktale In General; 2 Multicultural Folktale; 3 Russian Folktale; 4 American Folktale; 5 Irish Folktale; 6 Spanish Folktale; 7 Gypsy Folktale; 8 Chinese Folktale.

• Films: The Art of Folk-Telling;

Johnny Appleseed; Indian Folklore

• Kinesthetic Resources:

Floor Game on Folktale Beginnings and Endings

• Computer Packages:

Write Your Own Folktale

Better Writing: How to Do it!

- Programmed Learning Sequence: The Art of the Folktale
- Multisensory Instructional Package: Folktales

Gifted and motivated youngsters can elect to use materials that complement their perceptual strengths. As indicated here, choices may be made from among books, pamphlets, films, filmstrips, and videotapes for visual and/or auditory students; among tapes, recordings, and lectures for auditory learners; among Flip Chutes, Electroboards, Pic-A-Holes, multi-part Task Cards, Learning Circles, and table games for tactual youngsters (Dunn & Dunn 1992, 1993); and among Floor Games, interviews, trips, role playing, and so forth for kinesthetic students. Although many among the gifted enjoy two or more perceptual strengths (60 or above on the LSI), they often prefer a variety of instructional alternatives (60 or higher on Varied or Learning in Several Ways). The choice of resources appeals to nonconformists' inclinations and simultaneously provides the diversity that diminishes boredom.

3. *Small-Group Instructional Techniques* introduce and/or reinforce new and difficult information, permit further development of higher-level cognitive skills, and allow students to master the required material alone, in a pair, in a small group, or with a specialist, based on the individuals' sociological preferences (Dunn & Dunn 1992, 1993). (It is always permissible to complete a Team Learning [see Figure 3.1] or Circle of Knowledge [see Figure 3.2] independently.) Although many gifted youngsters prefer learning by themselves, with whom they choose to study is a developmental characteristic—one which emerges as a result of previous interactions with children and adults. Thus, giving bright students opportunities to learn with different people may help them develop an appreciation of others' abilities and an interest in working with them. On the other hand, be prepared that such groupings may reinforce many gifted students' perceptions of the relative ease and speed with which they can accomplish assignments independently.

4. *Activity Alternatives* require that students use the new and difficult information they have learned in a creative way by making something original (e.g., a poem, composition, script, crossword puzzle, scramble word game, Flip Chute, Pic-A-Hole, Floor Game, stage setting, dance, pantomime, an Electroboard, or an opera). Because the student has to make something, he or she engages in an activity; because he or she may choose the activity to be completed, this part of the CAP is called an Activity Alternative. Thus the Objectives describe what students are required to learn; the Resource Alternatives and Small-Group Techniques actually do the teaching; and through the Activity Alternatives, the new information is used or applied, which permits transfer and contributes to memory retention. Because the Activity Alternatives provide choices from among various sensory activities, students can use their unique talents, interests, and perceptual strengths when designing their original resources.

Figure 3.1
Sample Team Learning for Contract Activity Package

Team Learning: Folktales

1. _____   3. _____

2. _____   4. _____

Recorder: _____

Read the following passage and answer the questions at the end.

Folktales have been told around the world since before recorded history. They are an important part of the literature and culture of each group. Indeed, they often are the way that families pass along the stories of their lives from one generation to another.

One of the characteristics of folktales everywhere is that they often begin with a phrase like, "Once upon a time..." Many adults remember their childhood days fondly because that phrase, and others like it, was the beginning of a wonderful story, one they enjoyed very much. That phrase, "Once upon a time..." is the way people tell their children what happened a long, long time ago. Others phrases that mean almost the same thing are: "There once lived a ...." and "Long, long ago..." or "Once there was a ..." These phrases are ways of telling that the story that is about to be told did not happen recently; indeed, it is likely that the story happened many years ago-- perhaps centuries!

Another characteristic of folktales is that they usually have a "hero"-- a "knight in shining armor" who often "saves the day!" They also were unique because they often had animals in

Figure 3.1 (continued)

major roles (rather than people)! However, the animals in folktales had <u>human</u> traits; they could

<u>speak</u> with humans and be understood, they could act and move as humans, and sometimes they

really <u>were</u> humans who had been "bewitched"! The ability of animals to speak, act, and move

in the same ways humans do is called, 'personification"-- and that is a common characteristic

of folktales! A final characteristic of this form of communication is that folktales often used

"riddles"-- problems where someone had to be very "clever" in order to outsmart someone else--

and win a prize.

1. List at least three (3) characteristics of folktales. If you can add a fourth, you are
   exceptionally intelligent.

   _____

   _____

2. Explain what "personification" means.

3. Write the "opening line" (beginning) of a folktale.

4. Write one sentence that <u>illustrates</u> "personification".

5. Make up a mini-folktale that includes at least three (3) common
   characteristics of most folktales. Be ready to tape-record it by tomorrow
   morning.

   -or-

   Read any American folktale. Report on the way in which it reflects at least three
   characteristics of most folktales.

   -or-

   Add music to either an original or a historical folktale and <u>record</u> it for "posterity" .

45

Figure 3.2
Sample Circle of Knowledge for a Contract Activity Package

Circle of Knowledge: In 3 1/4 minutes, think of all the "opening lines" you remember that are common to folktales.

1. _____   2. _____

3. _____   4. _____

   Recorder: _____

5. *Reporting Alternatives* are ways in which students share the original resources they develop. Thus, gifted students—even those who prefer to learn alone—are required to interact with others to obtain feedback concerning the correctness of the Activity Alternative they create. Each Activity Alternative, what the youngster chooses to create, is shared with one or more classmates and/or the teacher (his or her Reporting Alternative). Thus, a CAP page lists the Objective at the top and several related Activity and Reporting Alternatives in columns below (see below). The student examines the choices permitted and elects to complete the one Activity Alternative for each objective that most matches his or her strengths—or the one that is most appealing.

Sample CAP Page on the Topic: Folktales

Objective: Explain the meaning of each of the following vocabulary words:

typical

heroine

hero

Brahmin

proverb

historical

heroic

trait

wile

grasping

greedy

ancient

exaggeration

characteristic

personification

riddle

culture

century

Activity Alternatives

1. Write an original folktale and either use each of these words in it *or* highlight the way you used their meaning in the story.

2. Make an illustrated dictionary and invite any two classmates to read it and check your words.

3. Write a poem in which you explain each of these words.

4. Make up a crossword puzzle with each of these words. Make three photocopies.

5. Make a Flip Chute and cards to teach all these words and their meaning.

Reporting Alternatives

1. Either read your folktale to two classmates *or* record it on a cassette and play it for two classmates. Have your classmates initial them to show that you used each word correctly.

2. Display your dictionary and show how you incorporated each of the above words.

3. Mount your poem on the bulletin board and invite people to read it and sign that it explained these words accurately.

4. Ask two or three classmates to complete the puzzle.

5. Share your Flip Chute cards with your friends in this class.

When students have completed one Activity Alternative for each Objective, they need to ask someone else to examine it and, if it is found to be 100 percent correct, to sign either the activity itself or a paper attesting to the accuracy of its information. When students are adult or teacher motivated (60 or above on those elements on the LSI), they may share their original resource with an adult rather than a classmate. Someone's signature on either the activity or on a paper indicates that, in that person's perception, the information is totally correct. Students are not evaluated on the attractiveness of the product but, rather, solely on the contents. Making an original activity is part of the learning process, and students are judged by what and how much they learn, not how they learn it. As concomitant skills, students engaged in CAP studies gradually learn to read carefully, evaluate, and explain differences between their perceptions and those of others.

People of any age may be gifted in one or more areas, but no one is gifted in every way. Thus, students may not all be creative, nor able to develop beautiful original resources. It is no less unfair to require everyone to be talented tactually and artistically than it is to require that all children be auditory and able to sit quietly during long periods of passive learning through lectures or readings.

6. *Assessments* (pre-, post-, and/or self-tests) permit students to bypass selected objectives by demonstrating previous knowledge and/or mastery. They also document what and how much each youngster has learned, and whether individual students are truly capable of teaching themselves effectively. When students using CAPs achieve well on that unit's posttest (the teacher establishes the minimum grade required, e.g., 90 percent), they apparently are capable of self or paired instruction. CAPs are inappropriate for students who do not achieve well with them.

Many of the gifted become bored with the repetition of instruction or assignments designed to teach classmates difficult material the gifted individual already has mastered. Thus, a pretest enables such students to bypass objectives they already have mastered.

Many gifted students, although self-structured, require feedback from the adults in their lives (60 or above on Authority Figure Present on the LSI). Thus, regardless of their self-confidence, such youngsters feel good about the grades they earn; they enjoy both performing well and the adult recognition that excellent scores provide. Other gifted youngsters, although secure in their ability, pressure themselves for a variety of emotional reasons. Some feel as if they are imposters and not as intelligent, able, outstanding, creative, or gifted as others believe they are. Some are perfectionists and want to achieve error-free grades in everything. Some enjoy learning unusual information and demonstrating their power to do so. Some want to impress others, others like competing against themselves, and still others are compulsive. Many have unusual levels of motivation and energy.

Thus, permitting these students to assess themselves so that they become aware of what they know, what they need to reinforce, and what they must continue to study serves a variety of sound emotional reasons. Certainly, it reduces the tension and pressure that just being classified "gifted" requires such young people to endure.

CAPs are attractive to motivated, persistent students who learn easily. Youngsters, particularly those with an essentially global processing style, are drawn to illustrations, anecdotes, humor, and symbols and to getting a general idea of the topic before needing to concentrate on its details. Thus, CAPs include many pictures, drawings, and, when possible, cartoons to attract student attention. When CAP designers can think of jokes or clever puns related to the CAP theme, they are inserted onto the pages in odd shapes such as rectangles, diamonds, triangles, or circles.

Use color and characters to add to the learner's understanding of the materials and to weave in comics, sayings, drawings, or quotations throughout the CAP pages. After students have used three or four CAPs, they should be encouraged to design their own by using their textbooks as the basis of the information for objectives, assessments, and small-group techniques. They can comb the library for a variety of Resource Alternatives and either develop their own Activity and Reporting Alternatives or choose from the 160 examples in *Teaching Secondary Students Through Their Individual Learning Styles* (Dunn & Dunn 1993). Non-conforming students, for whom CAPs are equally effective, thoroughly enjoy creating their own because of the many options that increase this type of youngster's appreciation of the instructional strategy.

If using CAPs with gifted students appeals to you, more explicit directions for designing them can be found in Dunn and Dunn (1993) and in a teacher in-service package on CAPs available from St. John's University's Center for the Study of Learning and Teaching Styles, which has developed a CAP bank during the past twenty years. That bank includes samples in many subjects at multiple grade levels.

Instructional Strategy 2: Programmed Learning Sequences (PLSs)

Programmed Learning Sequences (PLSs) are highly structured visual materials that teach a specific topic, lesson, or skill. They are well suited for teaching anything difficult in the curriculum because they are self-corrective, leave little room for error, and permit students to learn either independently or with peers. PLSs are designed for learners with a strong need for external direction (structure), who extract meaning by seeing either the printed words, illustrations, drawings, graphs, or tables (Dunn & Dunn 1992, 1993).

Because students with strong visual memory tend to learn most easily by beginning new instruction with visual resources followed by tactual and auditory or kinesthetic reinforcement, PLSs always include tactual devices such as Task Cards, Pic-A-Holes, or Electroboards attached to selected frames periodically for reinforcement of what had been introduced earlier (Dunn 1990a,b). These hands-on, self-instructional resources make PLSs responsive to tactual learners, too. Although CAPs are effective for many gifted students, a different type of gifted youngster tends to prefer the PLS. For those, it is highly appropriate. A tape cassette of the entire PLS is glued to its back for users either unfamiliar with the language or content, or who need assistance with the reading level, as in the case of gifted underachievers or students interested in advanced content.

A PLS always comes in a shape related to what it is trying to teach. For example, the material presented in Figure 3.3, the PLS on bookkeeping by Karen Robinson is usually presented in the shape of a ledger, whereas Bo Iglesia's PLS on how to read maps (see Figures 3.4) is shaped like a globe. Feeling the contour adds appeal for both visual and tactual students. Thus, a PLS on astrology might be shaped like an astronaut or a star; one on *Anne of Green Gables* might look like a house of that period; one on mitosis might be in the shape of a cell; and one on politics could be shaped like the White House.

A PLS has a dual title—an analytic, to-the-point title and a global subtitle that is as humorous as possible. Examples might include:

- Basic Bookkeeping: Making Dollars and Cents of It
- Measurement: The Long and Short of It
- Rocks and Minerals: A Hard Topic
- Mitosis: Breaking Up Is Hard to Do!
- Electricity: The Shocking Truth (or) Wouldn't Touch It with a 10-Foot Pole!
- Long Division: Divide and Conquer
- Photosynthesis: Light up My Life!
- Congress: A Capital Offense
- Decision Making: I May Be Wrong, But I'm Never in Doubt!

Because most computer software and books are analytic (step by step, building up through details into an understanding), they often do not hold global students' interest and attention. Thus, a PLS responsive to multiple learning styles begins with a short anecdote or story that explains the value of what must be learned and, as much as possible, relates the content to the reader's experiences (see Figure 3.5). Sometimes an imaginative story in the beginning is carried throughout the text and, at times, the character in the story actually teaches the PLS.

The PLS lists objectives that indicate to the reader (and listener) exactly what must be learned (see Figure 3.6 from "France: The French Connection" by Wendy Love). If new or unusual vocabulary will be introduced, that is listed on a separate frame (see Figure 3.7). Then, like a book, the material actually teaches the subject matter, but in very small doses (see Figures 3.8 and 3.9). The back of each frame—which is what the pages are called—gives the answers to questions previously posed on its front. Thus, after the global introduction, each frame teaches something new, the learner is questioned about what was taught on that frame and, on the reverse side, the answers are presented in both print (for the visual/analytic student) and illustrations (for the visual/global students). If the author has a sense of humor, the back of each frame also includes jokes and a bit of teasing about the content, which is very appealing to global

Figure 3.3
Sample Shape for a Programmed Learning Sequence on Bookkeeping

BASIC BOOKKEEPING
OR
MAKING DOLLARS AND "CENTS" OF IT

Bookkeepers are the scorekeepers for business. What is *business*? A
formal definition is "all commercial activities designed to sell goods
and services to customers at a profit." In other words, a group of people
that receives, spends, borrows, saves, or lends money is a business. This
could be from your paper route, to a drugstore to a manufacturing plant,
to a professional practice like a doctor's. Business is a game with many
players, where bookkeepers keep the score.

Bookkeeping is telling the owner of a business how much money the
business has made, how much has been spent, what is owned, what is
owed, and whether the business is getting better or worse.

You may be the owner of a business yourself someday, so it is
beneficial for you to understand basic bookkeeping

In this program, you will learn some basic terms and principles so that
you will be able to "keep the score" for a business.

By the time you have completed this program, you will be able to:
1. Describe a transaction and its relationships.
2. Distinguish between debits and credits.
3. Understand the concept of double-entry bookkeeping
4. Identify assets—the types of assets and their classifications.
5. Define equity—the different types and their classifications.
6. Illustrate the Accounting Equation.
7. Identify and describe a Balance Sheet

Please read each paragraph. Then write the correct answer with the
special pen tied to this program. Make sure to check your answers on
the back of each frame; you cannot continue unless you know the
correct answer. So try again and try to do better this time. If you have
answered them correctly, please continue on to the next frame.

When you finish this program, please wipe off all your answers with a
damp cloth so it will be ready for someone else to use.

Have fun and learn something new!

Figure 3.4
Sample Shape for a Programmed Learning Sequence on Reading Maps

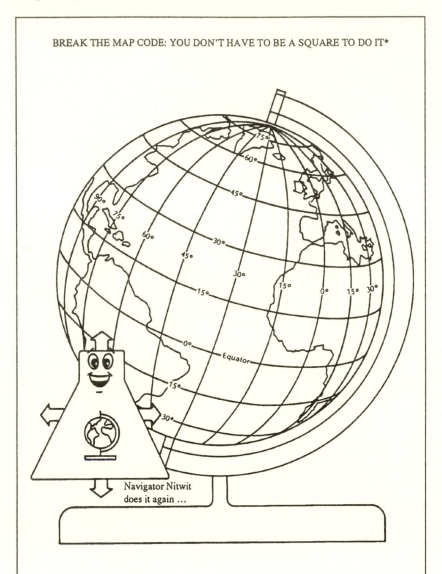

BREAK THE MAP CODE: YOU DON'T HAVE TO BE A SQUARE TO DO IT*

Navigator Nitwit
does it again ...

This Programmed Learning Sequence on "Break the Map Code" was designed by
Bodhilde Iglesias, a graduate student at St. John's University, New York, and a New
York City elementary school teacher.

Figure 3.5
Sample Introductory Frame for Programmed Learning Sequence on Bookkeeping

Frame 2

When you deliver a paper, that is a transaction. When you pay the
newspaper company, that is a transaction. When you collect from your
customers, it is a transaction. And when you pay the newspaper
company, the newspaper company pays its reporters and suppliers, and
the suppliers in turn pay their workers and suppliers. Each of these
instances (and the many others that accompany them) is a transaction. A
transaction is any business deal that involves money.

What is a transaction?

Back of Frame 2

A transaction is any business deal that involves money.

students (see Figure 3.10 from Maria Geresi's PLS "Magnets: The Power of
Attraction").

Every seven or eight frames, there is a short review that serves as an interval
test to show students how much of what needs to be learned they actually are
remembering (see Figure 3.11). Pre- and posttests evaluate the amount and
quality of total information being mastered. At the end of the PLS, the student
is reminded to rewind the tape (if that accompanying resource was used), erase
the answers that were written onto the laminated frames, and take the posttest
to see how much of the information has been retained and what needs additional
reinforcement (Dunn & Dunn 1993).

Examination of Figures 3.3 through 3.11 reveals how different this strategy
is from either a textbook or a CAP. Secondary students are taught to create
original PLSs either in pairs or in a small group (Dunn & Dunn 1993; see

Figure 3.6
Sample Objectives for Programmed Learning Sequence on France

By the time you complete this Programmed Learning Sequence, you will be able to:

1. Identify ten (10) French words for members of your family.

2. Name ten (10) basic French communication or greeting phrases.

3. List seven (7) articles of clothing in French.

4. Recognize and match five (5) French monuments with their French names.

5. Describe the significance of five (5) French monuments, the dates they were built, and their locations.

also Chapter 10); even elementary students can create mini-PLSs (Dunn & Dunn 1992; Chapter 10). However, before they can be expected to design a PLS based on the information either in a book or given to them by their teacher, students must have had experiences using three or four PLSs. Many teachers guide an entire class through the gradual development of a PLS. Thus, initially the youngsters learn in a group and eventually many outgrow the cooperative development of PLSs and create their own, either in pairs or by themselves.

Programmed Learning Sequences should be used only with gifted students who require a great deal of structure *or* with gifted underachievers who may not be performing well merely because of their inability to read or speak a language. PLSs also may be responsive to intelligent low-visual or slightly visually impaired youngsters who may hear the tape read the PLS to them

Figure 3.7
Sample Vocabulary Frame for Programmed Learning Sequence on Bookkeeping

These are some new words you will find in this program:

Vocabulary

Transaction	Any business deal that involves money
Journal	Tool for recording transactions
Chronological	In date order
Debit	On the left side
Credit	On the right side
Assets	Property the business owns
Liquidity	Easily turned to cash
Balance sheet	Financial statement showing assets, liabilities, and capital
Accounts Receivable	What customers owe
Inventory	Goods the business has for sale
Liabilities	A debt business owes to outsiders
Owner's equity	A debt business owes to owners
Accounts payable	What the firm owes
Wages payable	What the firm owes its employees
Initial capital	Money and assets the owner invests to start a business

initially; as they feel the PLS's shape and supplements, their understanding will increase gradually.

When students have strong interests in special areas (sports, art, music, dance, travel, sewing, photography, sculpturing, and so forth), but simultaneously evidence low motivation toward academics, core requirements can be taught through emphasis on whatever "turns them on." For example, the Center for the Study of Learning and Teaching Styles at St. John's University designed a PLS on "The Fast-Break Offense: Taking the Express to the Hoop." Ron Brunner, a coach in Buffalo, New York, designed a PLS to teach adults how to keep count in tennis and to teach his wrestling team to excel in that sport. By capitalizing on students' kinesthetic intelligence, he was able to develop a winning New York State team every year he taught them through their learning styles (Brunner & Hill 1992).

Figure 3.8
Sample Front and Back Frames for Programmed Learning Sequence on Bookkeeping

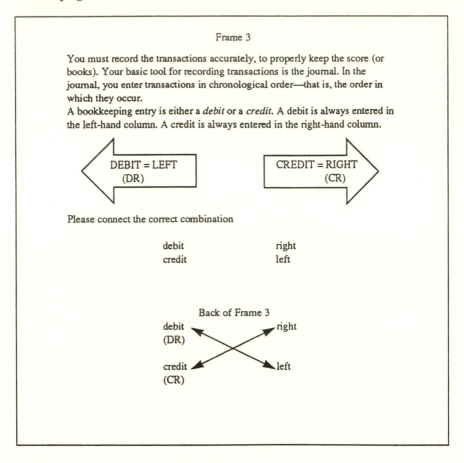

Frame 3

You must record the transactions accurately, to properly keep the score (or books). Your basic tool for recording transactions is the journal. In the journal, you enter transactions in chronological order—that is, the order in which they occur.
A bookkeeping entry is either a *debit* or a *credit*. A debit is always entered in the left-hand column. A credit is always entered in the right-hand column.

DEBIT = LEFT
(DR)

CREDIT = RIGHT
(CR)

Please connect the correct combination

     debit   right
     credit   left

Back of Frame 3
debit   right
(DR)

credit   left
(CR)

Instructional Strategy 3: Tactual/Kinesthetic Resources

Perrin (1984) and the data elicited from this research revealed that many gifted students enjoy instructional variety (60 or higher on the LSI scale Learning in Several Ways). Those youngsters often profit from the diversity of alternative instructional strategies. Although they do not necessarily require a hands-on approach (because they are capable of learning by listening to a lecture or by reading), many prefer active kinesthetic and/or tactual involvement.

Directions for Constructing a Flip Chute. Develop a Flip Chute (Figure 3.12) and a series of Flip Chute cards (Figure 3.13), each having a question on one side and an answer on the other, the flip side (Dunn & Dunn 1992, 1993).

Figure 3.9
Sample Use of Graphics for Programmed Learning Sequence on the Depression

Frame 12

Until the middle of the 1930s there was no system of unemployment insurance. If a person suddenly lost his/her job, he/she could not collect unemployment payments for a period of time until he/she found another job.

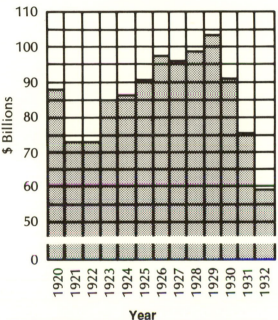

Gross National Product
1920-1932

Source: *Historical Statistics of the United States.*

(The gross national product, or GNP, is the total dollar value of all goods and services produced by a country in one year. It is considered a good measure of overall economic health.)

A program that did not exist in the United States until the mid-1930s was _____ insurance.

Figure 3.10
Sample Use of Humor and Illustrations for Programmed Learning Sequence on Magnets

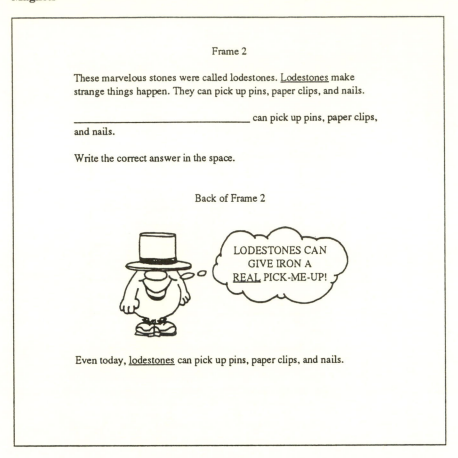

Suggest that gifted students use the Flip Chute and its cards to learn new and difficult information quickly and easily. For homework, permit the students one of three options: (1) make another tactual resource, such as a set of Task Cards, a Pic-A-Hole, or an Electroboard to teach the identical information, but differently and with illustrations; (2) use the new information they learned through the Flip Chute in a written composition, a short story, an operetta, or letter to a friend; or (3) convert that information into a Floor Game to teach or reinforce the body of knowledge.

The next day, the creative resource they develop for homework should be tested and used by two or three classmates to be certain all the information is correct. Students would have, for homework, the task of illustrating or

Figure 3.11
Sample Tactual Reinforcement Built Into Programmed Learning Sequence on France

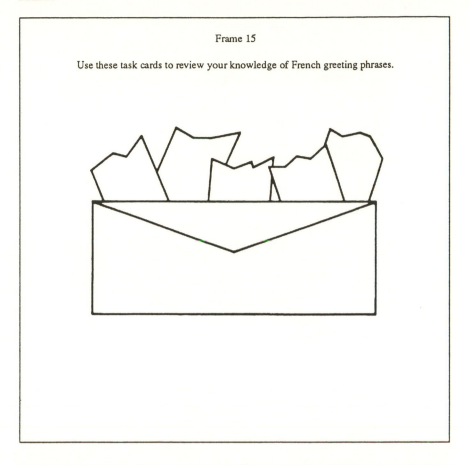

Frame 15

Use these task cards to review your knowledge of French greeting phrases.

finding pictures that represent the information on each card. They also could create their own cards with either the same, new, and/or different analogies.

Directions for Constructing a Pic-A-Hole. Figure 3.14 illustrates how the Pic-A-Hole card works. Figure 3.15 shows how to construct a Pic-A-Hole as an initial tactual resource for self, pair, or peer teaching (Dunn & Dunn 1992, 1993).

Directions for Constructing Electroboards. Figure 3.16 provides directions for constructing an Electroboard and Figure 3.17 shows a sample. Although most students pay rapt attention to what they are trying to learn as soon as the tactual component is added to instruction, Electroboards may be the single resource that consistently holds their attention. They require no more tactual involvement than Flip Chutes where an answer, once selected, is placed into the

Figure 3.12
Directions for Constructing a Flip Chute

Directions

1. Pull open the top of a half-gallon milk or juice container.
2. Cut the side folds of the top portion down to the top of the container.

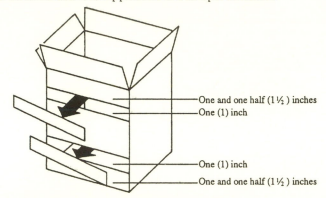

One and one half (1½) inches
One (1) inch

One (1) inch
One and one half (1½) inches

3. On the front edge, measure down both (a) 1½ inches and (b) 2½ inches. Draw lines across the container. Remove that space.
4. Mark up from the bottom (a) 1½ inches and (b) 2½ inches. Draw lines across the container. Remove that space.
5. Cut one 5 x 8 index card to measure 6½ inches by 3½ inches.
6. Cut a second index card to measure 7½ inches by 3½ inches.
7. Fold down ½ inch at *both* ends of the smaller strip. Fold down ½ inch at *one* end of the longer strip.

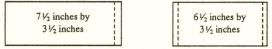

7½ inches by 3½ inches

6½ inches by 3½ inches

8. Insert the smaller strip into the bottom opening with the folded edge resting on the upper portion of the bottom opening. Attach it with masking tape.
9. Bring the upper part of the smaller strip out through the upper opening, with the folded part going down over the center section of the carton. Attach it with masking tape.

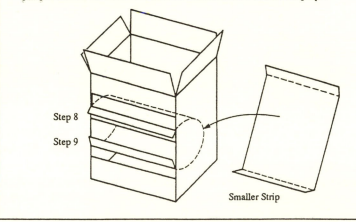

Step 8

Step 9

Smaller Strip

60

Figure 3.12 (continued)

10. Work with the longer strip, one end is folded down and the other end is unfolded. Insert the unfolded end of the longer strip into the bottom opening of the container from the outside. Be certain that the strip goes up along the back of the container. Push it into the container until the folded part rests on the bottom part of the container. Attach it with masking tape.
11. Attach the upper edge of the longer strip to the back of the container creating a slide. Secure it with masking tape about 5/8" from the top of the carton.
12. Fold down the top flaps of the container and tape them in place, forming a rectangular box.
13. Use small, 2 x 2½ inch index cards to write the question on one side and the answer upside down on the flip side. Notch each question side at the top right to insure appropriate positioning when the student uses the cards.

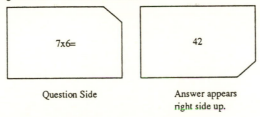

Question Side   Answer appears
                       right side up.

(Flip Chute directions were developed by Dr. Barbara Gardiner.)

Side View of Container

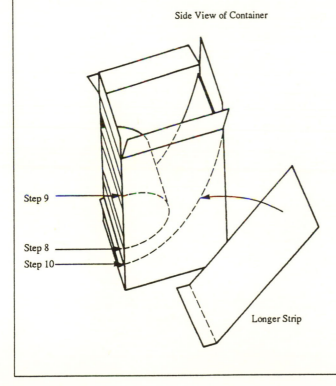

Step 9

Step 8

Step 10

Longer Strip

61

Figure 3.13
Sample Flip Chute Cards

What are the bottom two (2) chambers of the heart called?

Ventricles

The bottom two (2) chambers are the ventricles, the right and left ventricles.

What takes blood away from the heart and to other body parts?

Arteries

Arteries take blood away from the heart and bring the blood to other body parts.

What are the top two (2) chambers of the heart called?

Atria
(singular atrium)

Right and left atrium are the top two (2) chambers of the heart.

What membrane encloses the heart?

Pericardium

Pericardium is the membrane that the heart is enclosed in.

Figure 3.14
Sample Pic-A-Hole Card

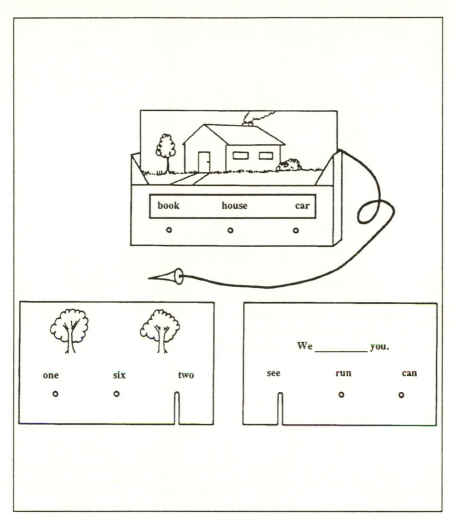

upper slot and merely needs to be caught as it emerges from the bottom opening. And, if anything, the Pic-A-Hole is more tactual, for students must choose the correct answer and then insert a golf tee into the correct hole, attempt to pull out the card, place it onto a nearby surface, and then reach for the cards and the tee again (Dunn & Dunn 1992, 1993).

SUMMARY

Use of the instructional strategies described and illustrated in this chapter will increase the pace of achievement and enjoyment of many gifted students who

Figure 3.15
Directions for Making a Pic-A-Hole

1. Cut a colorful piece of cardboard or poster board 24⅛ inches by 6½ inches.
2. Following the guide below, measure and mark the cardboard (on the wrong side) to the dimensions given. Use a ballpoint pen and score the lines heavily.

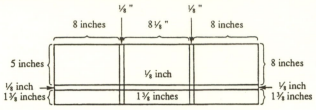

3. Remove the 1⅜ inch bracketed areas at right and left. Use a ruler and a razor or exacto knife to get a straight edge. The piece of poster board then should look like the following illustration.

4. Working on the wrong side of the center section only, follow the measurement guide given below.

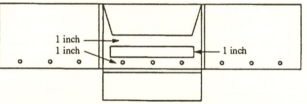

5. Remove the shaded areas with a ruler and razor or exacto knife.
6. Fold on all the drawn lines using a ruler as a guide to obtain sharp, straight fold lines.
7. Punch three holes as shown in the diagram.
8. Place an index card under the center section. Trace the openings onto the card. Remove the same areas from the index card. This will serve as a guide for placement of questions and answers, which can be written on 5 x 8 inch index cards in appropriate places. Punch holes.
9. Using 5 x 8 inch index cards, mark holes and punch them out. Use the guide for the placement of information.
10. Fold over the first side under the center section; then fold up the bottom flap; now fold over the last side. Paste or staple them together, being certain that the bottom flap is in between.

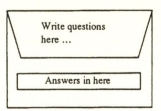

(Pic-A-Hole directions were developed by Dr. Barbara Gardiner.)

Figure 3.16
Directions for Making an Electroboard

Direction for Making an Electroboard

1. Begin with two pieces of either posterboard or oaktag cut into exactly the same size and shape.
2. List the exact questions you want the Electroboard to ask; then list their answers. Count the number of questions and divide the face of the left side of the Electroboard into evenly divided spaces so that the questions all fit on the left side.
3. Use a paper hole puncher to make one hole on the left side of the face of the Electroboard for each question you developed. Then punch corresponding holes *on the same horizontal level as the beginning of each question*—but on the *right* side; those holes are for the answers to the questions.
4. Print the questions and each answer separately in large, black, capital letters either directly on the oaktag or posterboard, or to secure very neat, attractive lines, onto *double*-line opaque white strips of correction tape. This tape can be obtained in most large stationery stores or directly from the Dennison Manufacturing Company, Framingham, Massachusetts 10701. When you are satisfied with the printing of the questions and their corresponding answers, peel the correction tape from its base and carefully place each question next to one of the prepunched holes on the left side of the developing Electroboard's face. Be certain that each is placed horizontal to the other and leaves even spaces between. Then peel off and place the answers onto the right side of the Electroboard near the other prepunched holes, but *be certain to randomize the answers so that none is on the same horizontal level as its matched question.*
5. Turn the oaktag or posterboard face over, and on its back create circuits made with aluminum foil strips and masking tape. Lay strips of aluminum foil "connecting" each question and its correct answer. Then use masking tape that is wider than the foil strips to cover each foil strip. Be certain to press both the foil and the masking tape cover so that they: (1) completely cover the punched holes and (2) remain permanently fixed.
6. Note the positions of each question and its answer so that you have a self-corrective guide in case one is necessary for substitute teachers or aides. Write the name and number (assuming you have several) of the Electroboard at the top of the code. Place into a secure place where access is available when necessary.
7. Using a continuity tester, which can be purchased in any hardware store, check every circuit to be certain that each is working. Do that by touching each question with one prong of the circuit tester and its related answer with the other prong. If the circuits were put together correctly, the tester's bulb should light. Experiment with touching several questions and *incorrect* answers (one at a time) to be certain that the bulb does *not* light.
8. Next tape the second, identically shaped and sized piece of oaktag or posterboard to the *back* of the first piece on which you have been doing all this tactile work; the second piece will serve as a cover to conceal the circuits so that your students do not know which questions are paired with which answers. Then tape the entire perimeter of both cards together, or connect the cards using double-faced tape. For the unit on France, the Electroboard was designed in the shape of France.

Figure 3.17
Sample Electroboard for France

otherwise would be restricted to traditional learning, a system with which many of them succeed academically but often lose their appetite for learning. By responding to student learning style strengths, we enable them to learn effectively and to enjoy the process. Extensive research indicates that many young people experience a reversal of their negative attitudes and poor achievement in school after their teachers begin providing instructional options through these resources (Andrews 1990; Brunner & Majewski 1990; Dunn, Beaudry, & Klavas 1989; Orsak 1990a; Perrin 1990; Sinatra 1990).

NOTES

The Contract Activity Packages, Programmed Learning Sequences, and tactual samples included in this chapter were excerpted from R. Dunn and K. Dunn, *Teaching Secondary*

Students Through Their Individual Learning Styles (Boston: Allyn & Bacon, 1993). The samples related to magnets and fairytales were from R. Dunn and K. Dunn, *Teaching Elementary Students Through Their Individual Learning Styles* (Boston: Allyn & Bacon, 1992).

Chapter 4

Counseling Gifted Adolescents Through Learning Style

Shirley A. Griggs

Dunn and Dunn developed a theoretical model of learning style, and Dunn (1989a) applied it to individualizing instruction for mainstreamed gifted children. She cited impressive evidence demonstrating that higher academic achievement and more positive attitudes toward school result when the learning environment matches the individual student's learning style preference. The Dunn and Dunn (1978) conceptualization and the empirical findings supporting it provide a strong rationale for the position that matching counseling approaches and individual learning style will increase and enhance counselee learning, growth, and development.

Griggs (1984, 1985, 1991) collaborated with the Dunns in applying the learning style model to counseling. The fundamental thrust of learning style-oriented counseling is eclectic. The counseling process begins with an assessment of individual needs and requirements for learning, including learning style preferences, and identifies a variety of counseling approaches that are compatible with them. Those adopting the approach recognize the validity of a vast array of counseling theories, maintain that no single approach can meet the needs of all counselees, and focus on selecting counseling interventions that match individual learning style. The learning style model of counseling should be introduced to practicing counselors after they are thoroughly knowledgeable concerning existing theories and techniques and the basic tenets of counseling and human development.

Although the learning style model is based on the premise of individual differences, research indicates that various special groups, including gifted children, are characterized by a core of learning style preference that distinguishes them from their peers not identified as gifted (Griggs 1984, 1985). Many gifted children will receive more help in coping with their special concerns in the social, personal, educational, and vocational spheres in a learning style-oriented counseling process.

The overall purpose of this chapter is to provide school counselors with information that will enable them to recognize the learning styles of gifted children and to utilize counseling interventions that match them. The specific objectives are as follows:

1. To increase counselor effectiveness with gifted and talented youth through identification of their individual learning styles;

2. To provide counselors with a schema for matching counseling techniques with the learning style preferences of gifted and talented youth;

3. To develop awareness among counselors regarding the special concerns of gifted and talented youth;

4. To review the research that supports a learning style approach to counseling gifted children; and

5. To discuss the findings of the international study of the gifted and talented in relation to counseling.

This chapter is divided into four sections. In the first section, the relationship of learning styles to counseling is addressed. Next, the learning style characteristics of academically gifted youth are identified. The third section of the chapter is devoted to the special counseling concerns of gifted adolescents. Finally, the findings of the international study of the gifted and talented are discussed in relation to counseling.

RELATING LEARNING STYLES TO EFFECTIVE COUNSELING

Interpretation of the Learning Style Inventory (LSI) (Dunn, Dunn, & Price 1985) is based on identifying distinct preferences—that is, those elements in which the standard scores are below 40 (low preferences) and above 60 (high preferences). If scores are in the middle range (41–59), there is no strong preference for the element and accommodations do not have to be made in terms of the learning environment. Learning alone versus peer-oriented and evening versus morning are two elements on a continuum. In these cases, scores below 40 indicate preferences for learning alone or in the evening; scores above 60 suggest peer or morning learners. Table 4.1 illustrates the interpretation of the LSI for counseling purposes.

Human development theories provide the framework for counseling students through their individual learning styles. Erikson (1950) has identified nine developmental stages. At each stage the developing person is required to cope with a specific psychosocial crisis. The acquisition of relatively positive versus relatively negative personality traits reflects the degree of success with which an individual has met these challenges. The stages, together with the psychosocial crisis postulated by Erikson for each stage, are as follows:

Table 4.1

Interpretation of the Learning Style Scales for Counselors

Elements	Score 20-29	Score 30-39	Score 40-59	Score 60-69	Score 70-80
Sound during Counseling	Always needs quiet when learning, doing homework. Use of silence in counseling facilitates understanding.	Usually needs quiet when Learning. Needs time for reflection in counseling.	Depending on the learning task, may prefer quiet or the presence of sound.	Some kind of sound (radio, recordings) enhances the learning process. Low tolerance for silence during counseling.	Consistently works in the presence of sound. Use of background music during counseling is suggested.
Light during Counseling	Always needs very low light. Eyes are sensitive and tire easily with florescent lighting.	Usually needs dim light to learn.	No strong preference for either low or high light.	Light area enhances the learning process.	Needs bright light and seeks out rooms with lost of windows when studying.
Temperature while Learning/Counseling	Prefers a cool room and may find it difficult to tolerate heat.	Usually seeks out a cool environment.	No strong preferences for temperature extremes.	Usually seeks out a warm environment.	Prefers a warm room and may find it difficult to tolerate cold.
Design during Counseling	Prefers informal design, such as circular arrangement in a carpeted area for group counseling.	Usually likes informality and diversity in design.	Depending on the learning task, may prefer formal or informal arrangements.	Usually feels more comfortable in a formal setting.	Prefers formal design; tends to work consistently in the same area at a desk/hard chair.
Motivation for Learning and Counseling	Exhibits low motivation for learning and may demonstrate resistance in counseling.	Tends to procrastinate; evidences difficulty in beginning tasks.	Vacillates between high and low motivation depending on the approaches used in counseling.	Generally highly motivated for learning and counseling processes.	Consistently well-motivated; accomplishes learning tasks with enthusiasm.

Table 4.1 (continued)

Elements	Score 20-29	Score 30-39	Score 40-59	Score 60-69	Score 70-80
Persistence during Counseling	Low level of persistence which may be evidenced by leaving counseling prematurely.	Somewhat limited time on-task; distractible.	Depending upon level of interest in counseling, may or may not persist until goals are achieved.	Generally commits self to counseling and endures until goals are achieved.	High level of persistence in counseling; works consistently to achieve goals.
Responsibility during Counseling	Is non-conforming; needs options and choices in counseling. May tend to blame others for own life circumstances.	Somewhat nonconforming; which may be evidenced in lateness or absence from sessions.	Vacillates between conforming and nonconforming behavior in counseling.	Generally follows through on commitment to counseling.	High level of responsibility in counseling; assumes responsibility for self and behavior.
High Versus Low Structure during Counseling	Responds to counseling approaches which utilize minimum structure and allow free expression (i.e., gestalt therapy).	Prefers counseling approaches which allow for minimum structure, i.e., client-centered counseling.	Prefers eclectic counseling approaches in which both active and passive techniques are utilized.	Prefers counseling approaches which define goals clearly and utilize structured techniques, i. e., behavioral counseling.	Strong needs for structured counseling approaches and concreteness, i.e., traitfactor counseling.
Learning or in Counseling Alone Versus Peers	Prefers to work things through alone; self-sufficient in many areas.	Generally prefers to resolve problems independently without peer counseling.	Depending on the situation, may seek help from peers resolve problems alone.	Generally an effective peer group member.	Peer-group counseling is the strongly preferred mode. Change is most likely to occur as a result of group activities.
Individual Counseling	Not a good candidate for individual counseling .	If given a choice, would not seek out individual counseling.	Depending upon the counseling approaches used, change may occur in individual counseling.	Generally comfortable and motivated in individual counseling.	Individual counseling is the strongly preferred mode.

72

Variety during Counseling; Sociological Structure	Generally uncomfortable with a variety of approaches; tends to favor a single mode of counseling.	Probably has a preference for a single counseling mode.	Depending upon the situation, may be open to a variety of counseling modalities.	Generally comfortable with diversity in counseling modes.	Prefers a combination of approaches in working through concerns, including alone, groups, and individual counseling.
Counseling Using Auditory Approaches	Tends to be "turned off" by talking approaches to counseling. Has difficulty listening and focusing on what is communicated.	Generally finds it difficult to participate in counseling if auditory approaches are used exclusively.	If the counselor perceived interesting and supportive, auditory approaches may be effective.	Generally auditory approaches during counseling are effective.	Responds well to auditory approaches; has good auditory memory and can recall conversations well.
Counseling Using Tactual Approaches	Tends to avoid doing things tactual, such as writing, picture drawing, etc.	There is limited interest in tactual approaches.	Does not have a strong preference for tactual approaches, but may find these approaches helpful on occasion.	Finds tactual approaches helpful when utilized during the counseling process.	Responds well to "hands on" approaches in counseling and the use of techniques such as puppetry, clay modeling, draw-a-picture, computer use.
Counseling Using Visual Approaches	Tends to be "turned off" by visual approaches in counseling such as bibliotherapy or the use of pictures or films.	Generally finds it difficult to absorb visual content.	Depending upon the situation, visual approaches may enhance counseling.	Generally finds visual approaches helpful in counseling; i.e., the use of modeling through videotaping.	Responds well to visual approaches; has good visual memory and can recall faces, scenes, places

Table 4.1 (continued)

Elements	Score 20-29	Score 30-39	Score 40-59	Score 60-69	Score 70-80
Counseling Using Kinesthetic Approaches	Very uncomfortable with kinesthetic approaches in counseling.	Prefers not to engage in action-oriented counseling strategies.	No strong feelings about kinesthetic approaches; discretion needs to be used.	Has a preference for action-oriented counseling approaches which involve body movement	Prefers counseling approaches that require body involvement such as role-playing and psychodrama.
Need for Intake during Counseling	Never has a need for intake while working.	Rarely utilizes food or drink while working.	Occasionally will use intake and find it enhances the learning process.	Often uses intake while learning.	Uses some kind of intake, such as food or drink, when working or learning.
Evening Versus Morning Energy Levels	Prefers evening hours for working, learning and studying.	Generally prefers the evening for working on tasks.	Time of day or night is relatively unimportant.	Generally prefers the morning for working on tasks.	Prefers morning hours for working, learning, and studying.
Late Morning Energy Level	Sluggish and low energy level around noon.	There is somewhat of a lull in energy level around 11:00 a.m.	Time is not a critical element here.	Generally prefers the late morning for working.	High energy level in the late morning hours.
Afternoon Energy Level	Afternoon is a poor time to schedule counseling activities.	Energy level begins to drop during the afternoon hours.	Time of day is not important; energy level is relatively constant.	Energy level begins to increase during the afternoon hours.	Afternoon is an excellent time to schedule counseling activities.
Mobility during Needed Counseling	Low need for mobility while in counseling; has the ability to sit for relatively long periods of times.	Generally prefers passive, low mobility, sedentary approaches learning or counseling.	Responsive to either passive or active approaches during counseling with no strong preferences for either.	Generally prefers action, high mobility approaches during counseling.	Prefers action-oriented approaches in counseling, i.e., roleplaying, mime, art therapy.

1. Infancy (0–2 yrs.)   Trust versus Mistrust
2. Toddlerhood (2–4 yrs).   Autonomy versus Shame
3. Early School Age (5–7 yrs).   Initiative versus Guilt
4. Middle School Age (8–12 yrs.)   Industry versus Inferiority
5. Early Adolescence (13–17 yrs.)   Group Identity versus Alienation
6. Later Adolescence (18–22 yrs.)   Individual Identity versus Role Diffusion
7. Young Adulthood (23–30 yrs).   Intimacy versus Isolation
8. Middle Adulthood (31–50 yrs.)   Generativity versus Stagnation
9. Later Adulthood (51 yrs.–)   Integrity versus Despair

Learning Style–Oriented Counseling in Secondary Schools

Students enrolled in secondary schools are predominantly in the fifth stage of development, in which the key feature is a search for identity. This stage is characterized by rapid physical changes, significant conceptual maturity, and heightened sensitivity to peer approval. The adolescent begins to think about the world in new ways that have profound implications for counseling and learning. Conceptual development results in a more flexible, critical, and abstract view of the world so that counselors can utilize techniques that involve deep levels of cognitive processing.

The fundamental question for the adolescent is: "Who am I and where do I belong?" Group identity and a strong sense of belonging facilitate psychological growth and serve as integrating forces. Negative resolution of these issues results in alienation, loneliness, and isolation. Adolescence has been described as a period of intense stress and turmoil. The adolescent is torn between a need to be a conformist and behave and think like peers or parents and a need to develop individuality and uniqueness.

Selected learning style elements remain relatively stable in individuals, such as a need for mobility versus passivity and temperature preferences, whereas other elements such as perceptual strengths, sound, and intake appear to follow the growth curve. Price (1980b) determined that preferences for tactual and kinesthetic modalities develop first, followed by visual modalities in the middle elementary school years, and lastly by auditory modalities in the late elementary and early secondary school years. Bandler and Grinder (1979) maintain that once the counselor has identified the counselee's favored representational system or perceptual strength and responded out of that system (auditory, visual, tactual, kinesthetic), feelings of trust and rapport increase. The development of auditory strengths during adolescence suggests that counselors can utilize a wide range of traditional, talk-through counseling approaches including reality therapy, client centered, cognitive, Adlerian, behavioral, and transactional analysis. For adolescents whose preferences are not auditory, a variety of interventions that accommodate visual, tactual, and kinesthetic preferences are outlined in Table 4.2.

Counseling Gifted Youth with Different Learning Style Preferences

A number of researchers have emphasized the importance of personal characteristics, such as learning style, in determining the effectiveness of one counseling method versus another. Kivlighan, Hageseth, Tipton, and McGovern (1981) asserted:

The literature on vocational counseling is replete with research in which no differences were found between various approaches in counseling. In most of the studies in which no differences between counseling methods were found, treatments were compared without regard to relevant personality variables of participants; the researchers implicitly made the uniformity assumption. (p. 319)

These investigators reported more desirable outcomes in group vocational counseling when treatment approaches and personality types (task-oriented versus people-oriented) were matched than when they were not. Similarly, Rosenthal (1977) studied the effectiveness of various counselor-training approaches on trainees with low versus high conceptual levels. He concluded that:

Comparing the results of one training method without considering trainee characteristics and learning style, as well as multiple assessment of skills, may lead to incomplete conclusions on the effectiveness of these methods. (p. 236)

Griggs, Price, Kopel, and Swaine (1984) studied the effects of group counseling on intellectually gifted sixth-grade students with different learning styles. Specifically, the study raised the following question: What are the effects of group counseling using career education interventions that are either compatible or incompatible with the learning style elements of low motivation and high need for structure versus high motivation and low need for structure? The study was conducted with a pre- and posttest experimental/control group design, using the Learning Style Inventory (Dunn, Dunn, Price 1985) to assess learning style and the Career Maturity Inventory (Crites 1978) and the Occupational List Recall Test (Westbrook 1972) as the dependent measures. A total of eight group counseling sessions were conducted with the same career education objectives but different counseling strategies. The results suggested that improvement in career awareness would be greater if students were matched to the type of counseling intervention compatible with their learning style preferences for structure and motivation.

There are a number of learning style characteristics that tend to be present in academically gifted learners. Counselors who learn to identify the learning style

Table 4.2
Secondary School Counseling Techniques and Compatible Learning Style Preference Patterns

Technique	Description	Compatible Learning Style Preference Patterns
Systematic Desensitization	An anxiety-reduction strategy involving: Verbal set (overview of technique). Identification of emotion provoking situations. Hierarchy construction. Coping responses. Imagery assessment. Scene presentation. Homework and follow-up.	Visual perception; analytical and deductive approach (left hemisphere).
Guided Imagery	The counselor asks counselees to relax, close their eyes, and create a mental picture of an event or experience. Clients share the imagery in an individual or group counseling session	Visual, auditory perceptual preferences; right brain dominant; average need for structure; varied sociological preferences.
Autobiographical Writing	The student writes an autobiography describing values, interests, goals, family, past events, etc., and shares it in a counseling session.	Tactual and auditory preferences; high structure; high responsibility.
Progressive Relaxation	In an individual or group counseling setting, the counselor directs students to tense and then relax all parts of the body progressively. Students are encouraged to apply this strategy in situations in which they feel anxious, tense, or nervous.	Accommodates either peer or adult sociological preferences; kinesthetic perceptual strength; need for high structure.
Metaphor, Parable, Allegory	Figurative language in which concepts are described symbolically or through stories or analogies.	Visual orientation; right brain dominant; global approach. May be utilized in individual, peer, or group counseling.
Free Writing	Counselees are instructed: "Conditions of tension, confusion, hostility, joy or excitement can be released through writing your feelings and thoughts freely. Keep a log of your writings to share in individual or group counseling."	Tactual perceptual strength; highly motivated and persistent; minimum need for structure.

and other personal-social characteristics of each child, and to select counseling strategies that match them, will be better able to help gifted learners.

LEARNING STYLE CHARACTERISTICS OF ACADEMICALLY GIFTED YOUTH

Although the elements of individual learning styles of gifted students may vary, several recent studies revealed a pattern of core preferences among the academically gifted in the United States that distinguish them from their peers (Griggs 1984). Gifted students are highly motivated (Kreitner 1981). They are self-motivated and independent learners (Cross 1982; Griggs & Price 1980; Price, Dunn, Dunn & Griggs 1981; Stewart 1981; Wasson 1980). Academically gifted youth are internally controlled (Cross 1982; Stewart 1981), persistent (Dunn & Price 1980; Griggs & Price 1980; Price et al. 1981), and nonconforming (Dunn & Price 1980; Price et al. 1981). Each of these preferences is discussed here, findings from the international study of the gifted and talented are reported, and implications for counseling these students are addressed.

Independent (Self) Learners

A number of studies conducted in the United States found that academically gifted students are self-learners who require a high degree of independence and autonomy when learning. They prefer large doses of independent study and generally become bored with routine and rote-memory tasks. These preferences may result in problems with authority, for these youth are frequently viewed as challenging, confrontational, and outspoken. The counselor's role as a consultant to teachers and parents is to support the student's independence and help adults deal effectively with student patterns of self-reliance. In the classroom, these students consistently prefer learning alone to the other sociological elements of peers or adults. In terms of counseling, they generally prefer individual counseling centered on self-management and self-monitoring rather than group counseling.

The international study findings partly support those previously reported for the academically gifted in the United States. Preference for learning alone was reported by the academically gifted in the United States and Israel, but not by their counterparts in the Philippines, Korea, Canada, and Guatemala. Gifted students, whose abilities were focused on domains other than the academic, indicated patterns in their preference for learning alone. Students talented in science from Korea, the United States, and Guatemala preferred learning alone, and those talented in literature from Israel, Guatemala, and the Philippines preferred learning alone. Science involves independent laboratory work and literature involves reading and writing, largely solitary activities.

Internally Controlled Learners

Previous studies of academically gifted United States students indicate that they are internally controlled or field independent. They usually are aware of their own needs, feelings, and attributes, which they experience as distinct from those of others (Witkin 1977). This distinction provides an internal frame of reference for dealing with other people and the environment in general (Perrone 1986). These students have a tendency to overcome the organization of the environment or restructure it. Generally, there is a pattern of relying more on self than on externals such as other people, chance, or luck. Field-independent children pursue active, experiental approaches to learning. This orientation has implications for counselors working with gifted students in such areas as decision making, career education, and moral development. For example, in the area of decision making, these students are more likely to generate options that are within their control and discount or fail to consider those options which involve heavy reliance on others or adherence to existing social practices or customs.

The international study of the gifted and talented did not investigate locus of control or field dependence/independence; therefore, no new findings are available in this area.

Persistent Learners

Persistence is highly correlated with indefatigability, long attention span, and ability to sustain interest and involvement over a period of time. Gifted students usually thrive on projects that demand persistence. They welcome challenging and complex tasks. Renzulli (1980) observed that gifted persons are highly product oriented. They attack a problem because they are attempting to produce a new and imaginative product. This suggests that the curriculum and the guidance program need to focus on high-level cognitive processing, reasoning, abstract thinking, and creative problem solving.

The international study revealed that academically gifted from the Philippines, Korea, and Guatemala are persistent. Also, five of the national groups talented in science, including all but those students from Canada, are persistent learners.

Nonconforming Learners

Nonconformity is associated with dissimilarity, innovation, divergent thinking, and creativity. Frequently, divergent thinking is the source of underachievement among the gifted, since traditional teachers tend to emphasize convergent thinking (Pirozzo 1981). There is overlap in the constructs of conformity and field orientation. The field-independent person is a nonconformist while, conversely, the field-dependent person is a conformist. Generally, gifted students tend toward nonconformity in terms of thought, attitudes, and behavior. Counselors need to recognize and support this uniqueness, which can take many forms.

The international study found that academically gifted from Israel and Korea were nonconforming, while similar populations from the United States and Guatemala were conforming. An additional contradictory finding was that the talented in science in the United States and Canada were less conforming than their nongifted peers, while their counterparts in Israel and Guatemala reported more conformity in comparison to the nongifted. The talented in music showed similar discrepancies, with those in the United States and Guatemala less conforming than the nongifted and those in the Philippines more conforming. Lastly, the gifted in social leadership from Israel, Guatemala, and the United States were more conforming than their nongifted peers.

It is difficult to interpret these disparate findings without a comprehensive knowledge of the philosophy of education in each of these culturally different nations. It is possible to speculate that some schools stress conformity and discipline in fostering gifted and talented youth, while others encourage nonconformity and innovation in working with a similar population.

Highly Motivated Learners

Highly motivated persons have a strong drive that propels them to action. They are capable of effecting changes within themselves with a minimum of counseling structure and counselor reinforcement. Gifted students are highly motivated in terms of academic achievement, self-growth and development, and learning. In helping these students change self-defeating behaviors (such as shyness, overweight, procrastination, or moodiness), the counselor generally will discover that counselee monitoring of change is more effective than counselor monitoring. Effective self-monitoring involves five important steps: discrimination of a response, recording of a response, charting of a response, display of data, and analysis of data (Thoresen & Mahoney 1974). In overcoming shyness, for example, gifted students can monitor themselves by learning to discriminate between shy versus assertive responses, recording each incident related to these behaviors, developing a chart to record these behaviors over a period of time, displaying the data so that they act as a reinforcer, and analyzing the data to determine patterns and circumstances that result in goal attainment.

The international study revealed that a significant number of the gifted and talented were more parent motivated and/or preferred to learn with authority figures present. Students with these preferences included the talented in dance (Israel, Korea, United States, Canada), music (Israel), social leadership (Philippines and United States), and drama (Guatemala).

In summary, research studies indicate that gifted academically and talented students have a core of learning style preferences that distinguish them as a group from other students, and that they differ by culture and by domain. Findings that many are independent learners, internally controlled, persistent, nonconforming, and highly motivated suggest that school counselors can use a broad range of techniques and strategies. These can focus on high-level cognitive processing, reasoning, abstract thinking, creative problem solving and self-monitoring. However, it is important to recognize that assessment should extend beyond group differences, for within the gifted group there are broad differences as well as similarities in terms of learning style preferences. Individual differences among the gifted suggest that counselors need to assess each individual's learning style preferences and devise interventions that are congruent with those specific preferences.

SPECIAL COUNSELING CONCERNS OF GIFTED YOUTH

Gifted young people need support to ensure healthy intellectual, emotional, and career development (Kerr & Miller 1986). There are some common concerns among significant numbers of academically gifted and talented adolescents, which are related to their unique characteristics and the ways they are perceived by other youths and adults. These concerns frequently become the content of counseling sessions. In my work in supervising counselors of the gifted, I have identified theme areas that present special problems for the gifted, including peer issues; expectations of teachers and parents; decision making; competition versus cooperation; possible feelings of isolation, uncertainty, and anxiety; and perfectionism.

Peer Issues

Everyone has the need for affiliation with others, but during the stages of puberty and adolescence, unusually high importance is placed on peer friendship and acceptance. Most young people do not want to seem "different" from their peers; they seek a sameness in appearance, dress, codes of behavior, values, language, and expression. One gifted student made the following comment:

I'm not a social outcast or anything, but sometimes I feel people my own age just don't understand me because I'm gifted. They tease me a lot. I wish my friends would accept giftedness as being a good thing. (Galbraith 1983)

Gifted children sometimes find it hard to find acceptance among peers because their goals and interests might be very different. Whereas gifted students are more popular than are less able peers at the elementary school level, this popularity diminishes significantly in high school, especially for academically gifted girls (Austin & Draper 1981). Such a readjustment of social status and the concomitant changes in behavior that may be required of bright adolescents may become a source of concern or anxiety. These problems may be compounded if the gifted adolescent is accelerated in school so that his or her classmates are two or more years older. Counselors can support gifted counselees by valuing their individuality and providing opportunities for the expression of feelings. These youngsters should be affirmed for striving to develop their uniqueness— part of the process of searching for an identity.

Expectations of Teachers and Parents

One of the hardest things for teachers and parents of gifted and talented adolescents to do is *not* to assume that emotional maturity will necessarily equal intellectual ability (Prichard 1985). Frequently, gifted children are expected to excel in every area, and they complain that adults expect too much.

Frequently, the school day is not organized to accommodate gifted youth and is typically divided into a number of periods of 30 to 50 minutes each. Exceptionally gifted youth have intense powers of concentration and typically learn by total immersion (Tolan 1985). Whatever subject claims their attention becomes an obsession until they feel that they have mastered it. They dislike repetition and drill, which constitute a sizable amount of time in regular classrooms. The counselor needs to function as an advocate of the gifted, stressing the importance of individual accommodation through directed and/or independent study.

Decision Making

The process of decision making may be problematic for the gifted because some excel in many areas simultaneously. Frequently, gifted and talented adolescents are overextended in terms of sports, studies, hobbies, and pursuit of the arts. At the secondary school level, they tend to assume leadership positions in the extracurricular program and are frequently involved with student government, drama, journalism, music, or language clubs. They may have difficulty selecting courses at the secondary school level, owing to broad interests and high aptitude in many disciplines. To some extent, the process of decision making involves identifying and delimiting options so that choices can be made from a smaller field. However, gifted youth frequently have difficulty with the focusing and delimiting process, so that decision making may be delayed. The role of the counselor is to help gifted youth engage in introspection in order to identify strong interests, aptitudes, and intellectual strengths so that options and choices are clearly identified and evaluated.

Competition versus Cooperation

Gifted youth generally respond well to academic competition in the form of grades, honors, contests, awards, and scholarships. They frequently possess the motivation, persistence, and task commitment necessary to excel in the academic areas. However, also of importance is learning to become an effective team member and to achieve excellence through cooperation with others. Gifted youth can become disenchanted in the process of working with a team when they perceive that the goal can be achieved more efficiently through their independent efforts. Counselors need to provide opportunities for group counseling of gifted and nongifted youth that bring about their working together to resolve crucial issues such as peer pressure, independence, dating, and loss. The gifted can benefit from such group work because the options and solutions generated in these problem-solving groups are often more creative and analytic than those provided by a single individual.

Dealing with Feelings

The emotional development of gifted youth is viewed by most school counselors as equal in importance to their cognitive development. Learning style preferences for nonconformity and independent learning may result in feelings of isolation and loneliness. Gifted youth can benefit from counseling aimed at helping them get in touch with their feelings and gaining insight into the differences between loneliness and solitude. Frequently, gifted and talented youth engage in solitary activities (reading, problem solving, contemplation) to a greater extent than their nongifted friends, and such activities provide sources of satisfaction and fulfillment, if not judged atypical or unhealthy by others.

Generally, the moral development of the gifted parallels cognitive development, and there is concern regarding social and political issues during adolescence. Gifted youth are likely to be more disturbed by social injustices and the threat of nuclear war because they often have reached a higher stage of moral development than their peers. Rather than experiencing a sense of despondency and despair, youth need to be helped to gain a sense of empowerment in working for change. Through bibliotherapy—that is, reading about persons who have effected positive social change—and involvement in community service through volunteerism, the gifted can become active in meaningful change.

Gifted adolescent girls are particularly vulnerable to the challenges of adolescence as their social and physical development begins to take precedence over their intellectual and academic endeavors. As a result of cultural stereotypes, gifted adolescent girls may be faced with conflicting social messages about success. Values such as marriage, femininity, physical beauty and poise, modesty, dependence, and unselfishness may be stressed before academic achievement and fulfilling, challenging career preparation (Blackburn & Erickson 1986). Most gifted women fail to develop their abilities to the maximum professional attainment as they respond to pressures to conform to specific sex roles and fear success as an isolating goal.

Talented adolescents are frequently faced with a need for exceptional self-discipline if they aspire to excel in their area of exceptionality. Aspirations of competing nationally and/or internationally in such fields as music, art, dance, creative writing, drama, science, and athletics often require long hours of daily practice, resulting in feelings of despondency provoked by denial of basic social and personal needs. Counselors need to be sensitive to the pressures that these adolescents experience from parents and mentors and help them to clarify their personal aspirations and goals.

Perfectionism

Too often, gifted young people believe that the only acceptable level of performance is perfection; effort is merely a means to an end. Thus, when perfection is not reached, even 97 percent may constitute failure (Delisle 1982). This need to be perfect can immobilize the adolescent, resulting in limited risk taking and the lack of initiative in personal, social, and academic arenas. Adolescents need to become involved in bibliotherapy. Through reading about the disappointments, mistakes, and failures of great and gifted persons, they can gain the insight necessary to realize that failure is an opportunity to learn and achieve at an ever higher level.

FINDINGS OF THE INTERNATIONAL STUDY OF THE GIFTED AND TALENTED

The most significant finding of the international study of the gifted and talented was a strong preference for learning through tactile and kinesthetic perceptions. In all nations in which the study was conducted, many gifted and talented students in the various domains indicated a preference for learning through tactile and kinesthetic experiences. This finding suggests that counselors of the gifted and talented need to employ action-oriented strategies and experiental activities in working with this population. Whereas elementary school counselors regularly employ kinesthetic-based activities in play media with children—using dolls, puppets, clay, and toys—secondary school counselors most frequently use talk-through counseling approaches, as exemplified in behavioral, reality, rational-emotive, and client-centered theories. However, based on the findings of this international study of the gifted and talented, these approaches are the least effective and counselors need to retool to meet the needs of this population.

A number of counseling strategies are identified and discussed here that are predominantly kinesthetic or experiential in design. These strategies include role play, psychodrama, movement therapy, and field trips.

Role Play

A technique designed to help counselees develop effective interpersonal skills is role playing. Within a small group of approximately eight students, an interpersonal situation that involves conflict is identified by a member. The group member, who has experienced the conflict, describes the situation and the persons involved. In the first role play, the student plays himself or herself and the counselor plays the antagonist using body movement, gestures, and facial expressions to convey feelings. After the group provides feedback and identifies the factors that contribute to a win-lose outcome, roles are reversed with the counselor modeling effective communication, using both body language and dialogue. Finally, the script is reenacted with the student demonstrating effective communication that results in a win-win situation.

Psychodrama

Created and developed by J. L. Moreno, psychodrama is a group technique that allows a counselee to act out past, present, or anticipated life situations in order to gain deeper understanding, experience catharsis, and develop effective skills. The psychodrama consists of a director (usually the counselor who produces the psychodrama), a protagonist (the student presenting problem), the auxiliary egos (significant others in the protagonist's life), and the audience (other group members). The psychodrama includes the warm-up phase (the director interviews key players in terms of problem and present awareness), the action phase (the protagonist reenacts the encounter with auxiliary egos dramatizing the event), and the sharing and discussion phase (the protagonist processes the experience) (Moreno 1983).

Movement Therapy

Movement experiences can facilitate change in the endocrine and muscular areas that result in changes in the psychological condition of the individual. The methodology used by movement therapists is varied and may include utilizing images, memories, fantasies, or body awareness as a starting point. Movement therapy in a school is not therapy per se, but a technique that facilitates self-awareness and sensitivity (Balazs 1982). An example of a movement therapy technique that might be used in group counseling is as follows:

Counselor: Think of a feeling, such as joy. How could we express joy with movement? Let's explore it. Choose a partner and face each other. Express joy with your hands— show a happy hand, happy fingers! Good! Now let's see your happy shoulders! Will you stand up now and dance with your partner, communicating in your dancing how much you enjoy it?

Discussion: Let's sit down for a moment and talk about how it felt to move with happy, joyful movements. (Balazs 1982)

Almost every emotion or feeling can be portrayed in movement, including joy, anger, distress, disgust, sadness, or frustration. Gifted and talented children find improvisation stimulating and the insight gained as a result of movement therapy makes the discussion and follow-up of the activity challenging.

Field Trips

One of the major developmental tasks of the adolescent is career decision making. During the high school experience, students need to become familiar with the world of work and begin to assess themselves in relation to job opportunities. Frequently, gifted and talented students have difficulty with decision making, owing to their multiple abilities and aptitudes, and de-selecting or eliminating possible career choices can be a painful process that is oftentimes delayed. Therefore, secondary schools need to develop strong career education programs that provide students with hands-on experience obtained through mentorship programs, field trips to businesses and industries, and cooperative programs that bring a variety of career role models into the classroom. After exposure to these career experiences, follow-up activities can be planned to accommodate the learning style preferences of individual students, including writing about the experience, preparing oral reports, and discussing student reactions in small groups. Actual job experience can provide the adolescent with some fundamental information needed for career decision making, such as a preference for working with people, data, or things; satisfying and dissatisfying job functions; and identifying important variables in the work setting that either enhance or impede work effectiveness.

CONCLUSION

School counselors are important in the lives of academically gifted and talented adolescents. Research findings indicate that gifted children have a core of learning style preferences that distinguish them from their nongifted classmates. However, the intragroup differences are greater than the intergroup differences. This mandates that we assess each child individually and select counseling interventions that respond to preferences. Counseling through individual learning styles can provide a powerful tool in helping each child achieve maximum realization of potential, both academically and personally (Griggs 1991).

Chapter 5

Giftedness, Creativity, and Learning Style: Exploring the Connections

Donald J. Treffinger and Edwin C. Selby

Three major goals are addressed in this chapter. First, we identify and summarize briefly some contemporary views of giftedness. Second, we consider a contemporary understanding of creativity. Third, we identify several significant connections among giftedness, creativity, and learning style.

In the last two decades, interest has grown substantially and rapidly in each of the three areas represented in the chapter's focal points—giftedness, creativity (and the more generic thinking skills theme), and learning style. The three broad areas share several common attributes. Each addresses a complex dimension of human performance. There have been many different, and sometimes incompatible or at least inconsistent, descriptions and analyses of each. There is a profusion of theories, models, viewpoints, systems, instruments (and just plain opinions, too) about each area. This has led to considerable controversy among proponents of one view or another and, all too often, to confusion among educators, trainers, or other practitioners who look to the experts in each field for guidance concerning applications. All three areas always stimulate spirited discussion among educators, trainers, researchers, or theorists, from those who are energetic proponents of particular models, to those who doubt the utility or very existence of any of them as identifiable constructs in the social or behavioral sciences. In each area, too, practitioners seek answers to questions about which research is unclear or perhaps even nonexistent; many approaches or models are extolled, some unhindered by the absence of any supporting evidence. Finally, each of the three areas has been the focus of much research, development, and training effort in recent years; thus, each area is in itself vibrant, dynamic, and challenging at many different levels of inquiry and application.

THE NATURE OF GIFTEDNESS

Our first task is to summarize briefly three important ways in which our ideas about giftedness are expanding. Significant paradigm shifts are evident in modern views of the nature of giftedness, in new views and models of identification, and in the nature of school programming (e.g., Dunn, Dunn & Treffinger 1992; Treffinger 1986, 1989, 1991a, 1991b).

Traditional views of the gifted child or the gifted person considered giftedness as a categorical index. Referring to someone as gifted designated their status or placement in a distribution of people, based primarily on test scores or some other objective, quantifiable criterion. Modern approaches view giftedness as a more complex, qualitative, and developmental construct. In this view, giftedness represents a set of potentials or qualities that are associated, over a sustained period of time (which may be measured in years, not weeks or months), with high levels of performance or accomplishment in any endeavor. *High level* implies quality of work, and frequently also suggests a contribution of creative merit—unique, unusual, or original work. *Performance* or accomplishment implies an end result (which may or may not be a concrete object or product) of worth to the person alone or, in the larger sense, for the enjoyment or benefit of others. The modern view does not associate giftedness with a label that will be applied only to a very small group of people acknowledged to be intellectually superior with respect to a fixed set of criteria. Instead, giftedness represents the fulfillment of talent or the realization of human potential. We do not hold that everyone is gifted, since it is obviously untrue that every talent in every person will be realized in high levels of accomplishment. But we do hold that everyone has significant potential, so anyone might find and develop talents in meaningful and impressive ways. In this sense, "time will tell," or history will determine whether or not it is appropriate to refer to someone as gifted. This view of giftedness leads to efforts to find and nurture the best in people, rather than use arbitrary formulas or criteria to sort, categorize, and label individuals.

Views and Models of Identification

A conception of giftedness that is inclusive, dynamic, and developmental necessarily creates a foundation for a new approach to identification as well. Traditional procedures focus heavily on using test scores, rating scales, or checklists to determine whether an individual belongs to the category of concern (in this case, the gifted). One attempts to judge whether or not a student is really gifted. Newly emerging paradigms hold that an entirely different set of questions must be considered, and that the fundamental purposes of identification must be reexamined. The questions focus more on efforts to find student strengths, talents, and sustained interests; to seek their best potentials; and thus to determine their needs. As we turn our focus away from identifying students for placement in a category, we shift toward a new focus on searching for needs, opportunities to expand student strengths, and ways to narrow any observed gaps between the student's needs and the services presently offered. This is more than just a diagnostic process, then; it is a formative or developmental process in which we attempt to recognize and nurture talents.

Nature of School Programming

The third major shift in contemporary gifted education involves movement away from a single, fixed program presumed to meet the needs of the gifted student (as though the student and the needs were the same, across all cases), and toward a richer, more diverse array of programming options. To the extent that we broaden our view of the nature of giftedness, and work to accomplish a more inclusive and flexible view of identification, we must be prepared to recognize the need for many and varied responses. Modern approaches to programming for giftedness involve identifying, supporting, and, as needed, creating a variety of different services to serve many students' needs in many ways. They move away from the resource room or pull-out program as a single mode of delivery, and increase the emphasis on working in, through, and then extending beyond, the instructional program and the regular classroom.

A CONTEMPORARY VIEW OF CREATIVITY

Whenever the word *creativity* comes up in discussion, it is likely to be used in as many different ways as there are people in the group. It would be helpful if everyone used the same definition, but efforts to stipulate or gain consensus are likely to encounter much resistance, since group members begin with different orientations and perspectives, leading them to emphasize different aspects of creativity. Rhodes (1961) proposed a structure of four major dimensions for understanding creativity: *person, process, product,* and *press*. Often referred to as the 4 Ps of creativity, these categories have helped many people to understand that creativity is a multidimensional or multifaceted phenomenon, and to clarify the assumptions and relative emphasis that one person or another employs to describe, define, measure, or nurture creativity. Rhodes's categories can readily be misinterpreted, however. The terminology of *press*, for example, has often seemed unclear. It also does not seem to serve as well today as in 1961, in light of the expanding body of theory and research on contextual or environmental factors that support or inhibit creativity and innovation. In addition, the term *person* may suggest a clearer, sharper distinction between "creative people" and others, who become by exclusion, "not creative people," than is appropriate today. A more contemporary view holds that creativity can be enhanced, nurtured, and expressed in a variety of ways by many people. Finally, despite their alliterative connection, the presentation of the 4 Ps does not illustrate clearly their interrelationships or the dynamics of a more holistic concept of creativity.

Figure 5.1
Components of Creative Productivity

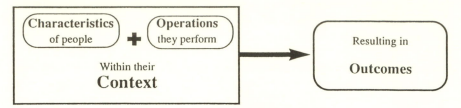

Treffinger, 1988, 1991©; Treffinger, Tallman & Isaksen, in press. Reproduced by permission.

An alternate, and perhaps more contemporary, description of the basic components of creativity may thus be valuable to consider.

One attempt at such an alternative is the COCO model (Treffinger 1988, 1991c; Treffinger, Tallman & Isaksen, in press), which is presented in Figure 5.1. This model describes four basic components, from which creative productivity results:

1. The *characteristics* that people possess and use, including, for example, their cognitive abilities, personal traits, intrinsic motivation, learning styles or psychological types, and creativity styles;

2. The *operations* or strategies and techniques they employ to generate and analyze ideas, solve problems, make decisions, and manage their thinking;

3. The *context* in which they must function, including the broad, stable influences often described as culture, the more specific and immediate or situational dimensions suggested by climate, the personal and interpersonal influences and skills involved in productivity (such as group dynamics, communication skills, and collaborative skills), and the physical setting or environmental resources or constraints in which people function; and

4. The *outcomes* that result from their efforts, which can be analyzed using a variety of specific criteria.

Learning Styles

Our understanding of giftedness and creativity has also been influenced by recent theory and research on learning style. As Dunn, Beaudry, and Klavas (1989) argued, all people approach new learning situations through their unique set of preferences or style, derived from both genetic influences and experience. Conti and Welborn (1986, p. 20) defined style as the pervasive qualities of a person that persist even as situations change. Miller, Alway, and McKinley (1987) differentiated between learning style, as a general or pervasive approach to dealing with learning situations, and learning strategies, or particular activities or techniques subsumed under a style. Researchers have identified an expansive array of factors or elements that may be used to describe or explain an individual's learning style. A number of theories and models for defining learning styles have been proposed, and inventories, checklists, and assessment instruments have proliferated. Unfortunately, not all of these have been accompanied by soundly designed, carefully conducted experimental studies of validity and reliability. Some instruments appear to be deficient in almost all the major criteria described as essential by the American Educational Research Association and American Psychological Association's standards for educational tests and measures. Such scales derive their appeal only from the charismatic presentations and energies of their developer-promoters, and as a result, the entire area of learning styles has been met with skepticism among some rigorous scholars. Davis and Schwimmer (1981) proposed criteria for assessing research-based learning style models. They argued that an effective model must be sufficiently broad to encompass many possible differences, yet sufficiently narrow to make possible the development of categories for analyzing those differences systematically. In addition, an effective approach must be well structured so it can be organized and communicated in a meaningful form, yet adequately flexible to incorporate findings from many sources. It must provide enough stability to define general preferences, but remain open-ended enough to provide for within-group differences.

Nonetheless, models and instruments have proliferated and have been reviewed and compared in depth in a number of sources (e.g., Claxton and Murrell 1987; Curry 1987; DeBello 1990; Dunn, Beaudry, and Klavas 1989; Dunn, DeBello, Brennan, Krimsky, and Murain 1981; Kirby 1979). Several approaches to studying personal types, styles, and preferences have been developed and supported by extensive research programs. Among those we consider to have the strongest base of supportive evidence are the Dunn and Dunn, and Price Learning Styles Inventory (LSI), Kirton's Adaption-Innovation Inventory (KAI), and the Myers-Briggs Type Indicator (MBTI). Our challenge in this chapter is to identify the significant connections among these three, to search for the important commonalities and thus clarify the implications of those connections for practice and future research.

Dunn, Dunn, and Price Learning Styles Inventory. The learning style model developed by Dunn and Dunn, and the related inventories developed by Dunn, Dunn, and Price, examine the person's learning style in relation to twenty-two dimensions classified into four broad categories: environmental, physical, sociological, and emotional. Their instrument yields scores for the specific variables associated with each of these dimensions, determining whether the variable is or is not a relevant factor for the person, is a preference (that is, desirable for the person but not necessarily essential for successful performance in demanding tasks), or is a factor of the person's style (that is, a consideration essential to successful performance, especially in new and challenging tasks). Not all twenty-two variables influence strongly any person's successful performance; the Dunns's research suggests that, for most people, approximately six to ten variables represent factors, or strong needs, within that person's self. Research on the nature of these styles, and their implications for learning and work performance, have been conducted from early childhood through adulthood, and have been reported in a wide variety of books (e.g., Dunn and Dunn 1978; Dunn & Griggs 1988b) and educational and psychological journals. The work of the Dunns and their associates in learning style has been evaluated very positively in several published national reviews of instruments purporting to assess learning styles (e.g., Curry 1987; DeBello 1990; Kirby 1979; Sewall 1986). (For extensive research bibliographies that are updated regularly, contact Dr. Rita Dunn, c/o Center for the Study of Learning and Teaching Styles, St. John's University, Grand Central and Utopia Parkways, Jamaica, NY 11439.)

Kirton Adaption-Innovation Inventory (KAI). Michael Kirton, of the Occupational Research Centre at Hatfield Polytechnic Institute in Great Britain, developed a theory proposing that individuals differ in their approach to creativity, displaying one of two general preferences. He distinguished between adaptors, who apply their creativity to bring about change and growth gradually or systematically, remaining within the accepted structure or paradigm; and innovators, who express and use their creativity through efforts to change existing paradigms or bring about entirely new and different structures. Kirton (1976) described a number of behavioral indicators that differentiate adaptive and innovative styles, and developed the Kirton Adaption-Innovation Inventory (KAI) to assess an individual's preference for one style or the other. Kirton's theory and instrument have been used as the focus for many research studies, in a variety of different sociocultural contexts and in a number of different occupational settings. These studies have resulted in the creation of a substantial body of published evidence generally supportive of Kirton's theory and of the psychometric adequacy of the KAI. The Adaption-Innovation theory and the KAI have also been described elsewhere by Kirton (1987, 1988), and reviewed extensively by Mudd (1987). (Bibliographies of recent publications and research in progress can be obtained from Michael Kirton, Occupational Research Centre, Hatfield Polytechnic, PO Box 109, College Lane, Hatfield, Hertfordshire, England AL10 9AB.)

Myers-Briggs Type Indicator. The MBTI was developed to translate the concepts of Swiss psychologist Carl Gustav Jung regarding personality types into a practical assessment methodology. Although the MBTI is a measure of psychological type, and thus not a learning style assessment in the same sense as discussed in this book, it reveals important differences among people and provides insights for understanding and working with them. The instrument represents an effort to help people understand their preferences and unique strengths; it is concerned with the "constructive use of human differences." The MBTI provides the person with feedback regarding his or her preferences in four major dimensions: Sources of stimulation (introversion or extraversion); ways of perceiving (sensing and intuition); ways of making decisions (thinking and feeling); and ways of dealing with the outside world (judging and perceiving). These four dimensions yield one of sixteen profiles, or "types," for each respondent. There is a very extensive body of research and interpretative literature regarding the

MBTI and its applications with adolescents and adults. An extensive technical manual is available (Myers & McCaulley 1985). (For information about the MBTI and the literature supporting it, contact: CAPT, The Center for Applications of Psychological Type, 2720 NW 6th Street, Gainesville, FL 32609.)

Distinguishing Level and Style

By far the most compelling area of common concern involves the need to differentiate level and style. Dembo (1988) pointed out that cognitive or learning style measures put value on a variety of traits and the degree to which those preferences are observed among individuals. In this way, they differ sharply from traditional ability measures, which focus on the value of possessing more of the particular dimension being measured. Traditional approaches to giftedness have emphasized, "How much ability does a person have? Does he or she have enough (of whatever we are looking for) to be designated gifted?" Similarly, many years of research have attempted to isolate the special characteristics of highly creative people, or to distinguish highly creative individuals from their less creative peers. We have emphasized the question, "How creative are you?" In both cases, we have viewed the problem as one of sorting and categorizing: highly gifted or creative, average in ability or creativity, and not very creative or gifted. Arguments have raged about distinguishing giftedness from genius; separating giftedness, creativity, and talent; or even about what specific scores should be used to establish appropriate cutoff points for these categories. Sternberg (1990) pointed out that a glaring difficulty in such efforts is that they inevitably become self-maintaining. Educators frequently assume that anyone beneath a certain cutoff point cannot be successful, gifted, or creative. Then they use that cutoff point to deny program opportunities to individuals below the cutoff. Thus, no students below the cutoff have the opportunity to demonstrate that they could succeed in those programs. This, in turn, reinforces the perception of their inability or lack of qualification. The evidence of experience in many fields—classroom teachers who report "unexpected" performances of students, social psychological research (e.g., Amabile 1989) describing the "extraordinary accomplishments of 'ordinary' children," or the ability of adult writers to accomplish creative work beyond their presumed level of "talent"(Block 1988)—affirms the importance of not remaining confined to preconceived, fixed notions of ability or level of creativity or giftedness.

Contemporary views of giftedness and creativity have thus been influenced powerfully by research and theory on styles; indeed, they have gained an entirely new agenda and strike new questions at their very essence. Through attention to style research and theory, the emerging questions with respect to giftedness are "How might my giftedness be expressed and developed?" "How might we discover, respect, and nurture the child's strengths and talents?" Instead of asking how creative a person is, we ask, "How are you creative?" But while it is very important to distinguish between level and style, and to recognize the importance of style in shaping modern views of both giftedness and creativity, we must also take caution not to force these distinctions into an oppositional, one versus the other view. Success and productivity arise from the confluence of level and style.

Another clear and very important message arising from the level-style issue is that the origins of talent and high-level creative productivity are complex and multidimensional. We should not expect a single score (nor even a single index that is a composite of several scores) to meaningfully differentiate people in relation to giftedness or creativity. Instead, it will be more valuable for us to build a profile of an individual's characteristics, abilities, styles or preferences, and interests. A comprehensive profile must also take into account various aspects of the individual's experiences and skills in using a variety of operations or strategies, the context in which the person functions, and the kind of outcomes toward which the person's efforts will be directed. The COCO framework (see Figure 5.1) suggests, therefore, that giftedness or creativity are not simply traits present or absent to some extent in a person. They are not fixed categories that you have or do not have entirely within yourself. Rather, they are extensively influenced by experience, setting, and outcome. Information about styles, which may be drawn from different instruments or approaches, can be important in relation to each of the COCO components; Figure 5.2 summarizes some of the key style questions for each component.

Considering level and style has thus had major impact on research and practice in the areas of giftedness and creativity. Figure 5.3 illustrates and summarizes some of the major distinctions between level and style in relation to four important areas of concern in giftedness and creativity. In Figure 5.3, note that one would ask very different questions, pursue very different goals, and employ different activities in each of the four areas of concern when operating from only one perspective or the other ("level versus style"). It is clear, however, that both perspectives add valuable information and insights, and that they are not necessarily incompatible. The key assessments, major emphases, principal goals, and key tasks from both level and style contribute in important ways to creative accomplishment. Our major concern, however, is that both giftedness and creativity have too often and for far too long been considered primarily, or even exclusively, from the level of perspective alone.

Keeping in mind the nature and extent of changes in our views of the nature of giftedness, identification, and programming, many specific connections with learning styles can also be identified. As educators seek to be more effective in recognizing and responding to the unique characteristics, strengths, and talents of individual students, and to developing instructional activities that are responsive to student needs, knowledge of learning styles can be extremely valuable. Taking students' individual learning styles into account provides a specific, theoretically sound, and research-based method for better recognizing student strengths and talents, and for identifying practical ways to make instruction engaging, challenging, and successful (Dunn, Dunn, & Treffinger 1992). Numerous studies in the early to mid–1980s used traditional "level" variables

Figure 5.2
Learning Styles and the Components of Creativity

Components of Creative Productivity	Connections With Learning Style
Characteristics	"How am I creative?" is a more useful question than, "How creative am I?" What are my strengths? How do I learn best? What is unique about me? How can I create a learning or working environment that will bring out my best? How do I channel and direct my creative energies? How am I different from those around me? How do I need them? What do I offer them?
Operations	In learning new processes or strategies, how might I use my style and preferences best? What techniques fit my style best? Why do some strategies seem to work better than others for me? What conditions make it most difficult for me to learn and use strategies? How can I use my natural strengths? Will I focus more on making things better or doing things differently?
Context	What environmental conditions seem to enhance or inhibit my performance? What internal conditions distract me, interfere with my efforts, or create barriers or obstacles for me? How can I establish and maintain the most productive environment? What would be the best team for me? How can I contribute best to a group?
Outcomes	What outcomes will result from my effort, and how will they reflect my style? Given my style, what form will my creative efforts most likely take? How will I know when I've reached my goal? What directions will best build on my natural strengths and preferences? Where will I be most likely to need the support and help of others?

Figure 5.3
Level and Style Concerns in Creativity

Dimension	Nature & Identification of Creative Talents	Implications for Nurture	Basic Tools for Diverging and Converging	Problem Solving
LEVEL	**How Creative Are You?** Key Assessments: Cognitive traits (e.g., fluency, flexibility, originality, elaboration.) Personality traits (e.g., Curiosity, risk-taking, preference for complexity, tolerance of ambiguity, resisting premature closure)	**Train people to be more like the "high creatives."** Major emphasis: To increase ability to produce "creative ideas" and/or to reason better, become more logical.	**Increase proficiency in using divergent or convergent thinking strategies or "tools."** Principal Goals: Learning how to get: •more ideas •better ideas "Stretching" for new or unusual ideas Improving logic, critical judgment	**Learning and applying a structured process for Creative Problem Solving.** Key Tasks: Learn CPS stages and techniques; Practice applying them; Use CPS with real problems. Focus: Enhance both quantity and quality of ideas.
STYLE	**How Are You Creative?** Key Assessments: • What directions will help you discover your strengths, talents, and best potentials? • In what ways will you invest your time, energy, efforts, and resources? • What are your strongest preferences? • What are your natural strengths or talents?	**Recognize Value, and Use Diversity** Different people prefer & use different methods; Maximizing the "fit" of people with environment, methods; Developing Your Personal Strengths and Talents	**How to select tools that enhance the person's confidence and fit his/her style needs?** Principal Goals: Flexibility in choosing and applying a variety of strategies; Different people may prefer different tools; (Possible pitfall: may overuse certain "comfortable" tools)	**How to "personalize" problem solving and enhance probability of successful application?** Key Tasks: Maximize tapping the strengths of individuals and creating a group that is both harmonious and productive. Learning how to make CPS a flexible tool that works well for you.

(e.g., intelligence or achievement scores, or measures of creativity thinking ability) to compare student learning style characteristics (Barbe and Milone 1982; Dunn and Price 1980a; Dunn, Bruno, & Gardiner 1984; Griggs and Dunn 1984; Griggs and Price 1980a, 1980b; Hanson, Silver, and Strong 1984; McEwen 1985; Price, Dunn, Dunn, & Griggs 1981; Ricca 1984; Stewart 1981; Wittig 1985). These studies posed questions that were quite predictable from the level perspective; they attempted to find the learning style dimensions critical for distinguishing highs from lows on one or more specific-level variables. Their findings, in general, revealed that students who were higher on the level measures differed from those who were low on the level measures in several ways. Higher-scoring students demonstrated:

- Well-integrated perceptual strengths, learning through varied channels
- Strength in tactile-kinesthetic areas
- Less preference for auditory or lecture-discussion methods
- Persistence, self-motivating, preference for quiet learning environment
- Preference for learning alone
- Independence (internal in locus of control, field independent)
- Nonconformity
- Preference for formal design in the learning environment
- Little need for external structure (i.e., structure created and/or imposed by others)
- Intuition in perception, seeking patterns, and exploring possibilities
- Common preference for "feeling" in decision making (weighing personal criteria, values, and relationships strongly as primary criteria)

Many important qualifications must also be noted, however. Despite these consistent significant differences between groups, the majority of studies also found that within-group variability was as great or greater than that between groups. It was evident that the high- or low-level groups were diverse, and not in fact strongly homogeneous. Developmental differences have also been found. Students at any particular age cannot be expected to be highly similar to others of similar ability level but of different age. Considered as a group, the unique insights among the studies also reinforced the important differences among learning style models and instruments. Varied approaches yielded differing information about the students. Finally, it must also be considered that, even though it is assumed that student self-descriptions of preferences are valid, the adequacy and accuracy of their perceptions may vary in relation to their personal and school experiences. For example, responsibility may be difficult to assess if one has seldom been given opportunities to make decisions and deal with their consequences. Self-directed learning skills, which may lead one to be more confident and positive about learning alone or independent study, can be taught. Student response to motivational efforts by teachers or authorities may be influenced by the skills and styles of the teachers with whom the student has actually worked.

Thus, we began to recognize that the most important contributions of these studies did not derive from enabling us to separate or differentiate groups based on level measures. Rather, these efforts led us to redefine the questions we were asking. It became clear that the importance of understanding styles arises from the insights those data give us into student uniqueness and personal strengths. Style research helped us to learn more about the variety of ways to understand student talents, interests, personal investments, and needs—the channels through which educators could seek and nurture competence and high-level creative productivity. It gave us keys to reaching people, not just novel ways to sort them.

To the extent that educators learn about their students' learning styles, and apply that knowledge to individualizing instruction, many students can be more successful in school. But more to the point, increasing numbers of students begin to discover their unique strengths and talents, and more teachers can better unlock and nurture the potential of those students. Style information may thus prove considerably more powerful for instruction than traditional level data. Rather than simply identify how much or how little ability one believes students to have, learning style measurements expand our understanding of the personal dynamics, motivations, and interests of the students. Quite simply, they give us a better way of charting a course to bring out the best in students. Knowledge of one's own learning style and preferences may also help enhance student self-esteem and confidence, and provide a foundation upon which to improve self-directed learning and independence.

Learning style awareness can also be a valuable component of our efforts to communicate clearly about, and to respect, the diversity inherent among people. Information about student learning style preferences is usually presented in a descriptive manner, emphasizing that all styles have their advantages and drawbacks—no one style represents the right or best way. The focus remains, properly, on the complementary strengths and needs among individuals and the uniqueness and strengths of each person. The vocabulary of style also provides us with a common language to analyze and discuss differences, permitting and supporting dialogue that is free from pejorative, emotionalized, or accusatory characterizations of others.

CREATIVITY AND LEARNING STYLES—SPECIFIC CONNECTIONS

These advances in understanding individual differences and personal preferences or styles are quite important for educators or trainers who work in the areas of thinking skills, creativity, and effective problem solving. Learning style models and assessment resources can help individuals better understand their own creative strengths. They can also enhance our efforts to individualize student efforts to learn methods and techniques for effective thinking and problem solving. Third, styles can help clarify and define several strengths or limitations that individuals may experience in applying thinking strategies or problem-solving processes. Fourth, knowledge of learning styles can be valuable in helping group members and their leaders or facilitators better understand and more effectively respond to all participants' unique needs and modes of functioning during work sessions.

Assessing Creative Strengths

The level-style issue has been the foundation for new work on creativity, just as it has influenced our views of giftedness. While how much creativity a person exhibits may be one worthwhile question, it is not the only one. It may be just as important—perhaps even more important from the educator's or trainer's perspective—to ask how the person expresses or directs her or his creative energy and efforts.

People's learning styles are likely to give us valuable information about the areas or directions in which they are likely to invest their creative efforts and attention. Styles may influence the way people:

1. Experience, recognize, and respond to challenges or barriers to creativity and problem solving;
2. Identify strategies for data collection, decision making, or interaction with others;
3. Define problems based on their individual perceptions;
4. Prioritize situations as interesting, challenging, or worthwhile prior to creating a problem-solving framework;
5. Plan and implement problem-solving strategies and frameworks;
6. Identify, select, and utilize both resources and strategies for creative thinking, critical thinking, and problem solving; and
7. Evaluate, analyze, and interpret ideas, action plans, and implementation.

Learning styles may also be useful to help people understand the psychological, social, emotional, and environmental conditions under which they are most likely to function effectively as they seek to put their creative thinking, critical thinking, and problem solving skills to work in group settings.

Individualizing Learning of Thinking Skills

Many training programs to nurture creative or critical thinking or effective problem-solving skills tend to present those skills in traditional formats such as texts, workbooks, or printed exercises and activities, and to rely heavily on directions, checklists, guidelines, or instructor-led group experiences or discussions. Contemporary knowledge regarding individual learning styles will enable us to improve instruction in thinking skills and problem solving by planning learning activities and comprehensive instructional programs that respond to student preferences and learning styles. Just as teaching through learning styles has been demonstrated to be effective in improving significantly the performance or achievement of students with learning difficulties, we believe that such instruction can also be effective in enhancing student growth at higher levels and in complex processes.

Identifying Possible Strengths and Limitations in Process Use

Isaksen and Treffinger (1985) proposed that Creative Problem Solving (CPS) involves three broad components of creative effort: understanding the problem, generating ideas, and planning for action. In each of these areas, styles can be useful in understanding the possible strengths and limitations that individuals may experience when working on problems. Using Kirton's Adaptor-Innovator distinction, for example, several possible advantages and potential challenges for both adaptors and innovators in each of the CPS components can be formulated; these are summarized in Figure 5.4.

Enhancing Group Process

Although we tend to view thinking as an individual activity, and surely it is such in many important ways, we should not overlook the fact that effective thinking and problem solving in the everyday world often involves working in a variety of formal and informal groups: brainstorming groups, quality circles, legislatures, committees, families, teams, classrooms, boards of directors, staff meetings. The quality and effectiveness of these group efforts will be influenced by many factors, including time, resources, values, and goals. It is important to recognize that effective groups learn and use deliberate methods and techniques for generating and analyzing ideas, and apply specific processes such as Creative Problem Solving for making decisions or solving problems (Isaksen and Treffinger 1985).

We also find, however, that the effectiveness of a group in using such methods and processes successfully is also influenced by the personal styles and preferences each person brings to the group, and the way those styles are reflected in the interactions among group members. Some relevant dimensions of style are reflected in a group's choices regarding environmental preferences (meeting early in the morning, late afternoon, or at night; providing snacks and refreshments or not; meeting in a conference room or office, or in someone's living room). Other dimensions of style manifest themselves in psychological or interpersonal concerns (the importance of specific goals and written agendas; degree of emphasis on closure for each specific item; focus on details and procedures or on broad values and patterns; emphasis on logical or rational criteria or values and human relations criteria in reaching decisions; emphasis on people issues or

Figure 5.4
Possible Strengths and Limitations of Adaptors and Innovators in CPS Components

Component I: Understanding the Problem

	Adaptor	Innovator
+	Sees the "boundary" and stays in it. Knows the system well—can generate data about it. Logical analyst. Identifies problems that exist within present structure	Looks broadly at issues and new directions. Draws from many fields or disciplines. Recognizes emerging issues and cutting edge concerns Looks beyond immediate context
−	Boundary may become a solid wall May get "stuck" in the current reality, Lack richness of vision Might not be open to unusual views Can be quick to criticize, may stifle discussion.	May not recognize or observe boundaries May get lost in the future state. Focus on big picture may lead them to overlook important details— play fast and loose with facts, specifics. Others may not see unusual connections the same way- question relevance/value

Component II: Generating Ideas

	Adaptor	Innovator
+	Generates ideas that are recognized as relevant to context; May generate fewer ideas, but find it easy to gain acceptance for them Focus on gradual, incremental change.	Generates profusion of ideas, many of which may be novel or unusual. May generate "visionary" ideas large scale breakthroughs.
−	Can be seen as rigid or unreceptive to new ideas or viewpoints. May seek closure before unusual ideas can be generated or developed. May find it difficult to defer judgment	Some ideas may be perceived as "off the wall" or unworkable. May find it too easy to keep generating more ideas, too difficult to seek closure. May find it difficult to converge and judge ideas.

Component III: Planning for Action

	Adaptor	Innovator
+	Knows how to get ideas through the important channels, how to prepare and present ideas. Recognizes possible obstacles within the system.	Develops unusual ideas which may be clever or humorous Sees many positives and potentials in new ideas
−	Feels uneasy when things seem to move "too far, too fast." May be threatened by ideas perceived to be radical or too far removed from established procedures and traditional methods Can get locked too tightly in place.	May disregard need to sell ideas, gain support, or make them workable. Can be impatient and expect immediate acceptance of new ideas. May interpret any questions or concerns as negative criticism May "flit" from one idea to another.

planning issues in different degrees; broad generalizations and commitments or detailed step-by-step plans). In many ways, then, the preferences each person brings to a group, and the ability of each group member to recognize, respect, and respond constructively to personal differences within the group, will have significant impact on the group's progress and success.

SUMMARY

In this chapter, we have proposed that giftedness and creativity are linked with, and enhanced in important ways by, an understanding of learning styles. Through recognition of different learning styles, our understanding of the nature, identification, and nurture of both giftedness and creativity has expanded. Of primary importance, we have learned that giftedness and creativity are not one-dimensional, fixed traits present or absent in individuals, but that talents and creative potentials can be recognized and developed in many people.

Chapter 6

Reaching Creatively Gifted Students Through Their Learning Styles

Mark A. Runco and Shawn Okuda Sakamoto

A great deal can be learned about the learning styles of gifted children by studying creativity. This is because creativity is one of the most important components of giftedness (Albert & Runco 1986; Milgram 1990a; Renzulli 1978). Granted, there is some debate about the actual role of creativity in giftedness. One of the early sections of this chapter reviews that debate. Our view is that all truly gifted children are creative, and in this chapter we offer predictions about the learning styles of these children.

These predictions are based on three areas of research. Each of these is reviewed here, in the following sequence. The first focuses on the personality traits that characterize creative children. The second covers the cognitive characteristics of creativity (e.g., divergent thinking, problem-finding and evaluative skills, and creative strategies). The third emphasizes educational preferences of creative children. These preferences involve relationships with teachers and peers (i.e., grouping preferences).

There is a great deal of convergence on these three areas of research, hence the predictions described herein are supported by several lines of research. The personality research leads to many of the same predictions as the cognitive research, and both are further supported by research on educational preferences of creatively gifted learners. Admittedly, the predictions from this research involve only a subset of the twenty-two elements of learning style noted by Dunn (1984). We are fairly confident about our predictions concerning emotionality (motivation, persistence, responsibility), sociological preferences (working alone, being self-motivated), and psychological inclinations (hemispheric preferences). The remaining elements of learning style (the immediate environment and physical characteristics of the environment) must await further research.

DEFINITIONS AND DIFFICULTIES

Learning style has been defined as "the way individuals concentrate on, absorb, and retain new or difficult information and skills" (Dunn 1984, p. 43). Learning styles may be inferred from students' reactions to the twenty-two elements described by Dunn (1984). Creativity is much more difficult to define. In fact, there are several controversies in the creativity literature concerning how to best define creativity, how to measure creativity, and even how to study creativity (Runco & Albert 1990). This may explain why so little research has focused on the learning styles of creatively gifted children. There is research on the enhancement of creative skills (Feldhusen, Bahlke, & Treffinger 1969; Runco 1986), but that work has more to say about strategies for increasing creative performance than it does about the learning styles of creative individuals.

With disagreement about the concept of creativity, it is not surprising that there is also disagreement specifically about the role of creativity in giftedness. This may explain why it is a relatively common practice to place children in gifted programs solely because of their performance on some index of conventional intelligence, like the IQ. This practice is unfortunate because IQ and creativity seem to be unrelated in the moderately high levels of ability (e.g., IQs between 120 and 145; Runco & Albert 1987). Hence many children selected for gifted programs based on IQ are almost certainly *not* creative.

We believe it is most realistic to view creativity as one component of giftedness. Perhaps creative skills will soon be assessed as routinely as IQ and academic achievement. For now, and given common assessment and identification practices, it is likely that there are students in gifted programs who are creatively gifted, but also students who are gifted in the sense of academic and conventional intelligence but not notably creative. In this case, our predictions about the learning styles of creatively gifted students apply to a subsection of the gifted population. They also apply to the subsection of the nongifted population that has creative potential.

Just as there may be relatively uncreative children in gifted programs, there probably are gifted children who have not been identified. Even when paper-and-pencil identifications are used, some creative children remain unrecognized. Teacher recommendations occasionally are used for identification, but these are somewhat subjective and potentially biased (Runco 1984), and again some creative children are overlooked. Additionally, there is evidence that suggests that teachers prefer intelligent children to creative children (Cropley, in press; Getzels & Jackson 1962). Although regrettable, this can be no surprise given what we know about creativity. Some of the traits that characterize creatively gifted individuals (e.g., nonconformity) can easily disrupt the typical classroom. Furthermore, many of the traits teachers seem to appreciate—characteristics of the so-called ideal student (Cropley, in press)—preclude creative thought and behavior. What are the traits which characterize creative individuals?

Creative Personality

Of the various approaches to the study and definition of creativity, the one that is the most helpful for the present purposes focuses on the creative personality. This approach is particularly helpful because many of the traits have obvious connections to several of the elements of learning style defined by Dunn (1984) and Milgram (1990a). For example, several of the traits of creatively gifted children and adolescents lead directly to predictions about grouping preferences (Dunn, Beaudry, & Klavas 1989) and preferences for the presentation of information (Dunn 1984).

Many of the relevant traits have been recognized since Wallach and Kogan (1965) conducted their seminal investigation of children's creativity. Wallach and Kogan contrasted highly intelligent children, highly creative children, and relatively unintelligent and uncreative children. A large number of group differences were uncovered. The creative group had high self-confidence, but was also disruptive and high in attention-seeking behavior. Wallach and Kogan suggested that the attention-seeking behavior was a reflection of boredom with conventional classroom activity and eagerness to propose divergent ideas. The highly intelligent children who were relatively low in creativity were highly motivated, but unwilling to take chances or express affective associations. They also were less tolerant of unconventional suggestions than the other children. These characteristics have also been revealed in more recent research (Albert & Runco 1989; Runco 1984, 1989).

The "eagerness to express ideas" noted by Wallach and Kogan might suggest that creative children would have grouping preferences involving their peers, but other very compelling evidence suggests that creatively gifted individuals prefer working alone. Creatively gifted individuals are, for example, highly autonomous, unconventional, and nonconforming (Albert & Runco 1989; Runco 1984, 1989). They also tend to be intrinsically motivated. All this suggests that creatively gifted students would appreciate and benefit from opportunities for independent work.

One of the reasons we are confident about this independent grouping preference is that autonomy and independence seem to be the most commonly noted creative traits in the literature. The autonomy of creative individuals seems to be both emotional and intellectual (Barron & Harrington 1981; MacKinnon 1978). Also relevant is that creative individuals have been described as introverted, withdrawn, reserved, preferring solitary to group activities; they often need to maintain distance from their peers (Barron & Harrington 1981; MacKinnon 1978; Perkins 1981).

Albert and Runco (1989) explained creative autonomy in terms of family background. They found that parents of gifted children allowed earlier independence than other parents, and this independence was associated with independence in the judgments by gifted children about appropriate behavior. It was also associated with divergent thinking, one index of the potential for creative thought (Milgram 1990a; Runco, in press-a 1991). Autonomous work may also be associated with the need for personal mastery of creative individuals and their disregard for regulations, high initiative, and intrinsic motivation (McClelland 1963; MacKinnon, 1978). For these reasons, educators should expect creatively gifted students to have a learning style and grouping preference for working alone.

Intrinsic motivation has been observed in a variety of gifted populations (e.g., Milgram, in press; Nicholls 1983), and has been experimentally tied to creative performances (Amabile, Goldfarb, & Brackfield 1990; Hennessey 1990). Intrinsically motivated tendencies support our first prediction for autonomous grouping preferences, and also lead to the prediction concerning what Dunn (1984) referred to as "sociological preferences." Most obviously, creative students would not require what Dunn described as "motivation by the teacher." Creatively gifted individuals will probably benefit most when allowed to make decisions about the topics and methods of study. Simonton (1988) argued that "informal education, especially self-education, is far more conducive to creative development than is the highly formal, even rigid inculcation of cultural dogma" (p. 123). This is not to say that creative students should be given free rein. It might be tempting to give children too much self-determination (Cropley, in press). Like independence, educators need to aim for optimal levels. We will return to this idea of optimal levels later. For now, the point is that creative students need to have decision-making options in their work.

Our predictions about independent work and intrinsically motivated activity are consistent with what Torrance (1970) described as "creative needs." Torrance noted curiosity needs, the need to meet challenge and attempt difficult tasks, the need to give one's self completely to a task, the need to be honest and search for the truth, and the need to be different, to be an individual. Torrance's notion of the need to be different is consistent with our first argument that creative children may prefer working alone. The need for a challenge, noted by Torrance, suggests that creatively gifted children require a variety of tasks during the school day, an idea further supported by Gruber's (1988) description of creative individuals' *networks of enterprise* and Gough's (1979) identification of a wide range of interests as common for creative individuals. There is undoubtedly an optimal level of variety and challenge (Csikszentmihalyi 1990).

There are other important personality characteristics in addition to autonomy, intrinsic motivation, and a wide range of interests; and many, many studies of the creative personality in addition to those cited above. In a widely cited review, Barron and Harrington (1981) identified the following personality characteristics:

High valuation of esthetic qualities in experience, broad interests, attraction to complexity, high energy, independence of judgment, autonomy, intuition, self-confidence, ability to resolve antinomies or to accommodate apparently opposite or conflicting traits in one's self-concept. (p. 453)

In a review of the literature specifically on children's divergent thinking, Runco (in press-a) noted the importance of an internal locus of control (Aviram & Milgram 1977; Houtz, Jambor, Cifone, & Lewis 1989; Sawyers, Moran, & Fu 1984), playfulness (Pellegrini, in press; Sutton-Smith, in press), and cognitive tempo (Broberg & Moran 1988). Of these, playfulness may be the most important for those interested in reaching creatively gifted children. In Cropley's (in press) words,

Play does not seem to serve any basic needs (such as obtaining food) but, despite this, children persistently engage in it . . . Furthermore, a number of psychological studies have shown that play activities are related to the degree of creativity shown by children. It seems that, in play, children try out behaviors that would not normally appear, for example, because pressure for correctness or for social acceptability are eased during play. When they play, children can also deal with the external world in purely personal ways, turning the locus of evaluation inwards. They can give their fantasy freer rein. Thus, play provides a situation in which many of the social and emotional blocks to creative thinking are not present.

Cropley (in press) was concerned about traditional educational settings, and criticized:

Strict sanctions against play are imposed in most classrooms. Work is regarded as something that is done in silence and with grim concentration. Play is regarded as something that goes on outside the classroom, that is probably noisy, and most important of all, something that never yields worthwhile results except of a recreational nature. Consequently, any looseness of associations, introduction of tangential ideas in an attempt to find a solution to a problem, humor, noisiness, or even show of enjoyment is highly suspect in a situation which has been defined as work. The idea that a problem could be solved by playing with it is rejected, and the fresh insights that can be obtained in this way are lost.

Ayman-Nolley (in press), Pellegrini (in press), Smolucha (in press), and Sutton-Smith (in press) each recently argued that play and creativity are functionally tied. Simply put, play allows uninhibited exploration and uninhibited divergent thinking. It also allows children to practice ideational flexibility and problem solving as well as unconventionality. Finally, play is fun, and thereby supports the affective states that are most conducive to creativity.

Play, like several of the personality traits noted above, seems to be tied to certain cognitive tendencies. This will be more obvious after a brief review of the cognitive characteristics of creative individuals. Although there are many theories of creative cognition (Runco, in press-b), we focus on ideational tendencies of creative children and hemispheric preferences.

COGNITIVE CHARACTERISTICS

Creative individuals seem to think divergently and strategically. In fact, divergent thinking skills may be the most commonly recognized characteristic of creative children (Milgram 1990a; Runco, in press-a; Wallach & Kogan 1965). These include *fluency* (the ability to generate numerous ideas), *flexibility* (the ability to think of a variety of ideas and to avoid cognitive rigidity and functional fixity), and *originality* (the ability to think of unusual or unique ideas).

Each of these divergent thinking skills is influenced by the instructional environment. They are, for example, influenced by the tasks or assignment themselves and the stimuli within the tasks. In particular, unfamiliar tasks tend to elicit more original ideation than familiar tasks and topics (Runco & Albert 1985b). This may be because ideational associations are fresh and not preconceived. For present purposes, what is most important is simply that creative children should have opportunities to think divergently. This can be accomplished by allowing latitude and flexibility in educational assignments. This, of course, is consistent with what was suggested earlier about independent work.

Runco (in press-b) argued that there are important ideational skills besides those involved in the production of an idea. There are, for example, several problem-finding and evaluative skills that are required of creative thinking. These are rarely recognized. This is unfortunate because evaluations and selections play such a large role in creative performances. Runco (in press-c) demonstrated that children who were original in their divergent thinking were also accurate when judging the creativity of ideas. Runco also suggested that evaluative skills develop with practice. They are, in this sense, sensitive to the instructional environment.

The problem-finding abilities of creative children may also be sensitive to the instructional environment. We refer to problem-finding ''abilities'' because problem identification and problem definition skills are each important (Chand & Runco 1991; Okuda, Runco, & Berger 1990). Creative individuals are not only good problem solvers; they also know when to use their skills and how to approach problems in a manner that will allow them to succeed (find a creative solution). This takes us back to our discussion of intrinsic motivation, for it is quite reasonable to assume that tasks that are identified or defined by students will reflect their own interests. Tegano, Sawyers, and Moran (1989) described how teachers can promote problem finding in the classroom. The key may be to allow opportunities for student input before problems and tasks are completely framed.

Milgram (1990a) suggested that divergent thinking skills are normally distributed, and that all children can generate ideas. However, for many children, finding original ideas is dependent upon simple associative process. Some individuals seem to rely on serendipity (Mednick 1962) when searching for original ideas and must generate a large number of ideas to find even a few original ones (Hocevar 1979; Runco & Albert 1985a). Creatively gifted individuals, on the other hand, can find original ideas without generating a huge pool of possibilities. In fact, their originality is not dependent upon their fluency (Runco & Albert 1985b). In a word, creatively gifted individuals are strategic in their ideation.

This is an important individual difference, for it supports the claim that creatively gifted students require autonomy to determine a method of work. Creatively gifted children use effective problem-solving strategies, and do so spontaneously. This may explain why they do respond in a dramatic way to explicit instructions (Runco, 1986).

Runco (1986) demonstrated empirically how gifted and nongifted students differ in their problem-solving strategies. He administered conventional, inexplicit instructions for divergent thinking tests, and then another divergent thinking task with explicit instructions. He asked students to consider only original responses. Group comparisons indicated that explicit instructions enhanced the originality scores of the nongifted and talented groups more than those of the gifted group. Presumably, gifted children recognized the strategy that was appropriate to the task without instructional aid, and hence did not benefit significantly from explicit instruction. In addition to demonstrating how one specific strategy influenced divergent thinking and problem solving, this research suggests that educators might not need to supply all the details and procedures for working on particular tasks.

In a manner of speaking, the role of evaluation and selection is confirmed by demonstration of explicit instructions. What is usually emphasized in explicit instructions is a method for selecting creative or original ideas, and any selection requires an evaluation. It might not be a critical evaluation. Runco (in press-c) uncovered individual differences in schoolchildren in their ability to evaluate the originality of ideas, and he suggested that the most creative individuals are both evaluative and valuative. Judgments by parents and teachers may also involve both valuation (appreciation) and evaluation (criticism) (Runco & Vega 1989). Educators should give the opportunity to practice critical evaluations, but also reinforce appreciative and valuative efforts.

Creativity and Hemispheric Specialization

Hemispheric preference is a popular topic in the cognitive sciences, and an important dimension of learning styles (Dunn, Beaudry, & Klavas 1989). Hemispheric preference (or hemispheric specialization) is also a topic found in the creativity literature (Denny & Wolf 1984; Masten 1989; Torrance 1982). Although the findings from this research are not uniform, Masten concluded that "there seems to be a positive relationship between creativity in general and having a right-hemispheric learning style" (1989, p. 752).

This research suggests that creative individuals tend to have a right-hemispheric preference. However, we wish to emphasize that recommendations should not focus on one hemisphere. We wish to emphasize this because research findings on hemispheric specialization are somewhat mixed, and worse yet, interpretations are often clouded. There is good work on hemispheric specialization and creativity (Al-Sabaty & Davis 1989; Burke, Chrisler, & Devlin 1989;

Hoppe & Kyle 1990), but sadly, the lion's share of the research on this topic is somewhat misleading.

Many psychologists are critical of how the research on hemispheric specialization is being interpreted and applied. As Gardner (1982) suggested, "claims about the division of labor between the two halves [of the brain] are becoming increasingly remote from what is known or even suspected" (p. 278). We *do* know that under certain circumstances, the two hemispheres of certain brains differ. Typically, the left hemisphere is given the responsibility for processing linguistic information, especially syntactical information, and it seems to be involved in classification tasks. The right hemisphere is primarily responsible for spatial information and "simultaneous processing." And yet there is evidence that "not all human brains are organized the same way; for example, many left-handers—and even some right-handers—turn out to have significant linguistic capacities in the right hemispheres" (Gardner, 1982, p. 279).

The central issue may be one of generalization. In his Nobel prize-winning research, Sperry (1964) described his work with a small group of individuals who had commissurotomies. Sperry's patients had certain proclivities, probably reflecting disconnected hemispheres, but these may not apply to those of us with connected hemispheres. (How many people do you know who have had a commissurotomy?) In fact, the earlier findings did not even entirely apply to Sperry's patients; there were notable differences among the patients within his sample. Additionally, Sperry's findings about the two hemispheres may not be widely applicable because he started with a select (epileptic) group of individuals.

The most reliable research indicates that the two hemispheres of the brain interact in creative performances. Educators should not, then, focus on "right brain" operations, nor deemphasize "left brain" operations. Creativity requires an integrated mode of thought. Hoppe and Kyle (1990) made the same point when they emphasized the role of the corpus callosum in creativity. In their experimental work, they found that creative individuals manifest a "bilateral integration of cerebral function," and they noted that commissurotomy patients (psychopathological individuals) had disrupted callosal transmission, and thereby decrements in emotional arousal and responsivity. Hoppe and Kyle hypothesized that this in turn directly inhibited creative thinking. These findings illustrate the importance of dual-hemisphere functioning. Relating this to Dunn's (1984) model of learning style and the "elements" mentioned above, our prediction about the learning styles of creative children is that they tend to have (or at least should use) interactive or dual-hemisphere preferences. Those interested in clear writings about hemispheric specialization should consult Gardner (1982), Hoppe and Kyle (1990), and Bogen (1975). Bogen discussed the utility of hemispheric theories specifically for education, and like Hoppe and Kyle (1990), cautioned about looking to only one hemisphere.

INSTRUCTIONAL PREFERENCES

In the previous sections of this chapter we described how personality traits and cognitive characteristics which describe creative children lead to certain predictions about learning styles. In the present section we change our approach and focus on a line of research. Rather than drawing predictions from characteristics of the individual creative student, below we draw predictions about learning styles from research on the learning environment. This includes both the social and the physical environment. Much of what we know about the environments most conducive to creative performance has some connection to what Dunn (1984) referred to as instructional environments.

Teachers

One of the most important aspects of instruction is the student-teacher relationship. Dunn (1984) suggested that some children appreciate learning with adults present, but earlier we suggested that creatively gifted students would probably prefer independent and intrinsically motivated work. The research on environments further supports that prediction, but also suggests that the argument should be qualified.

Many creative geniuses of the past have credited the positive influence of a teacher (Albert 1975; Ochse 1990; Simonton 1984; Zuckerman 1977). Creative achievers particularly appreciated teachers—and for that matter, peers, faculty, parents, or siblings—who acknowledged their academic interests, allowed them to work independently at their own pace, and challenged their thinking (Goertzel & Goertzel 1962). In her study of Nobel laureates, Zuckerman (1977) found that creative achievers gained tremendously from their teacher role models, and these mentors were found to be especially able in the field of interest. The creatively gifted student may be intrinsically motivated, but thrives on the support and encouragement for his or her independence in an area of interest.

Chambers (1973) found that the teachers who were appreciated by creative adults, when looking back at their own educations, were those who allowed independence, respected individuality, and reinforced originality. These teachers were also enthusiastic, and were available before and after school hours. Teachers thought to be detrimental to creative development were overly critical, unenthusiastic, rigid, and sarcastic. Simonton (1988) reported that the "best liked teachers" of creative individuals allowed their students to follow their own interests. This is once again congruent with what we know about the creative personality, for students are able to utilize their intrinsic motivations if given freedom to follow their own interests. Interestingly, in his discussion of mentors and achievement, Simonton (1987) suggested that the best models for children are similar to the children, but not too similar.

Numerous biographers have reported that creative geniuses of the past have performed very poorly in school (Goertzel & Goertzel 1962; Miller, in press; Simonton 1988, chap. 5). Similarly, Wallach and Wing (1969) reported that creativity is unrelated to academic grade point average. Simonton (1988) went as far as to describe the scholastic performances of creative geniuses as "often miserable." He questioned the efficiency with which educational practices serve creative skills, and reported that many creative eminent individuals had received only marginal formal education. Of course, other creative geniuses are very well educated, but even these individuals seem to draw very heavily on their informal education. In fact, the optimal level of formal education for high-level creative performance seems to be a year or two of college (Simonton 1983), rather than a graduate or even a baccalaureate degree. Simonton's explanation for this was that education tends to inculcate dogmatic modes of thought, which is antithetical to creative thought. It also is something that can be avoided by teachers. If educators can do this, they may even minimize or avoid the "fourth grade slump."

Fourth-Grade Slump and Conformity

At certain ages, children seem to be spontaneously creative. Preschool children are regularly original in their language, songs, insights, and of course play. It may be that these are unintentionally creative (Wolf & Larson 1981), but for whatever reason creative potential seems quite high in the early years. Unfortunately, many children have a "fourth-grade slump" (Torrance, 1968) that may be a reflection of the pressures placed on them to conform. For example, in classrooms, children are often asked to sit in neat rows, raise their hands before asking a question, and do their homework the way the teacher explains it. Perhaps by the fourth grade this pressure is internalized and reflected in the thinking of students.

Gardner (1982) described the drop during the school years as a reflection of a *literal stage* wherein children can only think and interpret in a conventional fashion. Smith (1990) offered a psychodynamic explanation for the same phenomenon. All explanations of the drop in creative performance seem to recognize that one cause is an increase in children's conventionality. The fourth-grade slump reflects the peak of conventionality (also see Kohlberg 1987; Rosenblatt & Winner 1988). Runco and Chand (in press) suggested that as children become more conventional, they become more selective when evaluating ideas, behaviors, and solutions. In this view, children do not lose the potential for creative ideation, but rather become both more critical (choosing only conventional and fitting ideas) and less appreciative (ignoring ideas and thoughts that are unconventional). In this sense, the fourth-grade slump is a function of changes in the evaluative and valuative skills described above.

What does all this mean for instructional environments? Given that children seem to imitate significant adults (Runco & Albert 1985a), it suggests first that parents and teachers must themselves avoid relying on conventional thinking. Surely adults cannot and should not entirely avoid conventional thought. Without some conventions it would be impossible to communicate or share. But conventional thinking and behavior can be balanced with original thinking and behavior. This balance is what students need, especially creative students.

Creatively gifted children may not change as much as other children during the fourth grade, and may be unconventional when other children are highly conventional. Perhaps this is why Wallach and Kogan (1965) found creative students to be disruptive in class. If educators want to reach the creatively gifted student, they may need to tolerate or even utilize this type of unconventional behavior.

We do not recommend an entirely indulgent or entirely open classroom, and do not suggest that children need to be left to their own devices. To reach the creatively gifted individual, educators should offer opportunities for self-education and independent work (and encourage extracurricular self-education), *and* have periods where cooperation and factual information is emphasized. Dogmatic ideas should be avoided, and intrinsically motivated work and nonconformity should be tolerated. It is a matter of balance, or optimization.

OVERVIEW AND CONCLUSIONS

The creatively gifted learner appreciates independent work, has a wide range of interests, and is curious and intrinsically motivated. He or she is capable of using both divergent and convergent thinking strategies, probably uses integrated (dual-hemisphere) brain functions, tends to be unconventional and nonconforming, produces original ideas, and is good at finding and defining problems or assignments that allow flexible thought. These personality and cognitive characteristics reflect an autonomous learning style. In the classroom, teachers should expect the creatively gifted student to prefer independence—from the teacher, in the choice of assignments and tasks, and in terms of social grouping. If the creatively gifted worked on assignments that are intrinsically motivating, educators can expect remarkable persistence from their creative students (Dunn 1984).

There are various elements of learning style about which we can say little, at least concerning the creatively gifted individual. There is, for example, no reason to expect whether or not a creatively gifted child would have time-of-day, mobility, temperature, noise-level, or auditory preferences. In fact, we are only aware of research associating creativity with a small subset of the twenty-two elements in Dunn's (1984) model. This points to the need for additional research.

Some of what was discussed here may suggest that creatively gifted students will benefit from an open classroom. And indeed, Hedges, Giaconia, and Gage (1981) reported that openness was moderately related to independence and creativity (and unrelated to achievement and anxiety). Forman and McKinney (1978) reported that students in open classrooms had higher vocabulary, reading, and mathematics scores than those in traditional classrooms, and there was some indication that ideational fluency was higher in the former. However, there was no difference between the two types of classrooms in terms of the originality scores from divergent thinking tests.

Our view is that an instructional environment that is responsive to individual learning styles is more appropriate for creativity than an entirely open classroom.

Teachers should not assume that students can be entirely independent, nor turn their classrooms over to students; rather, they should act as managers (Brophy 1986). Responsive and flexible education will allow students to follow their own interests, and develop skills to support their creative efforts (e.g., independence). In his writing about responsive education, Torrance (1970) noted that, with the creative child, the adult must avoid throwing that child's thinking processes off course . . . [Teachers should] guide him by providing a responsive environment . . . [and the] controlled freedom which seems necessary for productive, creative behavior (p. 15). This notion of "controlled freedom" is entirely consistent with our ideas about the need for educational flexibility (also see Roe 1952).

This argument is reinforced by looking at common definitions of creative products. Although there is debate on the most appropriate criteria for products (O'Quin & Besemer 1989), there is a consensus that creative products must be original *and* useful (Rothenberg & Hausman 1976; Runco 1988). Products or performances that are original or unique but useless are not creative; they are bizarre. In Guilford's (1968) terms, children need to learn to use both divergent and convergent modes of thought. In Bailin's (in press) terms, it is a matter of creativity being both novel and rule governed. Applying this to the educational setting, originality and divergence are desirable, and seem to flourish in a flexible environment. But rules and convergence are also necessary, and these require structured lessons. This may seem slightly simplistic given that valuable originality requires that the student is cognizant of directions in which he or she can search for worthwhile ideas. The point is simply that many creatively gifted students have skills that will be most effectively reached through structured lessons. Open education may be best for some skills and traits (divergent thinking, flexibility), but more structured education may be best for others (e.g., critical thinking, encoding and memorization of factual information).

A great deal of what was proposed here implies that educators need to monitor their expectations for children (also see Marjoribanks 1983; Runco 1989). Parents and teachers should also monitor their own behavior. Runco and Albert (1985) found strong correlations between parents and their exceptionally gifted children in divergent thinking abilities, and suggested that a great deal of the similarity was a result of modeling and imitation. Graham, Sawyers, and DeBord (1989) reached a similar conclusion in their work with teachers.

Throughout this chapter we emphasized the importance of balance. The creatively gifted child is not just a free thinker and rebel. He or she is capable of both divergent and convergent thought. He or she needs to evaluate and valuate. He or she needs to develop original thought, but also needs structure and factual information. He or she needs respect from mentors, but also needs to be challenged. Educators must strive for balance in the educational environment.

Great care must be taken with generalizations, especially those concerning creative children. This is because of the need for balance and because the creative population is a heterogeneous one. Walberg and Stariha (in press) suggested that:

The grouping of students has special relevance for gifted and talented students. Teaching students what they already know or are yet unready to learn wastes time and may harm motivation. For this reason, traditional whole-class teaching of heterogeneous groups can cause inefficiency and problems. Educators must consider how students are grouped and try to help the full range if they want them all to learn as much as possible. Well-defined subject matter and student grouping may be among the main reasons why Japanese students are world leaders in achievement. (p. 8)

Care should also be taken because we cannot isolate traits that are shared by all creatively gifted individuals (Gardner 1983; Gruber 1988). No one personality or motivational characteristic describes all creatively gifted students. Further, there are questions about trait-situation interactions and the stability of personality (Albert & Runco, in press; Dudek & Hall, in press; Helson 1987; Lindauer, in press; Rubin 1982). Some traits may only be manifested in particular situations, and some may come and go as a function of developmental stage. Perhaps most important are the domain differences in creativity (Csikszentmihalyi 1990; Gardner 1982; Feist, in press; Milgram 1990a; 1991a; Runco 1986). Some traits may be associated with creative potential in one area or specialization but not in others. In part because of their intrinsic motivation, creative individuals tend to devote themselves to art, music, science, mathematics, chess, or some other specific domain. A student interested in expressing him- or herself in art may prefer working alone, whereas a student with creative social skills and leadership would certainly not. Hence, not all creative children fit the profile presented in this chapter, and it is therefore vital to be aware of the heterogeneity and variability of the creative population, and avoid sweeping claims about the learning styles of creatively gifted children and adolescents.

Traditional education seems to offer students opportunities to work and express themselves in some domains—like Gardner's (1983) *logical-mathematic* and *verbal-symbolic* domains, but creative children (especially creatively gifted children) may only stand out and work to their potentials when working in unconventional domains (e.g., interpersonal, intrapersonal, kinesthetic). Gruber (1985) and Runco (1991) have even recommended that we watch for creative giftedness in the moral domain. Clearly, creativity is multifaceted, and creatively gifted students represent a heterogeneous group. For this reason, educators will need a variety of techniques. To reach the creatively gifted student, educators will themselves need to be creative.

Part II

The Impact of Culture on Learning Style and Giftedness

Chapter 7

The Learning Styles of Gifted Adolescents in the United States

Rita Dunn, Shirley A. Griggs, and Gary E. Price

Until this past decade, American education was held in high esteem by most citizens and served as a viable path on which low socioeconomic families could move toward eventual financial security in this society. The American dream was personified by individuals' ability to obtain both necessities and luxuries of their choosing by applying a concerted effort in school, earning appropriate grades and degrees, and using those as the key to open doors closed to people without an education. Despite that widespread belief, U.S. school systems always have been of uneven quality; diverse in philosophy, methods, standards, and discipline requirements; unequally effective for selected groups within their multicultural student populations; and dependent upon the talents, unique personality, creativity, and dedication of each educator.

For fiscal year 1988, average public education expenditures varied from $4,952 per student in wealthy states to $2,819 in poor states. Perhaps as a result, three out of four colleges and universities were required to offer at least one remedial course in fall 1989. Sixty-eight percent offered mathematics, 65 percent writing, and 58 percent reading. At institutions with a predominantly minority student body, 55 percent of the freshmen enrolled in at least one remedial course; at institutions with a predominantly nonminority student body, 27 percent of the freshmen enrolled in at least one remedial course. Despite the efforts of various institutions of higher education to help young entrants achieve a high academic level, approximately one-fourth of them were unable to provide passing grades for freshmen in remedial courses and about one-half were unable to provide passing rates by racial or ethnic breakdowns (College-level remedial education, 1991). Regardless of the number of students from a variety of geographical locations who have graduated from high school but are unable to be admitted into four-year colleges without upgrading their basic skills, "the public rates the schools in its own communities higher than it rates the schools nationally'' (Oliva, 1988, p. 104).

CHARACTERISTICS OF AMERICAN EDUCATION

Diversity of Control

Historically, school curricula, scheduling procedures, academic and discipline requirements, employment, promotion and dismissal practices, and instructional systems have been determined through either state or local control. The latter comprises boards of education, which were either elected by citizens or appointed by politicians, and the administrators those boards chose. Depending upon the relative power of the various members of each system's board of education, and the relative power of each superintendent of schools—the chief school officer of the educational enterprise, one or the other, or both—directed and ensured the quality of that system. Depending upon the relative power of the superintendent, in contrast to the convictions and personality of each building principal, teachers have had either relative independence, a fair amount of self-determination, or no choice at all concerning how, what, who, or with what they taught. A current emphasis in the United States on restructuring seeks, as one of its major goals, direct and ongoing decision-making power for teachers in selected aspects of school management (Geisert 1991). That focus emerged from an experimental program implemented in selected schools of Dade County, Florida—a program which, as of this writing, has provided little published data concerning either its short- or long-term effectiveness.

Periodic Trends, Multiple Programs, Limited Research Base

Widespread adoption of poorly researched and only partly executed ideas—whether they are innovations or the repackaging of previously tried and discarded strategies—is a second facet of American education. Because of state education department, legislative, or central office encouragement, many programs have been instituted that have had either *no,* or only very limited, research documentation of their effectiveness. Few can be observed other than in selected grades in a limited number of buildings; fewer can be observed in a variety of regional areas, which might suggest generalizability or widespread application. Despite those deficiencies, introducing new methods on a wholesale rather than on a limited experimental basis is a widespread phenomenon.

To exacerbate the problem, many schools have initiated two or more ''new'' approaches simultaneously, which prevents determination of the contributions of each to the total results. Those schools cannot know what works, what does not, and what in each case either stimulates, contributes to, or inhibits the outcome. Furthermore, where evaluation does exist, it often is conducted by staff either within or employed by the system that introduced the innovation—

not at all the objective scrutiny suggested by funding agencies. In addition, school systems rarely employ people skilled in evaluation strategies; thus the reported results may be questionable. Visits to innovative schools often yield high teacher enthusiasm—an asset!—without any hard data to support the approach, a detriment considering taxpayer funds, teacher energy, and the value of time. Another facet of this problem is that the innovations often are the pet projects of a single administrator or group, hardly unbiased champions.

These comments do not reflect an anti-innovation perspective. Where children do not succeed academically, do not enjoy learning, do not behave well while learning, or conceivably could perform better than they do, it is important to explore alternative approaches. However, it is equally important that innovation be considered *experimental*. New programs should be examined carefully for their applicability to an intended population and evidence of their effectiveness. They then should be tried one at a time on a small-scale basis to see whether they do produce the results their proponents ascribe to them.

Multicultural Student Populations

Another characteristic of U.S. schools is that they always have reflected students' multicultural backgrounds to some extent. However, as the birthrate among whites has declined, the proportion of minority children has increased. Nearly one-quarter of all children under age 15 currently are black and Hispanic (Edelman 1987), and they are the most likely to achieve poorly in school, become at risk, and drop out (Paulu 1987). In fifty-three major U.S. cities, the current minority will be the majority by the year 2000 (Rodriguez 1988).

The high rate of underachievement among minorities led Hale-Benson (1982) to advocate that teachers "teach to the learning styles of Black children" (p. 196). That deduction, however, was extrapolated from her knowledge of how African families reared their young (Dunn & Griggs 1990). Hale-Benson used no diagnostic instrument to identify "learning style" and left the construct itself essentially unspecified. Nevertheless, what Hale-Benson described as a black learning style was reported by Carbo, Dunn, and Dunn (1986) as a global, holistic, simultaneous, field-dependent style that is representative of how many young children of all racial and ethnic cultures approach learning. Two decades ago, Ramirez and Castenada (1974) reported those same traits when describing Mexican-American children, as did Guzzo (1987) in the study of Brazilian children, Crino (1984) in the study of young Caucasians, and Dunn, Gemake, Jalali, Zenhausern, Quinn, and Spiridakis (1990) when describing African-, Chinese-, Greek-, and Mexican-American fourth- through sixth-graders in New York and Texas.

Previous to the undertaking of this international research project but during the past decade, five independent studies were completed to determine whether significant differences existed between and among different cultural groups within the United States (Dunn, Griggs, Price, in press; Jacobs 1987; Jalali 1988; Lan Yong 1989; Sims 1988).

Subjects in these studies ranged from elementary to middle school children in rural, urban, and suburban areas of the United States who were of lower or middle socioeconomic status. The cultural groups represented within the United States were black, white, Greek, Chinese, and Mexican. Those studies compared the Learning Style Inventory (LSI) (Dunn, Dunn, & Price 1979, 1981, 1985, 1987) profiles among children from diverse cultural backgrounds. Although the findings within cultures were not always compatible, there were clear differences among the groups with respect to the pattern of characteristics the students reported (Dunn & Griggs 1990). Some of those differences might have been related to variations in geographic location, age, or achievement levels, but some were clearly physiological and/or psychological in nature (Dunn & Griggs 1990). For example, individual preferences for quiet, sound, alternative illumination, temperature, seating arrangements, perceptual strengths, chronobiological time-of-day energy levels, and mobility were reported as being biological by both Restak (1979) and Thies (1979). However, a need for learning alone, with peers, or with adults, self-versus-teacher-versus-parent-motivation, external versus internal structure, and a need for variety versus patterns and routines certainly could have been either cultural or experiential in derivation (Thies 1979). However, before selected variables may be construed as essentially cultural in influence, it must be noted that many people in each cultural group differ dramatically from each other, their spouses, and their siblings (Dunn & Griggs 1990).

Although learning style differences were repeatedly reported as existing among multicultural subgroups in the United States, the research in counseling and learning styles and the practical applications of both (Dunn & Griggs 1988; 1990; Griggs 1985, 1991; Griggs & Dunn 1988) suggested that there apparently were as many within-group differences as between-group differences. Accordingly, it seems that educators should place less emphasis on teaching to groups and more on teaching to individual learning style strengths. Such individual approaches have been demonstrated effective in increasing academic achievement, improving attitudes toward learning, and ensuring better behavior than previously among students at all grade levels (Andrews 1990a; Brunner & Majewski 1990; Dunn 1990c; Dunn, Beaudry, & Klavas 1989; Dunn, Bruno, Sklar, Beaudry, & Zenhausern 1990; Dunn, Della Valle, Dunn, Geisert, Sinatra, & Zenhausern 1986; Dunn & Dunn, 1992a; 1992b; Dunn, Dunn, Primavera, Sinatra, & Virostko 1987; Dunn, Giannitti, Murray, Geisert, Rossi, and Quinn 1990; Dunn & Griggs 1988b; Dunn, Krimsky, Murray, & Quinn 1985; Harp & Orsak 1990; Orsak 1990; Perrin 1990; Pizzo, Dunn, & Dunn 1990; Sinatra 1990).

Learning Style Variations

Extensive research conducted in the United States during the 1980s indicated that gifted and talented students have learning styles that differ from those of underachievers (Pederson 1984; Ricca 1983; Wasson 1980) and from each other (Coleman 1988; Cross 1982; Dunn & Price 1980; Kreitner 1981; Lan Yong 1989; Mein 1986; Paskowitz 1985; Perrin 1984; Price, Dunn, Dunn, & Griggs 1981; Stewart 1981; Vignia 1983). Differences were reported between the styles of learning disabled and average achievers (Madison 1984; Snider 1985); among different types of special education students (Dean 1982; Ignelzi-Ferraro 1989; Lengal 1983); and between secondary students in vocational education and those in comprehensive high schools (Fleming 1989; Tappenden 1983; Zak 1989) and those in industrial arts (Kroon 1985). Indeed, whether or not teachers responded to the diversity of styles among their charges appeared to determine the amount of academic success each student experienced (Andrews 1990; Dunn 1990b; Dunn & Griggs 1988b; Gadwa & Griggs 1985; Harp & Orsak 1990; Orsak 1990a, 1990b; Perrin 1990). Differences have also been noted among highly academically achieving students, however no previous study examined the learning styles of gifted versus nongifted adolescents and then compared the unique traits identified within each achievement and each talent group.

Underachieving Students

The United States requires education for all children to age 16 and allocates many tax dollars toward that purpose. Over the years, more adolescents have attended school than ever before. Many more females and minority students than previously now obtain four-year degrees and, of those, significantly higher numbers continue into professional careers. Indeed, the average pupil-teacher ratio dropped from 17.6 in 1987 to 17.4 in 1988–89; and that is extremely low compared to the pupil-teacher ratio in most industrial nations.

Recently, however, economic stress has exacerbated the problems of urban centers, their schools, and their residents. The lure of work and economic security through city social services has brought many poor, illegal residents to this nation's cities. As their numbers increased, so did the percentage of poorly achieving, at-risk, dropout adolescents. Although schools have always had students who neither enjoyed academic learning nor performed well, the hope of eventually obtaining good jobs and a higher standard of living than their parents had kept many striving to complete high school. There was no alternative for such youngsters; they had two choices: menial labor or a "decent job" through education. That lure no longer exists for urban adolescents. Instead, drug trafficking and lawlessness provide some teenagers with more money than their parents ever conceived of earning. Their surroundings often are pitiful—crime-ridden apartments in neglected ghetto buildings with poor sanitation and dangerous gangs, often dishonest police and politicians, the availability of easy money by working for criminals, and the dissolution of the family and, particularly, a strong father figure—all have contributed to the eradication of hopes their grandparents shared.

The Carnegie Council on Policy Studies (1979) suggested that the major concerns of education should be to reduce the number of dropouts and the rate of absenteeism, particularly among minority students. However, Boyer (1987) admonished that resolution of the dropout problem is not aided by an emphasis on school reform in terms of adding core requirements in mathematics, science, English and foreign language. Instead, he argued, more attention needs to be focused on how children learn—their learning styles.

Gadwa and Griggs (1985) reported on a Washington high school alternative program in which exactly that was done. Dropout and at-risk students were diagnosed for learning style predispositions. In that study, students exemplified many global characteristics—needing sound (music), low light, an informal design, short assignments with break time in between, intake while learning, and high peer motivation (Dunn, Bruno, Sklar, Zenhausern, & Beaudry 1990; Dunn, Cavanaugh, Eberle, & Zenhausern 1982). They also were not morning-alert learners and required a variety of instructional strategies rather than routines and patterns. Those data were supported through interviews with the students and by teacher appraisals and anecdotal records. In addition, student behaviors indicated that the Learning Style Inventory data had accurately described them and how they learned. Those identical characteristics were revealed in two other studies of dropout populations, Johnson (1984) in Maryland and Thrasher (1985) in Florida. They also paralleled Tappenden's (1983) findings for 2,000 secondary, vocational education students in Ohio. When the Gadwa and Griggs population of underachieving, dropout, and at-risk adolescents were taught through their identified learning style characteristics, they attended classes regularly, completed two and three times the number of credits in a single semester, and increased their achievement test scores significantly (Dunn & Griggs 1988b).

Increasingly, educators said that dropouts come to school without a "readiness" to learn; they appear less able and less disciplined than previous generations. In addition, they appear inattentive, sometimes emotionally or psychologically disturbed, and have many personal concerns. Originally this type of student was found mostly in urban centers; gradually they became more evident in the suburbs. Originally they were present only among the poor; gradually they reflected affluence. At first, these youngsters were few in number; slowly the few expanded to many. In the beginning, they were mostly among minorities; currently they are evident among majority populations; in addition, the minorities they initially reflected are becoming our majority populations in many cities. Originally they came from no-parent homes; for the past decade, they have been emerging from single-parent and two-parent homes.

As one outgrowth, alarmed citizens have formed committees to examine not society but its educational systems. In addition, a number of government, privately supported business and corporate groups, and legislative groups have examined the effects of education. Each has eventually proposed changes, all of which have previously been tried. Suggestions have focused on a variety of concerns such as lengthening the amount of time spent in school, increasing and more narrowly delineating the requirements for high school graduation, restricting course choices, and mandating specific studies. None of the reports has focused squarely on the single measure that previously had increased academic achievement among those students who had not functioned successfully in conventional schools—matching individual learning style strengths with complementary environments, methods, sociological groupings, and instructional resources. Not a single report has addressed what prize-winning research has demonstrated as the most effective strategy for increasing student achievement and attitude test scores: teaching to individual learning styles (Dunn 1990c; Dunn & Dunn 1992, 1993; Griggs 1991).

Seven learning style traits significantly discriminate between high-risk or dropout students in comparison to their counterparts who remain in school (Dunn & Griggs 1988b; Gadwa & Griggs 1985; Johnson 1984; Thrasher 1984). Many dropouts appear to need:

1. High mobility;

2. A variety of instructional resources, approaches, and sociological groupings rather than routines and patterns;

3. To learn during late morning, afternoon, or evening hours, but not in the early morning (Andrews 1990, 1991; Gardiner 1986; Lemmon 1985);

4. An informal seating design, not wooden, steel, or plastic chairs and desks;

5. Low illumination; bright lights make them hyperactive and unable to concentrate passively;

6. Tactual and kinesthetic introductory resources accompanied or reinforced by auditory and visual explanations; they tend to have poor auditory and visual memory (Andrews 1990, 1991; Bauer 1991; Kroon 1985; Weinberg 1983; Wheeler 1980, 1983); and

7. Multisensory instructional packages or their equivalent because, although they often do tend to be motivated, they cannot remember the factual information they are taught through conventional schooling (Bauer 1991; Drew 1992; Gardiner 1986).

Interest in Giftedness

Based on the literature and funding available from governmental agencies, it must be concluded that American education has evidenced more interest in the plight of underachievers and dropouts than in giftedness. Chapter One, Resource Room, Special Education, Dropout Prevention, and Alternative Education programs for poorly achieving youngsters exist in almost every school in the nation on a full-time, daily basis. Programs specifically designed for the gifted are available in relatively fewer schools and often are scheduled for one period, one afternoon, or at best and only in rare instances, one day per week. Providing for the gifted often is viewed as elitism, and responsiveness to talent (other than athletic prowess) has been minimal. Politicians deplore the superiority of other nations' children in mathematics, science, and languages, but bright students in the United States are rarely accelerated, rarely grouped together for stimulation and pacing, and rarely taught differently from their average-achieving classmates. Without opportunities to advance their education in ways that respond to their unique learning styles—which demand a great deal of independent learning, contracting, problem solving, real-life challenges, and in-depth studies—many gifted and talented adolescents in the United States often suffer boredom, repetition, and frustration in traditional schools.

RESEARCH METHODOLOGY

Subjects

This sample of U.S. gifted and nongifted adolescents was composed of the total group of students in each selected public secondary school in diverse geographical locations—the northeast, southeast, north-central, south-central, and northwestern sections of the country. For a detailed description of subjects by grade and sex, see Chapter 2, Table 2.1. In 1989, a list was obtained of the 43,000 principals who were then members of the National Association of Secondary School Principals (NASSP), the leading professional organization of its kind in North America. That list was subdivided into urban and suburban schools in each of six sections of the United States and the 50th, 100th, and 150th school in alphabetical order in each of those sections was identified. Letters were mailed to each of those principals requesting participation in this study. Of those who indicated willingness to participate, only those schools with identified gifted populations were included. The sample ultimately included students in grades 7–12 identified as gifted or nongifted by grade point averages (GPAs) and school classification systems and/or creativity based upon their scores on the Tel Aviv Activities Inventory.

Materials

Two instruments were administered during the course of this study: the Learning Style Inventory and the Tel Aviv Activities Inventory. Both were described in detail in Chapter 2.

Methods

During the summer of 1989, a list of the 43,000 secondary school principals was divided into six geographical locations and separated into urban and suburban schools. Every 50th, 100th, and 150th school in each section was identified and a letter was mailed to the principals requesting participation in this study. In early September 1989, the principals who had responded positively were mailed a second letter requesting overall demographic descriptions of their schools, the number of students in grades 7–12 for whom instruments would be needed, and the names of teachers or guidance counselors who would administer the questionnaires. Subsequently, samples of each of the three instruments and directions for administration were mailed to those persons. During the fall 1989 and spring 1990 semesters, the principals who had indicated willingness to have their schools participate in this study were mailed a sufficient number of each of the two questionnaires for all students in grades 7–12. Personnel were employed to collect additional demographic data and the grade point averages of each of the students, who then were identified as either academically gifted or nongifted on the basis of their GPAs and each school's classification.

Procedure

During the fall 1989 and spring 1990 semesters, the Learning Style Inventory (Dunn, Dunn, & Price 1989) and the Tel Aviv Activities Inventory were administered to the students during two separate periods by the teachers and counselors who had agreed to do so. To ensure confidentiality of the data, each subject was assigned a research participant number, which was the only identification used during the data analysis.

The Academically Gifted United States Adolescents

Grade point average is frequently the best indicator of academic giftedness. In this study, students with a GPA of 3.4 or higher (A = 4.0) were designated as gifted. Among the 674 students for whom these data were available, 126 (19%) had a GPA of 3.4, whereas 548 (81%) fell below this level. The results yielded by the stepwise discriminant analysis, using the Wilks' Lambda criteria revealed that a total of twelve LSI variables significantly entered the equation when comparing the gifted and nongifted.

Academically gifted students were highly motivated, preferred bright light, warm temperature, and learning alone, needed sound, were parent motivated, kinesthetic, and highly responsible (conforming). The nongifted students preferred a formal design, learning in the late morning, required a high degree of structure, and were auditory. In combination, this discriminant analysis indicated that twelve LSI variables produced a Wilks' Lambda of 0.928 ($df = 12$; p. 00001); 81.45 percent were classified correctly based on these twelve LSI variables.

These findings are mixed in view of previous research concerning the academically gifted. That the gifted are highly motivated and prefer to learn alone was validated by previous researchers (Dunn & Price 1980; Griggs & Price 1980b; Stewart 1981; Wasson 1980). The most surprising findings were that these gifted were highly responsible (conforming) and only kinesthetically strong. Previous research revealed that the academically gifted were perceptually strong, not only kinesthetically but also visually, auditorially, and tactually. However, the studies conducted by Dunn and Price (1980), Stewart (1981), and Wasson (1980) examined the learning styles of elementary students; the research conducted by Griggs and Price (1980) was with junior high school students. Although the gifted were perceptually strong in comparison with same-age peers, modality development is a biological variable that matures with age. Thus, it may be that more high school students experience increased perceptual ability than do younger students, and by the time they reach secondary levels, the gap among same-age students may not be as wide as the variance between the relative perceptual development of grade school youngsters.

Nonconformity is the opposite of responsibility, and previous research identified nonconformity as a characteristic of the gifted; but that, too, may have more to do with age and gradual adaptation to the requirements of schooling than to differences between the gifted and nongifted. Also, it is possible that nonconforming gifted students drop out of school.

Preferences for bright light, sound, and warm temperature and being parent motivated were not evident in previous studies—another possibility related to age and adolescence. Price (1980b) reported that the older the person, the more light that was needed, and that puberty was a period wherein the need for sound increases disproportionately, eventually returning to its previously normal level as the youngster emerged from adolescence (Price 1980a). Although Murrain (1983) found that more of her secondary students preferred warmth than cool, neither temperature nor being parent motivated were previously linked to giftedness. However, it is possible that nonconforming gifted students refuse to tolerate conventional school requirements and that the parent motivated among the gifted remain in school to fulfill the aspirations of their parents.

There are other possible reasons for the differences evidenced. In most of the previous studies, academic giftedness was defined as an IQ of 130 or above on the WISC-R or Stanford Binet, whereas in the present study, IQ scores were not available. Additionally, most of the previous studies were conducted within a single school, whereas these data were collected from many schools representing every geographic region of the United States. Finally, as indicated above, different age groups were examined. Research indicates that selected learning style elements such as mobility preferences remain stable over time, whereas other variables such as perceptual strengths and sociological preferences appear to follow the growth curve. Others, such as the need for sound and intake, appear to increase during adolescence but eventually return to their previous "normal" levels.

Learning Style Preferences by Specific Domain

A summary of the learning style preferences of U.S. students talented in science, social leadership, dance, music, art, literature, drama, and sports is presented in Table 7.1.

Science. The results yielded by the stepwise discriminant analysis using the Wilks' Lambda criteria presented in Table 7.1 revealed that a total of ten of the twenty-two LSI variables significantly discriminated between the creative in

Table 7.1
Learning Style Elements that Discriminate between Creative and Noncreative Adolescents in the United States by Specific Domain

Domain	Creative	Noncreative
1. Science	(n=413)	(n=551)
	*formal design	*responsible
	*warm	*auth fig present
	*alone	
	*structure	
	*low light	
	*persistent	
	*sound	
	*motivation	
2. Social Leadership	(n=164)	(n=849)
	*kinesthetic	*mobility
	*motivated	*warm temperature
	*formal design	
	*intake	
	*structure	
	*responsible	
	*bright light	
3. Dance	(n=189)	(n=268)
	*intake	*sound present
	*teacher motivated	*warm temperature
	*auth fig present	
4. Music	(n=344)	(n=550)
	*kinesthetic	*mobility
	*evening	*morning
	*responsibility	*persistent
	*late morning	
	*afternoon	

Table 7.1 (continued)

Domain	Creative	Noncreative
5. Art	(n=330)	(n=529)
	*tactual	*auth fig present
	*visual	*structure
	*several ways	*responsible
	*motivation	*formal design
	*light	
	*auditory	
6. Literature	(n=71)	(n=745)
	*afternoon	*warm temperature
	*light	*auth fig present
	*motivated	*parent motivated
	*several ways	*auditory
	*kinesthetic	*teacher motivated
7. Drama	(n=112)	(n=305)
	*structure	*afternoon
	*motivation	
	*teacher motivated	
	*kinesthetic	
8. Sports	(n=659)	(n=316)
	*parent motivated	*peer
	*alone	*several ways
	*kinesthetic	*auth fig present
	*intake	*sound present
	*visual	
	*afternoon	
	*tactile	

science and those adolescents not creative in science. As illustrated in Table 7.1, the 413 adolescents who were creative in science were highly motivated and persistent, required low light, sound, warm temperature, high structure, a formal design in learning, and preferred to learn alone. In contrast, the 551 adolescents categorized as noncreative in science were highly responsible (conforming) and preferred authority figures present while learning. It is understandable that, to excel in science, it is necessary to be motivated toward difficult academic concentration, but preferring structure, formal design, and learning alone are not typically adolescent characteristics (Price 1980b).

Conversely, are highly conforming students who concentrate on pleasing the teacher rather than exploring new answers, and who require authority figures present while learning, lacking the qualities necessary for excelling in science? These, of course, are questions that require future exploration, but the overall findings of this research concerning the learning styles of adolescents in the United States tend to support the premise that students with specific learning style traits tend to succeed in specific talent areas.

Leadership. The results yielded by the stepwise discriminant analysis revealed that a total of nine of the twenty-two LSI variables significantly discriminated between the leaders and nonleaders. As illustrated in Table 7.1, the 164 adolescents classified as talented in leadership were highly motivated, kinesthetic, responsible (conforming), required a formal design while learning combined with bright light, external structure, and intake. The 849 noncreative socially preferred warm temperature and mobility. When comparing the learning styles of the young people creative in science with their counterparts in leadership, the similarities between them include motivation, external structure, and formal design. No clear hemispheric preference is apparent for, according to Dunn, Cavanaugh, Eberle, and Zenhausern (1982), preferring a formal design and bright light would be analytic; intake would be global, although intake and kinesthetic strengths are highly representative of adolescents across the board.

Dance. Table 7.1 reveals that the discriminant analysis indicated that only five of the twenty-two LSI variables significantly discriminated between the creative and noncreative in dance. The 189 creative in dance were teacher motivated, preferred authority figures present (meaning that they wanted authoritative, rather than collegial, teachers and needed the feedback those figures could provide to them), and required intake. With the exception of needing intake (a widespread adolescent characteristic, although the noncreative in dance did not approach the levels of this creative group), the young people creative in dance revealed learning styles extremely different from their classmates who were creative in either science or leadership. The 268 noncreative in dance preferred warmth and sound while learning. Cody (1983) reported that average IQ students preferred studying in a warm environment.

Music. Table 7.1 reveals that the discriminant analysis indicated that eight of the twenty-two LSI variables significantly discriminated between the creative and noncreative in music. The 344 adolescents creative in music were responsible (conforming), kinesthetic, and preferred learning in the late morning, afternoon, and evening. In contrast, the 550 noncreative in music preferred learning in the morning, needed high mobility, and reported being persistent.

The musically creative shared the learning style characteristics of conformity with the socially creative, and nothing with the creative in science and dance. Kreitner (1981) also reported that musically gifted students in Ohio were extremely kinesthetic—not auditory as many music teachers had believed. It also should be noted that the musically creative constituted the first group of gifted with three energy highs during the day—late morning, afternoon, and evening. The noncreative in music shared the mobility needs of their counterparts in leadership, but were the first to evidence high persistence levels.

Art. Analysis indicated that ten of the twenty-two LSI variables significantly discriminated between the creative and noncreative in art. Although artistically creative students shared the learning style element of high motivation with their science and leadership counterparts, most interesting among their traits were their multiple-modality strengths, a trait characteristic of many high IQ students (Dunn & Price 1980; Griggs & Price 1980b; Kreitner 1981; Ricca 1983; Price, Dunn, Dunn, & Griggs 1981). These youngsters were visual, tactual, and auditory. Apparently, artistically gifted adolescents reach sensory maturity earlier than most young people, for among the general population, young children usually enter school with solely kinesthetic and/or tactual strengths. Strong visual memory develops among some by third or fourth grade at the earliest, although perhaps 10 to 12 percent of kindergartners have it. However, one-third of many high school boys remain tactual and kinesthetic only, and few adults reveal three perceptual strengths. Most have one; gifted students often have two or more.

The artistically creative adolescents also preferred bright light and learning in several ways, demonstrating a strong need for variety as opposed to patterns and routines. In this regard, they shared a preference for bright light with the socially creative, and their need for variety may reflect, somewhat, why they chose to become engaged in art. The 529 noncreative in this area required a formal design, external structure, authority figures present, and were responsible. The noncreative groups appeared to have only one quality other than a need for warmth and mobility in common, and this group of nonartists did not even share those traits with their counterparts. The only entity that became apparent was that each noncreative group was significantly different from the creative in that specific area.

Literature. Our analysis revealed that ten of the twenty-two LSI variables significantly discriminated between the creative and noncreative in literature. Those seventy-one creative youngsters shared the high self-motivation reflected by their science, leadership, and artistic counterparts and were kinesthetic (similar to the creative in music and social), preferred to learn in several ways (similar to their counterparts in art), and preferred bright light (like the artists and those with leadership skills). The 745 noncreative in literature once again preferred a warm temperature, were parent motivated, preferred an authority figure present while learning, were auditory, and preferred a warm environment.

Drama. Table 7.1 reveals that only five of the twenty-two LSI variables significantly discriminated between the creative and noncreative in drama. The 112 adolescents creative in drama were teacher motivated (like the creative in dance). Also, like their counterparts in literature, leadership, and music they were highly kinesthetic. In addition, those creative in drama required external structure (like those in social skills and science). When one reflects on the fields in which these creative students wanted and obtained external structure, they tend to be in drama and science where teachers provide direction; being socially adept requires adherence to socially imposed structures. In contrast, dancers, musicians, and artists, after their initial training and neophyte years, must be internally structured for that very quality is the gift they give to their professions. The 305 noncreative adolescents in drama preferred learning in the afternoon.

Sports. Eleven of the twenty-two LSI variables significantly discriminated between the creative and noncreative in sports. Table 7.1 illustrates that the 659 talented adolescents in sports were tactual, visual, kinesthetic, afternoon and self learners who also were parent motivated and required intake. The 316 nontalented in sports consistently required variety in learning, sound present, authority figures present, and peer learning.

Other Factors in Learning Style Preferences

We summarized the learning style preferences of creative and noncreative U.S. populations according to environmental, emotional, sociological, and physiological stimuli.

Environmental Stimulus

1. Sound present while learning was preferred by the academically talented and the creative in science (a global characteristic), whereas an absence of sound (or a need for extreme quiet) was preferred by those nontalented in dance and sports.

2. Bright light (an analytic characteristic), was preferred by those talented in art, leadership, and literature and the academically gifted, whereas low light was preferred by the creative in science.

3. Warm temperature was preferred by the academically gifted, the creative in science, and the nontalented in dance, leadership, and literature.

4. A formal design was preferred by those with leadership talent, the creative in science, and the nongifted in art and academics.

Emotional Stimulus

1. Being self-motivated was characteristic of analytics and those gifted in art, drama, leadership, literature, and science.

2. Persistence was strong among those creative in science and literature and the noncreative in music.

3. Being responsible on the Learning Style Inventory, which correlates with being highly conforming on the California Psychological Inventory (White 1981), was characteristic

of academically, leadership, and musically gifted students as well as the nontalented
in science and art.

4. Being externally structured was characteristic of those with scientific, dramatic, and
   leadership talents and the nonacademically gifted and the nontalented in art.

Sociological Stimulus

1. The academically gifted and those talented in science and sports preferred learning
   alone.

2. Although we herein are reporting the learning styles of only the gifted and talented,
   it seems important to share that, with the emphasis on cooperative learning in the
   United States, in this study, only the academically nongifted and the noncreative in
   sports were peer oriented.

3. Being teacher motivated was characteristic of the talented in dance and drama.

4. Wanting an authority figure present was reported by those talented in dance, and the
   nontalented in art, science, and literature.

5. Wanting instructional and sociological variety when learning, rather than routines or
   patterns, was indicative of talented art and literature students and the nontalented in
   sports.

6. Being parent motivated characterized the academically gifted, and those talented in
   sports as well as the nontalented in literature.

Physiological Stimulus

1. Students creative artistically were the only auditory learners found among this population of gifted and talented secondary adolescents. Instead, being highly visual
   characterized the sports and artistically talented; tactual strengths characterized the
   gifted in art and sports; and being strongly kinesthetic characterized the dramatically,
   musically, and socially talented, and the academically gifted.

2. Intake while learning was desired by the students talented in dance, leadership, and
   sports.

3. The musically gifted were the *only* late-morning gifted preferents; indeed, the only
   other late-morning students were the nonacademically gifted. Afternoon was preferred
   by the literature, music, and sports talented. Many of the musically talented adolescents
   preferred evening learning.

4. Needing mobility was characteristic of the academically nongifted.

CONCLUSIONS

Previous studies of the learning styles of various U.S. groups revealed differences within each group and between and among groups of various ages,
grades, achievement levels, and cultures. This investigation corroborated those
data but revealed interesting school-related findings.

For example, instruction in the United States begins between 8 and 9 A.M.
and tends to address core requirements "first thing in the morning," under the
assumption that most students are alert at that time. This study revealed that,

when these secondary school gifted and talented had time-of-day preferences, they were not for early morning learning. Instead, their most preferred time of day was late morning (music), afternoon (literature, music, science, and sports), and evening (musically talented). Given the achievement levels of these young-sters, imagine how much more proficient they would be if they were permitted to attend classes and take tests at their most—rather than at their least—preferred concentration periods!

Whereas virtually *all* instruction in the United States occurs through lecture, discussion, and/or reading, the gifted and talented in this study revealed strongly tactual (art, sports) and kinesthetic (drama, music, social, and academically gifted) preferences—senses *rarely* directly addressed instructionally in U.S. secondary schools. Only the gifted in art and sports were strongly visual. Again, our imagination is excited by the academic excellence that might be possible if either their instructors used—or these youngsters were taught how to teach themselves through—tactual and kinesthetic instructional resources (Dunn & Dunn 1992b; see also Chapter 3).

Secondary schools in the United States rarely permit students to nibble, snack, or drink juice or water while learning. That constraint appears arbitrary and capricious in view of the fact that the dance, social, and sports gifted and talented adolescents in this study cited the need for intake while concentrating as one of their primary requisites for learning.

The LSI revealed significantly higher motivation scores among this group of talented and gifted than among their nongifted counterparts. Previous studies revealed that the learning styles of highly and underachieving global students differed on only two elements of style: motivation and perceptual strength. These data tended to corroborate those findings.

During the past few years, many schools have embraced small-group proce-dures called Cooperative Learning, in the belief that most students learn better with peers than in large-group lessons. Examination of the learning styles of the gifted and talented revealed that most were not peer motivated. Indeed, those in dance and drama, were teacher motivated; dancers preferred authoritative feedback; the scientists, athletes, and those with a high GPA preferred learning alone; and sports and academically gifted were parent motivated. These data suggest that either independent Contract Activity Packages or individualized studies directed by their teachers would be more appropriate than small-group instruction for these gifted students, a finding reported by Perrin (1984) with first and second graders.

That so many nongifted and global students required mobility while learning is another characteristic that should be addressed by educators. On a daily basis, many teachers tell students to ''sit still,'' ''stay in your chair,'' and/or stop moving, rocking, or extending their feet into the aisles. Teachers apparently are unaware of Branton's (1966) findings verifying that when a person is seated on a wooden, steel, or plastic chair, approximately 75 percent of the total body weight is supported by only four square inches of bone. The resulting stress on the tissues of the buttocks often causes fatigue, discomfort, and the need for frequent postural change. Addressing the mobility needs of gifted students becomes perfunctory when they are permitted to teach themselves or learn together through Contract Activity Packages or independent studies, which also address their sociological needs.

NOTES

This research was funded by St. John's University's Center for the Study of Learning and Teaching Styles. The authors acknowledge the contributions of the National Association of Secondary School Principals (NASSP) and numerous administrators, teachers, students, and parents.

Chapter 8

The Learning Styles of Gifted Adolescents in Israel

Roberta M. Milgram and Gary E. Price

Israel is a country with a short history and a very long past. The name Israel conjures up in the minds of many people Biblical scenes of Bedouins and camels, of kings, judges, and prophets. People of many religions look to Israel as the Holy Land and see Jerusalem as the spiritual hub of the universe. By contrast, others see Israel as the modern, pulsating city of Tel Aviv, with its urbane population, elegant shops, and rich cultural life. The amazing thing is that both perceptions are accurate. Israel is a culture in which the old and the new have integrated to produce a unique blend. In the town of Ashkelon today the Philistines do not do battle with Samson but rather a small child also named Shimshon (Samson in modern Hebrew) does "battle" with his playmates on the school playground. The view of the Sea of Galilee that Jesus saw from the Beatitudes when he made his Sermon on the Mount is the same today except that today one sees water-skiers, seaside restaurants serving St. Peter's fish, and young people in nearby Tiberias doing what young people do all over the world.

Israel declared its independence and was admitted to the United Nations in 1948. The country was not born out of the ashes of the Holocaust in Europe, but that tragic event led thousands of Jews to come to Israel and had a significant effect on the personal-social development of subsequent generations of Jewish children born in Israel but living with parents and grandparents who bore the physical and psychological scars of the Holocaust.

Since its establishment, Israel has leaped into the twentieth century with accelerated intellectual, cultural, and technological development. The Jewish people have been known as the People of the Book. This is reflected in Israel in the enormous emphasis placed on religious studies by some segments of the population, who by their dress and life-style perpetuate the past, and by the extraordinary interest and support for music, art, and literature on the part of others. By the same token the People of the Book in modern times emphasize intensive development in the theoretical and practical aspects of science and technology.

An accurate picture of the world in which an Israeli child grows up must include the constant stress of war and terrorist attacks. In a country that has known six wars in forty-two years, a child is never free from the challenge of coping with the aftermath of the last war, the danger of the next war, or the ongoing hazard of terrorist activities. The Israel Defense Force is not a remote institution without impact on his or her life. Fathers are called for reserve duty each year for thirty to forty days until age 55. Each youngster knows that upon graduation from high school he or she will serve two to three years or more. Accordingly, the standards of behavior, advancement, and values of the Israel Defense Force have a potent effect on the personality development, including learning style, of Israeli children.

People born in Israel are called sabras. A sabra is a cactus, thought to be tough and prickly on the outside and soft and sweet on the inside. The sabra personality is reflected in such elements as independence, persistence, and non-conformity. Many children, however, do not follow the sabra model because, being born in other countries and only recently immigrated to Israel, they reflect the learning styles characteristic of their native land and/or their parents.

Is there a distinctive learning style that characterizes the children of a country that, since its birth over 40 years ago, has absorbed hundreds of thousands of immigrants from countries all over the world? What does Uri, born in Israel of parents who are tenth-generation Jerusalemites, have in common with Nadia, who arrived in Israel thirty-five years ago as a toddler with her parents from Morocco, or with Noam, born in Israel of American-born parents who immigrated to Israel twenty years ago, or with Stuart, born in Britain who came to Israel ten years ago, and with Sasha who came one month ago from the Soviet Union?

The learning styles of gifted adolescents in each country are shaped by the behaviors, feelings, emotions, attitudes, and values of the the people who constitute the culture in which each lives. Despite the enormous differences in background among the children in Israel, we believe that powerful cultural variables shape the behaviors, emotions, attitudes, and values of native-born and immigrant Israeli youngsters, and produce a learning style that is more or less characteristic of learners in Israel.

The Israeli individual portrayed here may appear to be very different from people in the United States. Nevertheless, Israel is a Western-oriented society that shares with the United States many child-rearing practices and values influencing cognitive and personality development and many attitudes and practices associated with urban socialization (Eisenstadt 1951, 1967). These include a permissive orientation in the home and the school, and an emphasis upon individual initiative, independent thinking, and the assumption of responsibility.

In previous research on personality variables, we found that junior high school

American and Israeli children were equally low in dogmatism and high in internal locus of control, when compared to children who had recently immigrated to Israel from the Soviet Union (Aviram & Milgram 1977). Both Western groups were highly similar in creative thinking and both were higher in creative thinking than children who grew up in the Soviet Union. By the same token, Israeli pre-schoolers were similar to American pre-schoolers on creative thinking (Milgram, Moran, Sawyers, & Fu 1987; Moran, Milgram, Sawyers, & Fu 1983). On this basis, one might expect to find considerable similarity in the learning style of children in the two societies, but since this question has not been examined empirically, it merits investigation.

In the current chapter, we not only compare learning style differences between learners in the United States and Israel across the board, but also examine learning style in gifted and talented adolescents characterized by the wide variety and range of abilities postulated by Milgram in her 4 × 4 model (1989, 1991a) within the Israeli group. Although the model provides the basis for expecting learning style differences based upon different categories and levels of abilities, the exact nature of these differences remains to be empirically determined.

This book is the first comprehensive cross-cultural investigation of learning style in adolescents in general, and in gifted adolescents in particular. The remainder of this chapter is divided into three parts. In the first part, the methodology and procedure of the study conducted in Israel are presented. In the second part, the distinctive learning styles of Israeli and American adolescents are compared. In the third part, the learning styles of gifted and nongifted Israeli adolescents as defined by Milgram's 4 × 4 model are analyzed as follows: high general intelligence, high grades in the school subjects of Hebrew Literature, Hebrew Language, Mathematics, and English (a foreign language in Israel), high divergent thinking ability, and high creative attainments in eleven specific domains: science, mathematics, computer, social leadership, dance, music, art, literature, foreign languages, drama, and sport.

RESEARCH METHODOLOGY

Subjects

The subjects were the entire student population (N = 985) in grades 7–12 of a Tel Aviv junior-senior high school. The distribution of subjects by grade and sex was presented in Chapter 2, Table 2.1.

Materials

Four instruments were administered. The Learning Style Inventory (Dunn, Dunn, & Price 1984), the Tel Aviv Activities Inventory (Milgram, 1990b), and the Tel Aviv Creativity Test (Milgram and Milgram 1976a) were described in detail in Chapter 2.

As reported in Chapter 2, Curry (1987) compared the Learning Style Inventory with twenty other measures of learning style and reported very high psychometric standards for this instrument. The test reliability of the Hebrew translation of the Learning Style Inventory was estimated by means of analysis of variance, a technique reported by Hoyt (1941) that is comparable to Kuder Richardson 20. The reliability coefficient range for seventeen elements was .62–.86. The range for four other elements was .54–.58, and only one element (Persistence) yielded a low reliability (.22). On the basis of these findings we concluded that the reliability of the Hebrew translation of the Learning Style Inventory was satisfactory.

In addition, two verbal subtests of the Milta Measure of General Intelligence (Ortar 1980)—General Information and Vocabulary—were administered in Israel. The intermediate level form of the test was administered to children in grades 7–9, and the adult level to children in grades 10–12. These two subtests were selected because of their high correlation with the total score as reported in the test manual (Ortar 1980). The Milta was scored, and IQ scores extrapolated according to the directions provided by the author.

Personal data (identity number, age, sex, and socioeconomic status) and school grades in Hebrew literature, Hebrew language, mathematics, and foreign language (English) were entered into the data base.

Procedure

The four instruments were group administered in two separate sessions according to instructions provided by the authors of the test instruments. In the first session, three instruments (Learning Style Inventory, Tel Aviv Activities Inventory, Tel Aviv Creativity Test) were administered with no time limits. In the second session two subtests of the Milta Measure of General Intelligence were administered with a five-minute time limit for each subtest as indicated in the test manual.

Two examiners were present in each testing session. The first author trained the examiners and supervised the test administration. In order to ensure complete security of the research data and to protect the personal privacy of the subjects, each subject was assigned a participant number that was used on the test forms and during all phases of data analysis.

RESEARCH RESULTS

Comparison of Israeli and U.S. Students

We first compared Israeli learners with a random sample of American learners drawn from a data base provided by Price Systems, Inc. We asked, "In what way are the learning styles of American and Israeli adolescents similar and different?'' A discriminant analysis was performed on the twenty-two elements for the two samples.

Results of the discriminant analyses that indicate on which of the twenty-two learning style elements one group was superior to the other and on which no difference was found between the American and Israeli samples are summarized in Table 8.1. For ease of presentation and analysis, the twenty-two elements were summarized according to logical groupings in Table 8.1 and in subsequent tables in this chapter. The groupings are Personality, Social, Environmental, Perceptual, and Time.

Israeli adolescents expressed a stronger preference than Americans to learn alone, without authority figures present and away from the watchful eye of teachers. They prefer less structure in learning tasks provided for them, thus leaving them free to interpret situations and assignments in their own way. These differences would appear to reflect the features of the independent sabra character described earlier.

On the other hand, Israeli adolescents are more conforming. They prefer a more formally designed classroom atmosphere and a quieter learning environment than Americans. Their lower scores on kinesthetic, tactile, and mobility elements indicate a lower preference for learning by means of active real-life experiences, manipulative materials, and frequent, free movement around the classroom. These scores are also consistent with their preference for less flexible attributes in the learning environment. The pattern of preferences of Israeli youngsters represents an acceptance of the status quo in the Israeli educational system and indicates a certain degree of satisfaction with things as they are.

The acceptance by students of many status quo features of the conventional Israeli classroom is in marked contrast to the widespread call for reform and revision of these features on the part of professional education circles in Israel. It makes one wonder if the changes called for would meet the needs of the consumers of education, the students, or the needs of producers of education, educational theorists, and professional practitioners.

Both Israelis and Americans are equally willing to learn by visual and auditory means, the more conventional teaching strategies.

The findings reported above for Israeli adolescents—greater independence on the one hand and preference for a more conforming learning environment on the other—appear to be contradictory at first glance. However, they may well reflect some of the diverse trends within Israeli national character—the individualistic pioneering spirit and the conventional characteristics of learners in a tight-knit society that shares a single religious orientation, as well as many basic attitudes and values. Although individual initiative is prized, children are socialized to function within the limits of a relatively insular society.

Americans reported a higher level of motivation to learn than Israelis. This finding is somewhat surprising in terms of the great importance that Israeli society attaches to education and transmitting the value of education to young people. Comparison of motivation scores of the two groups shows that both groups

Table 8.1
Learning Style Elements that Discriminate Between Adolescents in Israel and in the United States: Relative Contribution to Differentiation

ELEMENT	ISRAEL-U.S. DATE BASE COMPARISON
PERSONALITY	
OVERALL MOTIVATION	4
TEACHER MOTIVATED	1
PERSISTENCE	6
RESPONSIBILITY/CONFORMITY	5*
STRUCTURE	14
MOBILITY	13
SOCIAL	
ALONE/PEER	10
AUTHORITY FIGURES	16
SEVERAL WAYS	11
ENVIRONMENTAL	
NOISE LEVEL	2
TEMPERATURE	7*
DESIGN	3*
PERCEPTUAL	
TACTILE	15
KINESTHETIC	9
TIME	
LATE MORNING	8*
AFTERNOON	12

*Israeli learners higher that U.S. Data Base

reported high overall motivation to learn. The relative difference in level of motivation may reflect a cultural difference in talking about the importance of education. Children in the United States are more competitive and are encouraged to express their views freely. They are reinforced by their teachers, parents, and peers to say that they want to do well in school. Since no one would censure them for presenting these views openly, they speak their mind and report high motivation. Israel was founded on a socialist ethic and Israeli children are reinforced for being noncompetitive and to refrain from saying positive things about themselves and their values. They may have internalized the same high values about school and achievement, but publicly it is more acceptable to downplay their motivation to excel in school.

The preference of Israeli students to learn in the late morning rather than in the afternoon and in a warmer rather than a cooler temperature clearly reflects the geographic location in which these youngsters are growing up. Israel is a warm, if not a hot, climate with no snow or severe cold and only a little rain in the so-called winter months between December and February. Most schools are not yet air-conditioned and close early in the afternoon to avoid the hottest part of the day. The school and work day starts early with schools and offices opening at 8 A.M., and some schools open as early as 7 A.M. Many businesses close between 2 and 4 P.M. in order to cope with the heat. One may conclude that these students prefer what they are used to.

Learning Styles of Gifted and Nongifted Israeli Adolescents

This section deals with differences in learning style within the Israeli sample as a function of IQ, school grades, creative thinking, and eleven domains of creative performance (science, mathematics, etc.). These differences were examined by conducting fourteen separate discriminant analyses. Subjects were divided into gifted high intelligence and nongifted intelligence groups on the basis of their IQ test scores, and into gifted high scholastic achievement and nongifted scholastic achievement groups on the basis of their grade point average (Hebrew literature, language, mathematics, English). Subjects with scores in the upper 20 percent of each distribution were designated as gifted.

Gifted high-creative-thinking and nongifted lower-creative-thinking groups consisted of subjects with creative-thinking scores that were above and below the total sample mean on the Tel Aviv Creativity Test (Milgram 1980), respectively. The gifted group for creative attainment in the remaining eleven specific domains of creative performance consisted of subjects who gave positive responses to specified Activities Inventory items from among those in the relevant domains that clearly reflected relatively outstanding activity and/or attainment. One such item in science was: "Have you conducted an original scientific experiment? (Both the idea for the experiment and the implementation of the experiment were original and not a repeat of another experiment)." In literature, a suitable item was: "Have you ever written a literary piece that was published in a community newspaper (not school)?'' In mathematics, an item indicative of specific creative ability was: "Did you work out original solutions to mathematical problems (proofs for theorems or propositions not given by the teacher or textbook)?''

The learning style elements found to discriminate among the fourteen gifted and nongifted groups within the Israeli samples are presented in Table 8.2. It may be recalled, the results of these analyses provide us with a listing of the elements that distinguish between the two comparison groups in each instance and reflect the relative discriminatory power of each element, with the more powerful discriminators appearing high on the list with a rank of 1, etc.

Gifted High-Intelligence Children. Gifted high-intelligence learners reported stronger preferences for independent learning without peers or adult authority figures present. They are less motivated by parents and teachers, and are less conforming. These features are consistent with a preference for internal rather than external locus of control and reinforcement.

These gifted learners expressed a higher preference than nongifted for visual and kinesthetic-oriented learning, a lower preference for tactile learning activities, and no difference on auditory learning. These findings are consistent with earlier research in that high-IQ gifted children prefer learning through visual or kinesthetic means (Dunn & Price 1980a; Griggs & Price 1980a). On the other hand, the current findings on high-IQ gifted learners differ with those reported earlier in that the preference for tactile learning and against auditory was not found. This disparity is probably because previous research did not distinguish between high-IQ gifted and the other categories of giftedness. Our analyses, by contrast, were guided by the multidimensional 4 × 4 model (Milgram 1989, 1990a, 1991a) that posits four different categories of giftedness. It is likely that the differences postulated among gifted learners will be reflected in their perceptual learning style preferences.

In the preceding section on Israeli-American comparisons, we noted that Israeli children prefer to learn in the late morning rather than in the heat of the afternoon. Within the Israeli sample, gifted high intelligence children are even more reluctant to learn in the afternoon hours than the nongifted. This may be because they operate at a high level of concentration and resent the fatigue and discomfort caused by the afternoon heat more than nongifted children who demand less of themselves.

High-IQ gifted children expressed a tendency to favor eating and drinking while learning. In the Israeli group five of the fourteen gifted subgroups reported higher intake preference than nongifted. The five groups were identified as gifted by the criterion of IQ, mathematics, leadership, music, and literature. This preference was not noted in the American-Israeli comparisons, indicating that it is restricted to certain gifted Israeli categories and not others, and not to Israeli children in general.

Gifted high-intelligence children also prefer a warm temperature, a finding noted earlier favoring Israelis over Americans, but here differentiating further

Table 8.2

Learning Style Elements that Differentiate Between Gifted and Nongifted Learners in Israel: Relative Contribution to Differentiation

Element	IQ	Academic Achievement	Creative Thinking	Science	Math	Computer	Social Leadership	Music	Art	Dance	Drama	Sport	Literature	Foreign Language
Personality														
Overall Motivation	8	2*			1*	9		4		3	5			1*
Parent Figure Motivated	10	3		4	4		8	6	7					8*
Teacher Motivated	9	4*		8*	8*	8*	9*	5*	9*	12*		7*		
Persistence			5	6*		1				2*				5
Responsibility/Conformity	7			10*		6	2*			4*				9*
Structure			2						8					2
Intake	14*				5*	5*	3*	10*				1*	9*	
Mobility	5	6			6	10		8					4	
Social														
Alone/Peer	13	1		11*		5*							10	
Authority Figures	4	7	8	7	7	3		3*	5	1*			3	6
Several Ways				12							3*			
Environmental														
Noise Level	1*			5				7*	2*	5				7*
Light	6*				3	7*	4*		10*	7*	6			
Temperature							10*	2	3			4*	1	
Design			9	9	11*	4*				6		2*	8	
Perceptual														
Auditory	3*			2			5*				2*	5*		
Visual	11	6*					6		4					
Tactile	12*		1*	1*	2*	2*		1*	1*	9*	1*		6	
Kinesthetic			4*	3*			1*	11*	6*	10	4*	6	2*	
Time														
Evening/Morning			6							11*			5	3
Late Morning			7*		9*			12		8			7	4*
Afternoon	2		3		10*		7	9				3		10*

* Gifted higher than nongifted

within the Israeli sample. These children also prefer sound over quiet when they study. Three other gifted subgroups also preferred sound over quiet—music, art, and foreign languages. On the other hand, two other gifted subgroups—science and dance—preferred quiet over sound, and the remaining eight gifted subgroups had no preference either way as compared with their nongifted counterparts. We do not regard these differences as contradictory, but rather as indicating the importance of examining the correlates of giftedness according to the different categories and levels of the overall designation giftedness.

Interestingly enough, an almost identical breakdown obtained for the element of motivation, with two other gifted groups more highly motivated than nongifted (mathematics and foreign language), five less so (gifted intelligence, computer, music, dance, and drama), and the remaining six, no difference. Although the mathematical breakdown of the preferences was the same for motivation and sound, the specific gifted subgroups reporting high, low, or no differences in motivation were not the same ones. These findings as well highlight the utility of the 4 × 4 conceptualization of giftedness, and accentuate the idea that differences within the gifted group as a whole may be greater than those between gifted and nongifted.

Gifted High-Scholastic-Achievement Children. We next compared the learning style differences between children identified as gifted or nongifted using the criterion of high scholastic achievement. The academically achieving gifted were more highly self and teacher motivated and less parent motivated than their lower achieving peers. Moreover, in comparing the two groups, the academically achieving gifted expressed greater preference to study alone rather than with other children, did not require the presence of authority figures when they study, did not report the need for freedom to move about the classroom while learning, and preferred to learn visually. The pattern of preferences of high academic achieving learners that emerged is not surprising since it is clearly consonant with the kinds of attitudes that lead to successful performance in most conventional classrooms.

It is interesting to compare the high-ability gifted—that is, those with high IQ scores—some of whom achieve high grades in school and some who do not, with the high-achieving gifted—that is, those who by definition attain high grades in school. It is reasonable to view high academic achievement as reflecting both ability and motivation. Our findings support this notion in that we found youngsters gifted by the academic achievement criterion to be more highly self and teacher motivated than the lower-achieving comparison group. With the high-IQ gifted, the findings were reversed—that is, the higher IQ group was lower in self and teacher motivation than the lower-IQ comparison group. In addition, the higher-IQ group was less conforming, preferred to eat and drink when learning, and preferred more sound and higher temperatures. In addition to learning visually, the high-IQ gifted expressed preference to learn through experiences.

Taken together, the learning style preferences reported by the high-IQ gifted do not match the conventional classroom situation very well. These data provide some basis for explaining the academic failure of many highly able students as a result of the conflict between their preferred learning styles and the learning situations in which they find themselves.

Gifted Creative-Thinking Children. Gifted creative-thinking children differed from their nongifted counterparts on nine elements. They reported strong tactile and kinesthetic preferences, suggesting that they would profit from active involvement in experiential learning as well as from the opportunity to explore and handle a wide variety of materials as they learn.

These children prefer less structure in their school tasks, thus allowing each to define and interpret the tasks in his or her own way. By the same token, they prefer an informal learning environment, possibly with carpets, soft furniture, and the like. On the other hand, they are less persistent and feel less comfortable in the presence of authority figures. These findings would appear to substantiate some widespread, hitherto unproven views about these children. Finally, they also prefer to learn late in the morning, and not in the early morning or afternoon.

Eleven Domains of Creative Performance. The learning style elements that characterize adolescents gifted in one or more of the eleven areas are summarized in Table 8.2. These findings may serve teachers as a guide for understanding the needs of learners of each type that may appear from time to time in regular classrooms. Space limitations do not allow a detailed analysis of the learning style profile of each of the eleven subgroups. The discussion here of the profiles of high-IQ and high-creative gifted are designed to provide a model of how the data may be interpreted. Recognizing these learning style preferences provides valuable information to teachers and counselors in their efforts to differentiate curricula and to individualize instruction.

The most remarkable finding of the discriminant analyses of these eleven groups is that no two patterns of learning style are the same. As pointed out earlier, two groups (mathematics and foreign languages) are more highly motivated than their nongifted counterparts, whereas four others are less motivated (computer science, music, dance, and drama). Five of the eleven gifted groups were less motivated by a parent (science, mathematics, leadership, music, and art), whereas the gifted in foreign language were more parent motivated. With reference to formal design, gifted children in mathematics, computers, and sports prefer formal design more than their less gifted counterparts, possibly reflecting the structured equipment that all these fields require.

CONCLUSION

What conclusion can one draw from such complex and disparate information? These findings clearly demonstrate that the learning style profiles of gifted learners are not only conceptually but empirically distinguishable from one another. These findings apply to gifted learners in Israel. The data reported in each chapter on gifted learners in each of the other seven cultures in which our study was conducted will provide information about the similarities and differences in learning style of exceptional children across the world.

NOTES

We wish to thank Dalia Maoz, Israel Ministry of Education, Director, Central Region; Tziporah Lavi, Chief Inspector, Central Region; Shmuel Shimoni, Principal, Tichon Chadash Junior-Senior High School, Tel Aviv, Israel; Dalia Bashan, Acting Principal 1989–1990, Sharet Junior High, Kfar Saba, Israel; and the teachers and pupils of these schools for their generous cooperation.

Chapter 9

The Learning Styles of Gifted Adolescents in the Philippines

Joanne Ingham and Gary E. Price

A portrait of the Philippines and its people clearly would be depicted by a rich tapestry of intricate and distinctive reality. The geographical variability of the countryside and the historical influence of many different cultures, ethnic backgrounds, languages, religious beliefs, and outlooks on life, when woven together, make up the richness of Filipino society. The Republic of the Philippines, one of seven Southeast Asian countries, is an archipelago consisting of more than 7,000 islands, of which close to 800 are inhabited by a total of 60 million people. The intervening seas and the rugged, often inaccessible interior uplands have tended to isolate various groups from each other (Cutshall 1964). This isolation of tribes or communities led to the natural formation of a multitude of local dialects and customs and enhanced the role the family plays in shaping an adolescent's development and molding his or her values.

This diversity impacts on numerous aspects of the Philippine way of life. Filipinos speak more than eighty distinctly different dialects, eleven of which are spoken by enough people to qualify as a major language. Despite attempts during the Marcos regime to mandate Philipino as the language of the Philippines, there is no true national language (Gochenour 1990). English is considered the second language and, most notably, the language of instruction. As a visitor to the area surrounding Manila, the first author did not encounter difficulty communicating in English. In fact, the Philippines is one of the largest English-speaking countries in the world (Cutshall 1990) because of American influence after the Spanish-American War.

As a result of powerful geographical, cultural, and language differences, the family and community play a central role in the lives of Filipinos. Among Filipinos, the individual exists first and foremost as a member of a family. The family has been a permanent, vital element in the entire life of the person; all share intimately in each other's comings and goings, failures and triumphs (Gochenour 1990).

Several other values are deeply embedded in the cultural orientation and play a forceful role in Filipino life. Authority is always assumed to be present. In the home it is the eldest; in religion it is the priest; in school it is the teacher; at work it is the properly designated supervisor or those senior in rank. Individual Filipinos seldom claim for themselves full and final authority on any matter (Cutshall 1964). Filipinos prize harmony in relationships. The ultimate ideal is one of complete harmony between individuals, among the members of a family, among the groups and divisions of society, and of all life in relationship with God (Gochenour 1990). In addition, Filipinos respect tradition.

These cultural values of family, authority, harmony, and respect for tradition have shaped the development of Philippino adolescents. Consequently, they also have impacted on the emotional and sociological preferences these youngsters exhibit while engaged in new learning and creative expression.

The United States intervened in the Phillippines in the early 1900s during the Spanish-American War, and one of the lasting American contributions of that period was the creation of the educational system. The American emphasis on mass public education has been deeply internalized into Filipino social life. Having a diploma has become essential for a good job in the Philippines today (Steinberg 1989). As in the United States, schools have been primarily government-sponsored or church-sponsored institutions, and have educated millions of students from kindergarten through college.

Education and intellect are reflected in the Filipino's dress and manner of speaking. Filipinos admire mental work far more than physical work. Overseas employers see Filipinos as assets because of their familiarity with English and their academic and technical training. Education also enhances one's social status significantly, and is perceived as a means of raising the entire family's circumstances in this poor Third World country. As such, it is highly valued. Students are expected to study hard, although the rigors of learning may vary considerably from one school to another (Gochenour 1990). When one has reached a point of some intellectual accomplishment, it is not something to be passed over lightly. The neighbors share the news; the local paper may carry the story. If one is well educated, Filipinos expect that person to talk, act, and dress the part. Accordingly, there exists substantial family and societal pressures for students to succeed academically.

The Ateneo de Manila University is a Jesuit school. It is located northeast of the capital city of Manila, in a beautiful tropical setting in Loyola Heights, Quezon City, Philippines. Quezon City has been home to the university since 1952.

The Ateneo de Manila High School is one of the integral parts of the university campus, as is the Grade School, School of Arts and Sciences, Professional Schools of Business and Law, and Graduate School. The administrators and faculty of the high school speak with pride of the institution's reputation for attracting the country's outstanding male students. Students compete to be accepted as first-year students and work hard to complete the fourth year and to graduate.

The curriculum is shaped by several factors. Ateneo de Manila High School is a Filipino school and, as such, seeks to prepare its students to make a critical difference in the currents and ideas that direct the growth of the Filipino culture. Ateneo is also college preparatory and seeks to prepare the student academically for a productive career. As a Jesuit school, students also receive a solid religious education.

The enrollment of this urban high school, considered to be the premier high school in the Philippines, is approximately 1,800 male students. It has a staff of ninety-two faculty, four guidance counselors, two assistant principals, and one principal. Because of the tropical climate, the classrooms open to the outside lawns or squares for coolness. Paths connecting buildings and classrooms have been covered overhead as protection from the hot sun and the torrential downpours during the rainy season. The rooms have been arranged in a traditional manner and look very much like a typical conventional American classroom. Desks and chairs have been formally organized into rows all facing the front of the room where the chalkboard is located.

To sum up, the Filipino adolescent is defined as a learner and is shaped by the values and traditions of the culture and by the conventional educational system formed ninety years ago by the American politicians and instructional leaders of the time. These forces become evident as the results of the study show.

RESEARCH METHODOLOGY

Subjects

The Philippine subjects were the entire student population (N = 1,750) of a private, all-male Catholic high school located in Quezon City, Philippines. As in the United States, Catholic high schools typically are single-gender institutions. The students are described by their year in school as first year through fourth year, equivalent to the American classification of grades 9 through 12. Filipino students, however, enter high school one year younger than American adolescents; consequently, they range in age from 13 years to 15 years of age. The distribution of subjects by grade and age was presented in Chapter 2, Table 2.1.

When comparing the learning style preferences of the Filipino versus the American adolescents, learning style data were used from the whole population of 1,750. A sample population of 379 was selected for investigation of academic and creative giftedness. The sample population consisted of a random selection of three homeroom classes for each of the four academic years (twelve homeroom classes total). The sample, therefore, included the following student representation: first year = 102; second year = 98; third year = 95; and fourth year = 84, for a total sample of 379 students. This represented 21.6 percent of the total population.

Materials

The two instruments administered during the course of this study were the Learning Style Inventory (LSI) (Dunn, Dunn & Price 1989) and the Tel Aviv Activities Inventory (Milgram 1987). Both instruments were described in detail in Chapter 2.

The internal consistency or reliability of the LSI for the Philippine population was estimated by means of analysis of variance, a technique reported by Hoyt (1941) that is comparable to Kuder Richardson 20. The reliability coefficient range of twenty elements was .62–.88. The range of the other two elements was .50–.51. On the basis of these findings, we concluded that the reliability of the LSI for the Filipino population was satisfactory.

Method

During the first week of May 1990, the high school faculty and administrative staff participated in an in-service training program focused on learning style theory and its application. The teachers and guidance counselors were trained in the administration and interpretation of the LSI profiles. As a result of the positive response to the concepts and strategies, the principal was willing to participate in the study as a means of learning more about the learning style preferences and creativity patterns of his students, as well as to contribute to the body of knowledge in these areas.

Procedure

Between June 18 and June 26, 1990, the beginning of the Philippine school term, first the LSI and then the Tel Aviv Activities Inventory were administered to the students during two separate homeroom periods.

Homeroom teachers, trained by the first author, administered the instruments to the students. A member of the Guidance Department was trained in the administration of both instruments and served as the local project coordinator of the administration and collection of the data. To ensure confidentiality of data, each subject was assigned a research participant identity number. Only this number was used during data analysis.

RESEARCH RESULTS

Comparison of Filipino and American Students

We first compared the learning style preferences of 1,750 Filipino students with the preferences of a comparable sample of American students drawn from a data base provided by Price Systems. Table 9.1 shows the rank order of those learning style variables that significantly discriminated between the two groups.

The results yielded by the stepwise discriminant analysis indicated that eighteen of twenty-two learning style variables produced a Wilks' Lambda of 0.580 (p <.00001) and 80 percent were classified correctly based on the eighteen variables that account for approximately 41 percent of the variance.

Overall, the adolescents in the American sample preferred a warmer learning environment, preferred learning through their auditory and tactile modalities, were more late-morning preferenced, and preferred more sound in their environment when learning as compared to the Filipino youngsters. Perhaps the tropical climate of the Philippines influenced those students to prefer a cooler, as opposed to a warmer temperature, when concentrating.

The Filipino students preferred less intake than those in the American sample. The Filipino learners also preferred to learn more through their visual and kinesthetic senses, wanted bright light, preferred to learn more in the early morning and afternoon. In a tropical climate, the mornings and afternoons typically are cooler. Siestas in the late morning to early afternoon are part of the Filipino tradition.

In addition, the Filipino students were more teacher motivated and preferred to learn more in a variety of ways than did the American sample. The Filipino adolescents also were more parent-figure and authority-figure motivated than the American adolescents. The greater preference for working with authority figures was consistent with the value system of the culture to defer to authority figures and family.

The Filipino students were more persistent, preferred learning in a more formal design, and were more motivated than their American counterparts. Finally, the Filipino students preferred more structure when they received assignments than did the American sample.

Learning Styles of Academically Gifted and Academically Nongifted Filipino Adolescents

For the purposes of this study, those students who ranked in the top 20 percent of the sample with respect to overall scholastic achievement were categorized as academically gifted; the remainder were categorized as academically nongifted. Filipino students included within the top 20 percent had achieved an overall grade point average (GPA) equal to or greater than 3.7 on a scale of 4.0. Those whose GPA was less than 3.7 were categorized as academically nongifted.

Ten learning style variables significantly discriminated between the academically gifted and academically nongifted samples. The discriminant analysis indicated that ten of twenty-two learning style variables produced a Wilks' Lambda .904 (p <.00001) and 81.79 percent were classified correctly based on these ten variables.

Table 9.1
Learning Style Elements that Discriminate Between Adolescents in the Philippines and in the United States: Stepwise Order and Mean Scores

Stepwise Order	LSI Variable	American Students (N = 1750)	Filipino Students (N = 1750)
1	Temperature	15.46	10.54
2	Requires Intake	17.95	15.45
3	Kinesthetic	25.38	27.21
4	Light	13.05	14.44
5	Tactile	17.20	16.95
6	Auditory	13.88	13.23
7	Evening-Morning	15.92	17.31
8	Afternoon	16.75	17.49
9	Late Morning	11.49	11.20
10	Teacher Motivated	19.64	19.84
11	Noise Level	14.01	12.63
12	Visual	8.81	9.51
13	Learn in Several Ways	13.56	13.58
14	Parent Figure Motivated	17.29	17.74
15	Persistent	16.82	16.96
16	Design	10.04	10.76
17	Motivation	31.82	32.84
18	Structure	12.83	13.21

Those categorized as academically gifted were more motivated, preferred less structure and learning in the afternoon, were more visual, were more parent motivated, were more persistent, and preferred bright light when learning new and difficult information. In addition, the academically gifted preferred to learn less through their auditory sense, preferred a less formal design, and preferred intake less than their academically nongifted counterparts.

Previous investigations have examined the learning styles of academically gifted American students. Each revealed significant differences between their characteristics and those of academically nongifted American students (Cody 1983; Cross 1982; Dunn & Price 1980; Griggs 1984; Griggs & Price 1980; Stewart 1981; Wasson 1980). Among those traits that tended to characterize the American academically gifted are independence, internal control, persistence, perceptual strengths, nonconformity, and motivation. The findings of the Filipino academically gifted are similar with respect to the learning style elements of motivation, persistence, perceptual strength, and structure. It must be noted that students who are both auditory (remember three-quarters of what they hear) and visual (remember three-quarters of what they read or see) are more likely than those who are not auditory or visual to retain difficult academic information, and thus be identified as gifted according to the criteria of academic achievement.

Rodrigo (1989) conducted research with Filipino first-grade pupils at the Ateneo de Manila Grade School, comparing the learning style preferences of students classified as academically below average, average, and above average. The results indicated that the above-average and average students preferred a quieter environment than below-average students. Above-average students preferred the afternoon and visual stimuli, whereas below-average students preferred auditory stimuli. It was interesting to note that these findings, although having utilized a younger population, were corroborated by the results of this study.

Learning Styles and Measures of Creative Performance

Research examining the learning style preferences of gifted and nongifted learners traditionally has considered the gifted as academically gifted. However, concepts concerning giftedness and intelligence have been further refined. A gifted child has been described as being gifted in specific domains or intelligences. Milgram (1987) characterized adolescents as gifted in one or more of the domains of creative performance (science, drama, art, music, sports, literature, dance, leadership). Gardner (1983) theorized that one can be intelligent in one or more of the seven intelligences (musical, linguistic, logical-mathematical, spatial, bodily-kinesthetic, interpersonal, and intrapersonal). This phase of the study sought to examine whether or not those Filipino adolescents classified as gifted in specific domains of creative performance, as measured by the Tel Aviv Activities Inventory, possessed distinct learning style patterns characteristic to each domain.

Table 9.2 reveals how Filipino students responded to the nine category areas

Table 9.2
Learning Style Elements that Discriminate Among Creative and Noncreative Filipino Adolescents by Specific Domain

Domain of Creative Performances	Item Ratio Needed to Show Creative Engagement	Ratio of Creative to Noncreative Filipino Students	Stepwise Order Of Discriminate Analysis For LSI Elements; (P) Preference For Creative Group
Science	4/8	130/221	Tactile (P) Auditory Lrn Sev Ways Formal Design (P) Evening (P) Teacher Motivated Persistence (P)
Social Leadership	8/11	41/313	Intake Light (P) Kinesthetic (P) Formal Design Auditory (P) Mobility Parent Motivated (P) Afternoon Auth Fig Present (P) Motivation (P)
Dance	2/2	20/76	Intake Afternoon (P) Tactile (P) Structure Kinesthetic (P) Motivation (P)
Music	4/9	86/261	Kinesthetic (P) Structure (P) Late Morning Morning (P) Temperature (P) Responsible (P)
Art	4/8	112/224	Kinesthetic (P) Auth Fig Present Persistent Intake Tactile (P) Formal Design (P)

Table 9.2 (continued)

Domain of Creative Performances	Item Ratio Needed to Show Creative Engagement	Ratio of Creative to Noncreative Filipino Students	Stepwise Order Of Discriminate Analysis For LSI Elements; (P) Preference For Creative Group
Literature	5/6	53/254	Light (P) Persistent Responsible (P) Temperature Morning (P) Alone (P) Ln Sev Ways (P) Teacher Motivated Auditory (P) Visual (P)
Drama	2/4	39/109	Tactile (P) Teacher Motivated Sound (P) Intake Late Morning Parent Motivated Persistent
Sports	4/6	100/266	Late Morning Structure Auditory (P) Evening (P) Motivated (P) Auth Fig Present (P)

of the Tel Aviv Activities Inventory. The table was constructed to provide for ease of reading and interpretation. For instance, by noticing the domain of science, the reader can see that, to be included in this creative engagement area, the student had to respond positively to four or more of the eight inventory items. A total of 130 respondents indicated that they had a creative affinity for this domain. The last column of the table reveals the stepwise order of the LSI elements, which significantly discriminated between the creative and noncreative students for the science domain. The *P* in parentheses after the seven LSI elements indicates whether the 130 science creative-affinity students preferred that element more strongly than the 221 students who did not show a creative affinity for the science domain. Thus, the reader can note the 130 science-affinity students preferred four of the seven LSI elements in relation to the science domain. By inspecting the results for each of the nine category domains of the Tel Aviv Activities Inventory, the LSI preference for those students who had a creative affinity for that domain can be determined.

The discriminant functions for the eight category domains of the Tel Aviv Activities Inventory were all highly significant. The grouped cases that were accurately categorized by group as creative versus noncreative in the eight domains ranged from 68 percent to 89 percent.

Science. Those adolescents considered gifted in science preferred to learn more through their tactile (hands-on) sense, preferred a more formal design, and indicated that they were more persistent than were the nongifted students in science. Further, the gifted preferred to learn less through their auditory sense, preferred to learn less in a variety of ways, were less morning preferred, and were less teacher motivated than were their nongifted peers.

Leadership. The individuals who were high in the social area expressed many preferences. The gifted preferred less intake, brighter light, preferred to learn more through their kinesthetic and auditory modalities, wanted a more informal design when learning, preferred less mobility, were more parent-figure motivated, wanted authority figures present, and were more self-motivated. In addition, the gifted further preferred to learn less in the afternoon, whereas individuals in the nongifted group preferred to learn more in the afternoon.

Dance. Those students classified as gifted for dance indicated they preferred to learn more in the afternoon, preferred to learn more through their tactile and kinesthetic senses, and were more motivated than the nongifted group in dance. Those who were classified as gifted for dance also preferred less intake and less structure than their nongifted counterparts.

Music. Those students classified as gifted in the domain of music indicated they preferred to learn more through their kinesthetic sense and preferred more structure than their nongifted counterparts. In addition, they preferred to learn in the morning and preferred a warmer environment. In addition, those classified as gifted in music also indicated they preferred to learn less in the late morning and indicated they were less responsible or conforming than the nongifted sample.

Art. Those adolescents classified as gifted in the domain of art indicated they preferred to learn more though their kinesthetic and tactile senses, were less persistent, and preferred a more formal design when learning than the nongifted in art. The gifted group also preferred authority figures present to a lesser extent and preferred intake less than the nongifted sample.

Literature. For each of the ten variables, the gifted sample indicated stronger preferences than the nongifted group. The gifted preferred more light, were less persistent, more responsible, and preferred a cooler learning environment. In addition, the gifted adolescents preferred to learn in the morning, alone, and in several ways. Further, the gifted were less teacher motivated and preferred to learn through their auditory and visual modalities as compared with the nongifted students.

Drama. The students classified as gifted for drama were less teacher and parent motivated, preferred less intake, and preferred to learn less in the late morning than the nongifted sample. In addition, they indicated they were less persistent than those classified as nongifted. The gifted adolescents also preferred to learn using their tactile sense and wanted more sound present when learning new and difficult information as compared to the nongifted group.

Sports. Those adolescents classified as gifted for sports wanted less structure, preferred to learn more through their auditory sense, and were more motivated than the nongifted sample. The gifted preferred to learn less in the morning and late morning, and wanted authority figures present less so when compared with the nongifted sample.

CONCLUSIONS

Gifted learners are characterized by stronger preferences than their nongifted peers for learning through auditory, tactile, and kinesthetic senses in eight of the nine domains of creative activity investigated. This finding is consistent with other studies of gifted American learners as cited above. Because these students possess many perceptual strengths, they are able to learn easily from an extensive array of instructional methodologies.

The current findings represent a significant addition to our knowledge about the learning styles of gifted Filippino learners. The learning style elements that characterize adolescents as gifted in the nine domains of creative performance are different. No two patterns are the same. Acknowledging and respecting these differences can provide valuable information to administrators, teachers, counselors, and to the students in planning courses of study to meet individual needs and developing beneficial study habits and routines. However, while no two learning style patterns were identical, several observations can be made.

In five of the eight creative performance domains, the Filipino gifted learners preferred bright light and a formal design when learning as compared with the nongifted sample. These preferences represent an advantage for gifted youngsters because they match the characteristics in conventional classrooms, which frequently have bright fluorescent bulbs overhead and are furnished with desks and chairs. On the other hand, gifted students were less teacher motivated than their nongifted peers, a preference not generally accommodated in a conventional classroom.

To sum up, we found numerous differences in learning style preferences between adolescents in the United States and in the Philippines and between gifted and nongifted learners in the Philippines. Moreover, the differences in learning style among gifted learners in the Philippines are greater than the similarities and reflect differences in definition and criteria of giftedness. These findings constitute additional support for the argument that one should not categorize gifted learners solely on the basis of their IQ scores or grade point averages (Milgram 1987; Gardner 1983) or discuss learning style patterns without considering the learner's cultural background and without identifying a specific domain of giftedness.

Chapter 10

The Learning Styles and Creative Performance Accomplishments of Adolescents in Guatemala

Richard Sinatra, Eva Sazo de Mendez, and Gary E. Price

Guatemala, the third largest country in Central America, is a land rich in history and natural beauty. The Mayan Indian civilization flourished in Guatemala long before the Spanish arrived in the sixteenth century. More than 48 percent of the Guatemalan people are descendants of the Mayan Indians, and roughly half of the current estimated population of 9.5 million still follow a traditional Indian life-style. Another 40 to 50 percent of the current population is of mixed Indian and Spanish ancestry. These people are called Ladinos; they speak Spanish and follow more modern customs, influenced by the West.

While most of the Ladinos live in cities or towns, the Indians live in small country settlements or in rural towns. Most of the Indians are poor and uneducated, and follow an agrarian way of life. The Ladinos constitute the middle and upper class and control the government and business activities of the country.

Guatemala is largely a mountainous country. Most of its people live in the rugged highlands of the central part of the country. The climate is tropical, but modified by the high altitude of the mountain ranges and volcanic peaks. Whereas Spanish is the official language of the country, several Indian languages and dialects of the Mayan family are widely used. Many Indians speak both Spanish and an Indian language; however, a large number of Indians speak only one of the Indian languages. Overall, the people are predominantly of the Roman Catholic faith.

According to Guatemalan law, primary education is free and compulsory for children between the ages of 7 and 13. However, there are not enough schools or teacher positions available to attend to the large number of eligible children, so only 55 percent of the eligible population attends primary school. From this number, 15 percent go on to high school. Very few of the country's teachers speak the Indian languages and some remote rural areas have no schools at all. School attendance is much higher in the cities than in rural areas.

While it is estimated that half the Guatemalan population cannot read and write, the literacy rate is only about 15 to 20 percent among the Indians in rural areas. For urban Ladinos, the literacy rate is approximately 70 percent. Education is, therefore, regarded as a privilege in Guatemala. For those who reach high school and complete it, success has been achieved. Very few students continue their education in one of the country's five universities.

High schools, encompassing grades 7 through 12, can be characterized in a number of ways. Most important is the way they are subsidized. Public schools are supported by the government. The students come from low-income families. With an average of 60 students per class, these schools lack the facilities and resources that most public school students enjoy in the United States. Students attending the private schools, called *colegios,* are supported by tuition fees. The students come from families in the medium to higher socioeconomic levels. High schools may have a religious orientation, predominantly Catholic; a male or female orientation; a rural or urban orientation; or a Ladino or Mayan cultural orientation.

In this chapter we examine the learning and thinking styles of Guatemalan adolescents found in a cross-section of the country's high schools. We selected schools and subjects that reflect the cultural, linguistic, and economic diversity of the population cited above. By the same token, we examined a range of schools found in rural and urban areas rather than concentrating on a fixed population in one high school.

RESEARCH METHODOLOGY

Subjects

The subjects were 664 adolescents (363 boys, 281 girls, and 20 undeclared) in grades 7 to 11, from seven schools in Guatemala. The characteristics of each school, its student body, and the number and grade level of the students selected to participate in the study are presented in Table 10.1. The table indicates that many more students attended each school than were represented in this study. However, a representative sample of the student population of each school was achieved, along with a range of grade levels. Moreover, 49 adolescents from two Mayan high schools, the Instituto Andres Curruchiche and the Instituto San Antonio Las Flores, provided a sample representative of the Indian culture.

Because of the diversity of the schools themselves and of the student populations attending each school, the seven schools are briefly described below.

The Centro de Usos Múltiples. The Centro de Usos Múltiples is a nonreligious, coeducational public school that offers some experimental programs. The school has a technical orientation in that students are prepared to assume a livelihood or profession. They are trained to become electricians, foundrymen, cooks, hair stylists, or mechanics. About fifty students attend classes in each of the various programs.

The Colegio Americano. The Colegio Americano is patterned after the American educational system. It is located in the capital, Guatemala City, and is private, coeducational, and nonreligious. It attracts students from a high socioeconomic background; the wealthier families send their children to this school. Ninety-six percent of the student population is of Ladino-Hispanic culture. There are from twenty-five to thirty students per class. The school has numerous resources to offer students, such as computers, a library, and multimedia equipment. Students have a longer day than those in most other institutions; classes start at 7:30 A.M. and end between 3 and 4 P.M. The Colegio has an advanced program at the eleventh- and twelfth-grade levels; students who seek entry must pass exams and interviews at the tenth-grade level. The students selected for the advanced program come from the Colegio and from many other schools of Guatemala, and youngsters from low-income families may be granted scholarships to the advanced program. Many of the fifty-nine students from the Colegio participating were enrolled in the advanced program. Only seven students had a grade point average below 2.0.

The Instituto Andres Curruchiche. The Instituto Andres Curruchiche is a public school located eight-five kilometers from the capital in the country of Comalapa. To reach the school, it is necessary to drive eighty kilometers on a primary road and the rest on an unpaved road that winds through mountainous terrain. The Instituto is in a rural community in which the primary language is Cackchiguel. Female students still wear regional dress. Classes, on the average, include sixty-two students.

The Liceo Guatemala. Only eighty-six of the seventh-grade students at the Liceo Guatemala participated in the study. The Liceo is an urban, private institution with a religious orientation. The average size per class is sixty-six students who come from a middle socioeconomic background. These students had participated in activities of social projection, which aided them in the creative performance questions in contrast to students who attended the Colegio Americano.

The Instituto Pedro Arriaza Matta. The Instituto Pedro Arriaza Matta is a public school that holds classes in the evening because most of its student body works during the day. The students are generally from families of very low income, and the adolescents have to be wary of the adverse social and crime conditions of the capital city. The high delinquency and crime rate has caused this school to decrease in population from 1,500 students in 1987 to fewer than 500 students in 1991. Students start classes at 7 P.M. and finish by 10 P.M. which gives them a relatively short amount of time in school. Attendance is irregular, partly owing to the traveling arrangements students must make to get to and from school.

The Instituto San Antonio Las Flores. The Instituto San Antonio Las Flores was founded cooperatively by the mayor, parents, and teachers of a poor, rural municipality called Chinautla. Until very recently, Chinautla did not have a high school. The mayor, however, convinced residents of nearby Mayan villages that the interests of their children would be best served by the area's addition of a high school. Furthermore, teachers at the elementary school wanted educational opportunities for their students beyond the sixth grade.

Using the elementary school as the facility, the community opened a high school two years ago. It opened with one seventh-grade class (twenty-nine boys and one girl) and added a class each year. The second year, fifty-four seventh- and eighth-grade students attended with most being male once again. This year, the high school will expand into the ninth grade and it is hoped it will attract additional students.

Most students work in the morning and attend the high school classes between 1 and 4 P.M. Some get to and from school each day by taking a bus along the road to the capital city, but many students walk the two to four miles each way to attend the high school. With the environment being generally hostile to education, teachers show great dedication and sacrifice. The institute student population has been growing in hope of improving the conditions and moral values of this community.

Instituto de la Asunción. The Instituto de la Asunción is a school dedicated to teacher preparation. It is a private, urban, religiously oriented school attended by females from middle- to high-socioeconomic families. Of the 118 students who participated in this study, only one had a grade point average below 2.0. A characteristic of this school is student success. If students have low grades or attitude problems, they are asked to leave. Graduates of the school are among the most talented, brilliant, and dedicated in Guatemala.

Materials and Procedures

Each participating high school completed a questionnaire that resulted in the description analysis found in Table 10.1. Three instruments were completed at the end of the 1990 school year by all 664 students who participated in the study. They were the Learning Style Inventory (Dunn, Dunn & Price 1989), the Tel Aviv Activities Inventory (Milgram 1987), and a student questionnaire. A full description and discussion of the instruments may be found in Chapter 2. All instruments were translated into Spanish and generally completed during one school day. One of the researchers either directly administered or trained the teachers of the participating students to administer the instruments at each school site.

The Student Questionnaire. Each student completed a questionnaire that requested the student's overall grade point average and grades in the five subject areas of mathematics, science, Spanish, English, and social studies. Since the school year was almost over, the grades reflected the student's work during that year. Students reported their grades in percentage figures; for instance a grade in mathematics would be 85 and in English 76. It was interesting to note that many of the Mayan students had higher grades in the content subjects and lower grades in the two language subjects, English and Spanish.

The researchers converted each student's general grade point average from the averaged scores of all subjects into a scale ranging from 1.0 to 4.0. A 1.0 grade point average was equal to a 60 percent total average, whereas a 4.0 was equal to a 100 percent average. The 3.5 score was calibrated at a percentage average 86 or 87 and a 2.0 score was equal to an average of 70 percent.

Table 10.1 reveals that of the 664 students, a total of 121 students or 18 percent of the study population fell below the 2.0 average. It was believed that the inclusion of these students would provide a balance for ascertaining the styles of the high achievers—those above the 3.5 grade point average (GPA).

RESEARCH RESULTS

The key statistical procedure used in this study was the discriminant analysis as described in Chapter 2. We first compared the learning styles of Guatemalan and American adolescents, next compared the learning styles of high versus low academic achievers, and finally analyzed the learning styles of creative versus noncreative learners.

Comparison of Guatemalan and American Students

The learning style preferences of the 664 Guatemalan students were compared with the preferences of a similar number of American students randomly selected from a data base provided by the third author. Table 10.2 shows the rank order of learning style elements that significantly discriminated between the groups. The Guatemalan students were further grouped into Mayan and Ladino Guatemalan categories to provide for an even more detailed analysis of learning style patterns.

Twenty-one of the twenty-two LSI variables significantly discriminated at the .00001 level between American and Guatemalan subjects. Only the LSI element, teacher motivated, failed to enter the stepwise discriminant analysis. A Wilks' Lambda of .44 was produced for the discriminant analysis of the twenty-one comparisons for the American and Guatemalan or Ladino students, and a Wilks' Lambda of .93 was achieved for the discriminant analysis of the twenty-one comparisons for the American or Mayan students. Table 10.2 reveals the stepwise order of the LSI elements that discriminated between the groups and shows the mean raw score for each element.

Table 10.3 indicates the way each of the population groups compared and contrasted in their learning style preferences. When no wording appears for a learning style element for any one group, the group preferred that element in a moderate way compared to the other two groups. By inspecting the mean raw scores for that element on Table 10.2, the reader can determine the relative standing of the middle group to the other two groups. For instance, for the

Table 10.1
School and Subject Characteristics of Guatemalan Subjects

	SCHOOL CHARACTERISTICS			SUBJECT CHARACTERISTICS	
School Name	General	Socioeconomic Status (SES) and Language Characteristics	Number and Grade Range of Secondary (Adolescent) Students	Number	Grade Levels
1. Centro de Usos Multiples	Public, urban, coeducational	Middle to low SES 60% Hispanic/	500; Grades 7 to 10	258 Total (72 below 2.0 GPA)	7-9
2. Colegio Americano	Private, urban (located in capital city), coeducational ,non-religious	Very high SES, 96% Hispanic	500; Grades 8 to 12	59 Total (7 below 2.0 GPA)	9-11
3. Instituto Andres Curruchiche	Public rural, coeducational, non-religious	Middle to Low SES, 100% Mayan	540; Grades 7 to 12	31 Total (4 below 2.0 GPA)	7-9 10 and 11
4. Liceo Guatemala	Private, urban, male, religious	Middle SES, 99% Hispanic	1500; Grades 7 to 12	86 Total (32 below 2.0 GPA)	7
5. Instituto Pedro Arriaza Matta	Public, urban, coeducational, non-religious, evening classes only, (located in capital city)	Very low SES, 40% Hispanic 60% Mayan	450; Grades 8 to 12	94 Total (32 below 2.0 GPA)	9
6. Instituto San Antonio Las Flores	Semi-private, rural, coeducational, non-religious, cooperative enterprise of local community	Very low SES, 100% Mayan	54; Grades 7 and 8	18 Total	7-8
7. Instituto de las Asunción	Private, urban, female,religious; school dedicated to teacher preparation	Middle to High SES 100%Hispanic	750; Grades 7 to 12	118 Total (1 Student below 2.0 GPA)	7-9
			Total Subjects	664	

166

Table 10.2
Learning Style Elements that Discriminate between Adolescents in Guatemala and in the United States: Stepwise Order and Mean Scores

Stepwise Order	LSI Variable	American Students (N=664)	Mayan (N=49)	Guatemalan Students: Guatemalan/Latino (N=615)
1.	Temperature	17.75	14.22	13.64
2.	Evening-Morning	15.61	22.45	20.53
3.	Requires Intake	17.82	10.12	13.65
4.	Visual	8.64	9.71	10.15
5.	Auditory	13.66	15.39	14.57
6.	Auth Fig Present	11.96	12.06	10.66
7.	Motivation	31.29	32.41	30.85
8.	Design	10.12	13.59	11.86
9.	Late Morning	11.24	11.94	10.65
10.	Light	13.09	11.39	12.91
11.	Afternoon	16.59	16.57	16.54
12.	Persistent	16.75	15.84	16.39
13.	Par Fig Motivated	17.11	18.20	17.06
14.	Structure	12.48	14.57	13.18
15.	Responsible	12.84	13.35	13.69
16.	Tactile	17.09	19.02	17.23
17.	Kinesthetic	24.89	25.96	25.49
18.	Needs mobility	14.28	12.24	12.95
19.	Silence Sound	13.90	11.82	12.92
20.	Learning Alone-Peer	22.11	20.16	20.79
21.	Learn in Sev Ways	13.28	12.57	11.95

Table 10.3
Learning Style Element Preferences for the Three Student Groups

Learning Style Element	American Students (N=664)	Mayan Students (N=49)	Guatemalan/Latino Students (N=615)
1. Temperature	prefer most warmth		prefer most cool
2. Evening-Morning	learn in evening	prefer early morning	
3. Requires Intake	most intake	least amount of intake	
4. Visual	least visual		most visual
5. Auditory	least auditory	most auditory	
6. Authority Figure Present		most prefer	least prefer
7. Motivation		most self-motivated	least self-motivated
8. Design Preferred	least formal design	most formal design	
9. Late Morning		prefer most	prefer least
10. Light	prefer brightest	prefer less light	
11. Afternoon	prefer slightly more		
12. Persistence	most persistent	least persistent	
13. Parent Figure Motivated		most by parent fig	least by parent fig
14. Structure preference	least structure	most structure	
15. Responsible/Conforming	least responsible		most responsible
16. Tactile	prefer least	prefer most	
17. Kinesthetic	prefer least	prefer most	
18. Needs Mobility	needs the most	needs the least	
19. Noise Level	prefer sound	prefer quiet	
20. Learning Alone-Peer	learn with peer		learn most alone
21. Learn in Several Ways	prefer the most		prefer the least

learning style element of temperature, the American students preferred the most warmth (mean = 17.75), the Guatemalan or Ladino students preferred the most cool (mean = 13.64), while the Mayan students with a mean of 14.22 were closer to their Ladino counterparts. For the element of preferring to learn best in the evening or morning, the American students indicated a strong preference (15.61) for learning in the evening. The Mayan students revealed that they most preferred to learn in the early morning (22.45). By inference, with a mean score of 20.53 for that element, the Guatemalan or Ladino students were more closely aligned to their Mayan counterparts. This alignment by the two Guatemalan groups is verified by the ninth and eleventh LSI elements to enter the discriminant analysis. Readers can continue in this way to compare the means of the three groups as shown in Table 10.2 in relation to their preferences for twenty-one LSI elements as shown in Table 10.3.

Comparison of Guatemalan High and Low Achievers

Overall, 664 Guatemalan students participated in this study. There were 363 males (55%), 281 females (42%), and 20 students (3%) who did not indicate gender on their inventory instruments. The distribution of students by grade and sex was presented in Table 2.1 in Chapter 2. Please note that the majority of students were young teenagers between the seventh and ninth grades. Only 55 students were at the tenth and eleventh grades and two-thirds of these older students were male.

For the purpose of this study, the high achievers in academic performance were those Guatemalan students who achieved a grade point average (GPA) of 3.5 or better in their averaged academic subjects. Those students who achieved an average of 3.4 or lower were categorized as academically nongifted. There were 118 students in the academically gifted population and 541 students who achieved below a 3.4 average in their school grades.

Nine learning style elements significantly discriminated between the two academic achievement groups. The discriminant analysis revealed that an overall Wilks' Lambda of .952 was produced (p <.0002) for nine of the twenty-two LSI variables. The high academic achievers were more responsible (conforming) and more persistent in their learning habits than the low academic achievers. Furthermore, the high-achievers preferred to learn more in the afternoon and in a warmer environment. When compared to their academically nongifted age peers, they prefer to use a kinesthetic rather than an auditory modality. The academically gifted also prefer less structure in their assignments and a less formally designed classroom environment, but they do not apparently require freedom to move about the classroom as they wish.

The next analysis of the data sought to determine the degree of giftedness or creative activity in the eight specific domains of creative performance as measured by the Tel Aviv Activities Inventory. Table 10.4 reveals the learning style preferences of Guatemalan students—both Ladinos and Mayan—who reported

Table 10.4

Learning Style Elements that Discriminate between Creative and Noncreative Guatemalan Students by Specific Domains

Domain of Creative Performance	Item Ratio Needed to Show Creative Engagement	Ratio of Creative to Noncreative Guatemalan Students	Stepwise Order Of Discriminate Analysis For LSI Elements; (P) Preference For Creative Group
Science	4/8	175/405	Tactile (P) Responsible (P) Requires Intake (P) Peer Oriented Formal Design Afternoon (P) Persistent (P) Morning (P) Needs Mobility (P) Kinesthetic (P)
Social Leadership	8/11	148/487	Responsible (P) Self-Motivated Kinesthetic (P) Structure Formal Design Visual Tactile (P) Needs Mobility Requires Intake (P) Learning Alone (P) Afternoon
Dance	2/2	71/174	Needs Mobility Structure (P) Teacher Motivated Late Morning (P) Persistent Sound (P) Kinesthetic (P) Morning
Music	4/9	131/410	Tactile (P) Sound Requires Intake (P) Needs Mobility Formal Design (P) Afternoon Light Responsible (P)

170

Table 10.4 (continued)

Domain of Creative Performance	Item Ratio Needed to Show Creative Engagement	Ratio of Creative to Noncreative Guatemalan Students	Stepwise Order Of Discriminate Analysis For LSI Elements; (P) Preference For Creative Group
Art	4/8	239/352	Tactile (P) Requires Intake (P) Structure Authority Figures Sound (P) Persistent (P) Parent Figure (P)
Literature	4/6	48/420	Persistent (P) Learning Alone (P) Visual Kinesthetic (P) Evening (P) Needs Mobility (P)
Drama	2/4	126/160	Structure Parent Figure (P) Authority Figure(P) Requires Intake Morning Auditory (P) Sound (P) Persistent (P)
Sports	4/6	331/261	Parent Figure (P) Afternoon Motivation Auditory

171

being creative versus noncreative in the eight domains measured in the Tel Aviv Activities Inventory. Table 10.4 was constructed for ease of reading and interpretation. For instance, by noting the domain of science, the reader can see that to be included in this creative engagement area, the student had to respond positively to four or more of the eight inventory items. A total of 175 students of 580 respondents indicated that they had a creative affinity for this domain. The last column of Table 10.4 reveals the stepwise order of the LSI elements that significantly discriminated between the creative and noncreative students for the science domain. The P in parenthesis after the ten LSI elements indicates whether the 175 science creative-affinity students preferred that element more strongly than the 405 students who did not show a creative affinity for the science domain. Thus, the reader can note that the 175 science affinity students preferred eight of the ten LSI elements in relation to the science domain. By inspecting the results for each of the eight domains of the Activities Inventory, the learning style preference for those students who had a creative affinity for that domain can be determined.

The discriminant functions for seven of the eight domains of the Activities Inventory were highly significant. The percent of cases that were accurately categorized by group as creative versus noncreative in the eight domains ranged from 55 to 90 percent.

While not as meaningful as the LSI preferences noted for each group for each creative inventory domain, an overall trend was noted among the preferences of domain-affinity students versus students who did not have domain interests. Four LSI elements were preferred for four of eight Activities Inventory domains by the creative-affinity students. These were a preference (P) for tactile and kinesthetic involvement, requiring intake, and exhibiting persistence. In three of eight Activities Inventory domains the LSI elements of responsible (conforming/nonconforming), morning or late morning, sound and parent-figure-motivated were preferred by creative-affinity students.

CONCLUSIONS AND IMPLICATIONS

This study provides interesting insights into the learning styles and creative performance of Guatemalan adolescents. The seventh through eleventh grade students who reported accomplishments and/or affinities for at least two of the eight category domains of the Tel Aviv Activities Inventory were persistent (four domains) and responsible (conforming) (three domains); preferred tactile (four domains) and kinesthetic involvement (four domains); and preferred to learn with sound (three domains) and in the morning or late morning (two domains).

By understanding the learning styles of creative adolescents, educators may be able to enhance their creative accomplishments to an even greater degree. Milgram (1990a, in press) has noted that creative performance items can reveal a student's activities and accomplishments in domains outside of school and serve as predictors of attainments in adult life. The activities considered relevant are freely chosen by the student and are not related to the fulfilling of traditional school requirements such as the earning of grades or credits. This belief regarding creative affinities is consistent with Gardner's theory of multiple intelligences (1983). He noted that one can be intelligent in the areas of music, linguistics, logical-mathematical reasoning, spatial reasoning, bodily-kinesthetic reasoning, and interpersonal or intrapersonal reasoning.

More questions are raised than are answered by the present results, however. First, we attempted to test a representative sample of the country's adolescents in order to include students from both the Mayan Indian and Ladino or Hispanic cultures. However, from the two institutes attended by Mayan students, we were able to include only forty-nine complete cases. These students, moreover, were generally in the high academic range of their classes. Therefore, the results of comparing Guatemalan Ladino students with the American students for LSI element preferences, as shown in Tables 10.2 and 10.3, are probably more globally meaningful than the results for the Mayan students.

Second, Guatemalan high achievers in both cultural groups were characterized as those students who achieved a grade point average of 3.5 in their averaged academic subjects. A total of 118 students were found to fall into the high academic group as compared to 541 Guatemalan students who fell below a 3.4 index. The researchers noted, however, when averaging student grade point averages from five academic subjects that many students had relatively high grades in mathematics, science, and social studies and appreciably lower grades in Spanish and English. Since the Tel Aviv Activities Inventory tapped creative performance affinities and accomplishments in such areas as science, social leadership, art, and literature, it may be far more meaningful to correlate the eight domain areas of the inventory with extremely high grades in specific academic subjects. In this way, creative affinity for a domain can be compared to academic accomplishment. For the Mayan adolescents in particular, this type of analysis may be quite meaningful. In their culture and community, art and artistic crafts are predominant activities. In Chinautla, where the Mayan adolescents attend the Instituto San Antonio Las Flores, girls learn the art of pottery and have had their pieces exhibited in many museums of the world.

Finally, the majority of adolescents in this study were seventh through ninth grade students. The secondary school grades in Guatemala extend from the seventh to the twelfth grades. No twelfth graders were represented in this study and only fifty-five students were at the tenth and eleventh grade levels. When comparing learning style preferences with creative accomplishments for adolescents, it may be far more meaningful to compare first- and second-year high school students (grades 7 and 8) with fifth- and sixth-year high school students (grades 11 and 12). Since education at the higher levels of schooling in Guatemala is achieved by students who are persistent, motivated, or come from privileged families, differing profiles could emerge from lower-grade high school students as compared to upper-grade high school students.

Chapter 11

The Learning Styles of Gifted Adolescents in Korea

Bernadyn Suh and Gary E. Price

Korea is a small nation on a peninsula in the heart of the Far East. Since early history it has been a battlefield for the rivalries of Japan, China, and Russia. Americans came to know Korea primarily through the tragedy of the Korean War. It is a country of rugged beauty. The Koreans are a vigorous people, quick to show their pleasure and resentment. Korea, "a shrimp among whales," according to an old Korean proverb, is still suffering on a daily basis from the cruel game of power politics as a hot spot in the cold war. The Koreans are a people separate from the Chinese and Japanese, although they have absorbed and adapted many cultural features from their neighbors. For example, in the educational system, national examinations for admission and graduation have been instituted. The Korean students come from homes where education is highly regarded. Even during the Korean War, the Korean people were certain that their young children were educated.

After 1950, the growth in enrollment at all levels of education was dramatic. Primary schools expanded rapidly, and secondary and tertiary systems of education were expanded. The six years of primary education were made compulsory in 1949, and essentially full enrollment at the primary level was achieved by the early 1960s. Since then, the main growth has been in secondary education. During the 1960s, the expansion of three-year middle schools was particularly rapid. These middle schools now provide academic education to a large proportion of the twelve- to fifteen-year-olds and have been extended to all but the most remote rural areas. Literacy of those over twelve, estimated to have been 22 percent in 1945, rose to about 90 percent in 1975. Girls still receive less education than boys, but the gap is narrowing.

Only primary education is tuition free. This willingness to pay high fees reflects the traditional respect for education in Korean culture and the expectation that an investment in an individual's education will yield a high rate of return. The reliance on fees for much educational financing has encouraged private institutions to respond to the rising demand for schooling. Private schools are of negligible significance at the primary level, but become increasingly important at each higher level of study.

Class size is large, and learning depends heavily on rote memorization, at least at the lower levels. Such a system cannot provide individual attention or opportunities for personal creativity considered by many people as essential to education of high quality. Teachers appear to manage the large classes without excessive problems, disciplinary or otherwise.

Excessive competition among students has been another threat to the quality of the educational process, especially where advancement from one educational level to the next depends on admissions examinations. Before 1968, entrance into middle schools was based on examination results. A small number of middle schools appeared to offer much greater promise of eventual admission to the best high schools which, in turn, offered better prospects of acceptance by the most prestigious university departments. Consequently, impending examinations distorted the educational objectives of the final two years of elementary school. To remove these distortions and to counter elitism, the government abolished the examination for entrance into middle schools in Seoul in 1968 and to all middle schools in 1970. Children in each school district were assigned by lottery to an individual school, whether public or private.

Enrollments at all ages have grown much more rapidly than the population. This growth, in turn, has raised the education and skills of average Korean citizens to a much higher level than in the majority of other developing countries. Yet despite all that has been achieved, the situation appears far from satisfactory to many Koreans. For instance, although the situation has been steadily improving, only 80 percent of middle school students advanced to high school in 1981.

The Korean government has a long-standing commitment to compulsory and basically free middle school education. The near universality of primary education achieved by the early 1960s provided an abundant pool of easily trainable, low-cost workers for labor-intensive industries.

At the primary level, the thrust of programs was to reduce the size of classes and to improve schools. But even classes of sixty students, the norm for most primary schools, were large by international standards, and overcrowding was extreme in metropolitan schools. Criticism of middle and high school programs focused on the inadequacy of instructional materials and the pace of inclusion of instructional technology. The school population continued to shrink until the early 1990s, when children of those born in the postwar baby boom passed through primary and middle school. Having 70 to 75 percent of the students complete twelve years of education was a goal, and meant that Korea would have one of the most extensive systems of formal general education anywhere.

To sum up, the following are the major characteristics of the Korean educational system at each age level:

Pre-school education: Optional and primarily privately run with emphasis on socialization skills.

Kindergarten education: Public or private, teaching basic letter recognition, basic computations, singing, and dancing.

Elementary school education: Public for six years. There are no entrance exams and the students are computer-assigned by lottery to the different schools by their school districts.

Middle school education: Public, approximately 60 percent, and private, 40 percent, for three years. Students are selected by state administered standardized tests.

High school education: Public (40%) and private (60%) varies from city to city. High school continues for three years and includes the following three curricula:

1. College preparatory schools (some are coed);

2. Vocational schools (includes industrial, commercial, agricultural, and fishery curricula);

3. Special high schools for elite students only, including science and foreign language high schools; junior college for two years stressing vocational training; college for four years; graduate school for two years.

RESEARCH METHODOLOGY

Subjects

Subjects were ninety-two students of eleventh (N = 45) and twelfth (N = 47) grades, all males, in the Haesung High School, a Catholic school located in Jeonju, Korea. The main sources of income in the town of Jeonju are small businesses and agriculture. The school is a college preparatory school with a student population of 1,316 students in twenty-four classes. The average class size is approximately fifty-three students.

The subjects all qualified for enrollment by attaining a rank in the upper 10 percent of their regular class in the general achievement tests. The subjects met in advanced study of English and mathematics for one hour in the morning before regular classes. Students learned English and mathematics intensively, with specially prepared materials, one subject each day, alternately. Most students were highly motivated and aspired to attend prestigious colleges in Korea.

The subjects were from working-class homes where they were highly motivated to take advantage of the educational opportunities. As mentioned above, secondary education is not compulsory and parents are required to pay tuition for their children to attend. Consequently, extensive pressure is exerted on students to succeed academically. Competition is keen and discipline is firm. The parents sacrifice their own comfort and conveniences to ensure that their children will have the educational opportunity to enter the most prestigious Korean colleges.

There are no big businesses or large-scale enterprises in the town. The students are from economically limited situations, but are upwardly mobile and aspire to use education as the vehicle for social advancement.

Materials

Two instruments were administered. The Learning Style Inventory (Dunn, Dunn, and Price 1989) and an English translation of the Tel Aviv Activities Inventory (Milgram 1987). The two instruments were described in detail in Chapter 2.

Procedure

The two instruments were group-administered in English in two separate sessions by Mr. Eun-Jong Kwak, a Korean teacher who has taught English for more than thirty years. The students studied English for more than five years and were proficient in it.

RESEARCH RESULTS

Comparison of Korean and American Students

We first compared the learning style characteristics of adolescent learners in Korea to a comparable random sample from the United States. There were ninety-two subjects in each group.

The means and stepwise order of the eleven learning style elements that significantly discriminated between learners in the United States and in Korea are presented in Table 11.1.

The first variable to enter the discriminant equation was design. Overall, the Korean students preferred a more formal design than the U.S. students. This may be because they are used to hard wooden desks and chairs. The second variable was persistence. The U.S. students were more persistent than were the Korean students. The third variable was intake. The U.S. students preferred more intake than did the Korean students. Again, this may have been reflected of cultural habits where American students have easy access to food. The fourth variable was temperature. Overall, the Korean students preferred a warmer environment than did the U.S. students. The fifth variable was authority figures present. Overall, the U.S. students preferred more authority figures present than did the Korean students. This finding is interesting, as the Korean classroom was highly structured and teacher directed, but the students did not prefer teachers present as much as the U.S. students. The sixth variable was mobility. The U.S.

Table 11.1
Learning Style Elements that Discriminate between Adolescents in Korea and in the United States: Stepwise Order and Mean Scores

Stepwise Order	LSI Variables	American Students (N=92)	Korean Students (N=92)
1	Design	12.18	16.58
2	Persistent	17.10	15.94
3	Requires Intake	14.30	10.53
4	Temperature	12.65	13.49
5	Authority Figure Present	10.93	9.48
6	Need Mobility	13.49	10.94
7	Motivation	32.94	32.12
8	Learning Alone-Peer Oriented	20.39	21.56
9	Afternoon	16.29	15.27
10	Structure	12.55	12.68
11	Learn in Several Ways	13.10	12.58

students indicated that they needed more mobility than did the Korean students. Again, this could reflect cultural differences where mobility is acceptable in the United States. The seventh variable was motivation. Overall, the U.S. students indicated that they were more motivated than were the Korean students. Perhaps the difference is in intrinsic versus extrinsic motivation. The eighth variable was learning alone or peer oriented. The Korean students indicated they preferred to learn more with peers than did the U.S. students. The ninth variable was afternoon. Overall, the U.S. students indicated that they preferred to learn more in the afternoon. The tenth variable was structure. The Korean students indicated that they wanted more structure than did the U.S. students, and overall, Asian education is highly structured. The eleventh variable to enter the discriminant equation was learning in several ways. The U.S. students preferred to learn in several ways socially than did the Korean students.

Learning Styles of Academically Gifted and Academically Nongifted Korean Adolescents

For the purposes of this study, those students who ranked in the top 20 percent of the sample with respect to overall scholastic achievement were categorized as academically gifted; the remainder were categorized as nongifted. Korean students included in the academically gifted group were those who had achieved an overall grade point average (GPA) of 4.0 (N = 46). Those whose GPA was less than 4.0 (N = 46) were categorized as academically nongifted. Eleven learning style variables discriminated between the academically gifted and academically nongifted samples.

Those categorized as academically gifted were more persistent and expressed greater preference to learn visually and kinesthetically and with more structure than their nonacademically gifted peers. The gifted needed less mobility and were less conforming than the nongifted. They were also less parent-figure motivated and less desirous of having an authority figure present than the academically nongifted. There was also a difference between the gifted and nongifted as far as the time of day during which they prefer to learn, with the gifted preferring early and late morning and the nongifted preferring the afternoon.

Learning Styles of Creatively Gifted Korean Students

Learning style differences were compared in gifted and nongifted learners in the following eight specific creativity domains: science, social leadership, dance, music, art, literature, drama, and sports. The results are shown in Table 11.2.

The discriminant functions for seven of the eight domains of creative activity were significant. The percent of cases that were accurately categorized by group as creative versus noncreative in the eight domains surveyed ranged from 70 to 100 percent.

Structure was preferred by gifted learners in four out of eight creativity domains. Tactile, afternoon, parent-figure motivation, and kinesthetic were preferred by the gifted in three domains. Learners gifted in each of five creativity domains preferred cooler temperatures and those gifted in three domains preferred dimmer lighting while they learn.

Science. The results yielded by the stepwise discriminant analysis presented in Table 11.2 revealed that a total of six variables significantly entered the discriminant equation in the area of science. The first variable was persistence. Overall, the gifted students were more persistent than the nongifted students. This seems logical that the gifted would have more task commitment. These data parallel those of previous researchers, all of whom reported gifted students'

Table 11.2

Learning Style Elements that Discriminate between Creative and Noncreative Korean Learners by Specific Domains

Domain of Creative Performances	Item Ratio Needed to Show Creative Engagement	Ratio of Creative to Noncreative Korean Students	Stepwise Order Of Discriminant Analysis For LSI Elements; (P) Indicates Preference For Creative Group
Science	4/8	36/48	Persistent (P) Tactile (P) Temperature Alone (P) Structure Light
Social Leadership	8/11	11/78	Motivation (P) Auditory Visual (P) Warm
Dance	2/2	2/11	Light Auth Fig Present (P) Several Ways Morning (P) Sound (P) Afternoon (P) Visual Auditory (P) Kinesthetic (P) Needs Mobility (P) Parent Fig Mot (P)
Music	4/9	28/58	Kinesthetic (P) Structure (P) Learn Alone (P) Evening (P) Visual (P) Late Morning (P) Auth Fig Present (P)
Art	4/8	26/39	Temperature Tactile (P) Afternoon (P) Light Structure (P) Parent Fig Mot (P) Teacher Motivated (P)

Table 11.2 (continued)

Domain of Creative Performances	Item Ratio Needed to Show Creative Engagement	Ratio of Creative to Noncreative Korean Students	Stepwise Order Of Discriminant Analysis For LSI Elements; (P) Indicates Preference For Creative Group
Literature	5/6	1/80	Parent Fig Mot Learn In Sev Ways Structure Auditory Afternoon (P) Kinesthetic (P)
Drama	2/4	7/20	Temperature Parent Fig Mot (P) Structure (P) Noise Level (P) Peer Oriented (P) Teacher Motivated Kinesthetic
Sports	4/6	7/69	Peer (P) Tactile (P) Structure (P) Temperature (P)

persistence and task commitment. The second variable was tactile. Gifted students preferred to learn more through their tactile preference than did nongifted students. The third variable was temperature. Overall, the gifted students preferred a cooler environment than did the nongifted students. Interestingly, this differs from the Israeli gifted, who preferred a warmer environment, which may be reflective of geographical location. The fourth variable was learning alone or peer orientation. Overall, the gifted students preferred to learn more alone and the nongifted preferred to learn more with peers. These results agreed with findings that the gifted are more internally controlled and self-directed. The fifth variable was structure. Overall, the gifted students preferred less structure than the nongifted students. The sixth variable was light. Overall, the gifted students preferred learning in lower light and the nongifted preferred learning in brighter light.

Social Leadership. There were eleven gifted students and seventy-eight nongifted students in the social area. A total of four variables significantly entered the discriminant equation (as indicated in Table 11.1). The first variable was motivation. The gifted students were more self-motivated than the nongifted. The second variable was auditory. The gifted revealed a significantly lower preference for learning by listening than did the nongifted students. The third variable was visual. Overall, the gifted students preferred to learn more through their visual preference than did the nongifted students. It may have been that their visual preference contributed to their ability to learn through academic readings more than the nongifted. The fourth variable was temperature. Overall, the gifted individuals preferred a cooler environment than the nongifted individuals.

Dance. Table 11.2 reveals that the discriminant analysis indicated that there were two in the gifted group and eleven in the nongifted group. The first variable was light; gifted students preferred lower light than did the nongifted students. The second variable was authority figures present. The gifted wanted authority figures present more than the nongifted. The third variable was learning in several ways. Overall, the gifted preferred to learn less in varied ways than did the nongifted. The fourth variable was time of day: evening or morning. Overall, the gifted students preferred to learn more in the morning than did the nongifted students. The fifth variable was noise level. Overall, gifted students preferred to have sound present more than the nongifted. The sixth variable was time of day: afternoon. The gifted students preferred to learn more in the afternoon than did the nongifted. The seventh variable was visual. Overall, the nongifted group preferred to learn more through their visual preference than did the gifted. The eighth variable was auditory. The gifted students preferred to learn more through their auditory preference than the nongifted. The ninth variable was kinesthetic. In dance, the gifted students preferred to learn more through their kinesthetic preference than the nongifted. The tenth variable was mobility. Overall, the gifted preferred more mobility than the nongifted. The eleventh variable was parent figure motivation. The gifted students were more parent figure motivated than were the nongifted.

Music. The next comparison is for the learning style preferences of the musically gifted and nongifted. There were twenty-eight in the gifted group and fifty-eight in the nongifted group. The first variable to significantly enter the discriminant equation was kinesthetic. Overall, the gifted students preferred to learn more through their kinesthetic preference than did the nongifted. The results of this Korean sample agreed again with those of the Israeli sample and those of Wasson (1982) and indicated that the gifted preferred active involvement. The second variable was structure. The gifted students preferred more structure than did the nongifted. The Korean students were goal directed and concerned with the demands of a highly structured classroom. The third variable was learning alone or peer oriented. Overall, the gifted students preferred to learn more alone than did the nongifted. As noted earlier, the Korean gifted were internally controlled and self-directed, which would enable them to learn alone. The fourth variable was time-of-day energy level. Overall, the gifted preferred to learn more in the evening than did the nongifted. The fifth variable was visual. Overall, the gifted preferred to learn more through their visual preference than did the nongifted students. Most Korean gifted are avid readers and learn extensively through observations. This visual orientation is an important asset. The sixth variable was late morning. Overall, the gifted students preferred to learn more in late morning than did the nongifted and evidenced high energy levels twice during the day. The seventh variable was authority figures present. The gifted students did not want authoritative feedback as much as the nongifted students and instead preferred learning with collegial people. Again, these findings agreed with data that revealed that the gifted are self-directed and self-motivated.

Art. The next comparison in Table 11.2 was for the learning style characteristics of the Korean artistic gifted and nongifted. There were twenty-six in the gifted group and thirty-nine in the nongifted group. The first variable was temperature. Overall, the gifted students preferred a cooler environment than did the nongifted students. The second variable was tactile. Overall, the gifted students preferred to learn more through their tactile preference than did the nongifted. The third variable was afternoon. The gifted preferred to learn more in the afternoon than did the nongifted. The fourth variable was light. Overall, the gifted students preferred lower light than did the nongifted. The fifth variable was structure. Overall, the gifted students preferred more structure than the nongifted. The sixth variable was parent figure motivation. The gifted students were more parent motivated than were the nongifted. In Korean culture, emphasis is placed on teaching children to respect their parents. The seventh variable was teacher motivation. Overall, the gifted students were more teacher motivated than were the nongifted students. To succeed academically, the Korean students must want to meet the demands of their teacher.

Literature. The next comparison is for the gifted and nongifted adolescents talented in the area of literature. There was only one person in the gifted group and eighty in the nongifted group. The frequencies of selecting seven in literature, with a total score of seven, was one. Seven had a frequency of four. Sixteen had three. Twenty-nine had two and twenty-eight had one in this area. Again, the small sample size reduced the meaning of these data. The first variable was parent figure motivation. The gifted were less motivated than were the nongifted. The second variable was learning in several ways. The gifted preferred not to learn more in several ways than did the nongifted group. The third variable was structure. The gifted preferred to learn with less structure than the nongifted. The fourth variable was auditory. The gifted did not want to use their auditory preference as much as the nongifted. The fifth variable was afternoon. The gifted preferred to learn more in the afternoon than did the nongifted. The sixth variable was kinesthetic. The gifted preferred to learn more with their kinesthetic preference than did the nongifted.

Drama. The next comparison is for gifted and nongifted adolescents in drama. The first variable was temperature. The gifted students preferred a cooler environment. The second variable was parent figure motivated. The gifted were more parent figure motivated. The third variable was structure. The gifted preferred to have more structure. The fourth variable was noise level. The gifted preferred sound present more than the nongifted. The fifth variable was learning alone versus peer oriented. The gifted preferred to learn more with peers than the nongifted. The sixth variable was teacher motivated. The gifted were less teacher motivated than the nongifted. The seventh variable was kinesthetic. Overall, the gifted students preferred to learn less through their kinesthetic sense than did the nongifted but the actual mean difference was only .09 of a point.

Sports. The next is a summary of learning style preferences of Korean gifted and nongifted students in sports. The first variable was learning alone vs. peer oriented. The gifted preferred to learn more with peers than the nongifted who preferred to learn more alone. The second variable was tactile. The gifted preferred to learn more through their tactile preference than did the nongifted. The third variable was structure. The gifted students wanted more structure compared to the nongifted. The fourth variable was temperature. The gifted wanted a cooler environment compared to the nongifted.

CONCLUSION

We have learned in this study that the Korean students have specific preferences for learning. They have distinct learning style profiles. We need to understand these differences and maximize the opportunities for all children to develop their fullest potential to contribute to the common good for life on this fragile planet. In a comprehensive cross-cultural study of Asian children with American children, Stigler and Stevenson (1991) concluded that, "Although the number of children in Asian classes is significantly greater than the number in American classes, Asian students received much more instruction from their teachers than American students" (p. 17). This is a very interesting finding and the authors further cite examples of Asian teachers handling diversity and allowing students to reconstruct their view of learning through concrete interactions with the learning environment. "According to this view, knowledge is regarded as something that must be constructed by the child rather than as a set of facts and skills that can be imported by the teacher" (p. 20). So, Piaget was right in many ways. Each person has to construct his or her view of reality based upon his or her interactions with the environment. The culture one grows up in has direct impact on this view of reality and one's learning style.

Chapter 12

The Learning Styles of Artistically Talented Adolescents in Canada

Mary Rue Brodhead and Gary E. Price

The high school molds itself around a small knoll, one of the few to be found in this Ontario city. The school's circular driveway sweeps around to the main entrance, a bank of nondescript fire doors. This unpretentious entrance does not prepare the visitor for the large foyer filled with spectacular oil paintings, sculptures, photographs, and other forms of innovative artistic expression, or for the sound of an orchestra practicing on the large stage in the adjoining auditorium. Posters advertising a dance production, a musical performance, an athletic event, or perhaps a play are displayed on all available wall space. The school vibrates with creative energy.

The high school was established as a magnet school for artistically talented students by the board of education. The program has been expanded to include students from approximately seventeen other Ontario boards of education. The arts program offers broad instruction in the visual arts, music, drama, and dance, as well as the regular required curriculum. As of September 1990, 425 of the 842 students attending the school were officially in the arts program. Except for their arts credits, these artistically talented students attend the same classes as students in the regular high school program.

Students apply to be accepted in their preferred area at the end of the eighth grade. They are chosen for both their artistic accomplishments and potential; the interview process is extensive and rigorous. Visual arts students prepare a portfolio; dance, music, and drama students perform a selection of pieces illustrating their ability. All applicants spend two days in workshops designed to enable the teachers to assess each participant's potential to learn new material. The final step in the admission process is an individual interview with teachers. Recommendations from arts teachers are important; grades, though a factor, carry less weight in the selection process than the other criteria. Though the auditions are stressful for these young adolescents, it has been observed that the process of self-evaluation and analysis that is required enhances their self-knowledge and understanding.

The staff, students, and parents have a strong commitment to the value of the performing arts. In the first two graduating classes, 98 percent of the students in the program went on to complete their Ontario academic courses (pre-university); 80 percent continued into postsecondary education (half in the arts) and only 2 percent dropped out of high school. The school grades of many arts students improve as they advance in the program.

An emerging body of research supports the value of an arts program (McLaughlin 1990). Findings indicated that arts programs not only increase the student's expertise within a particular field but also encourage creative and intuitive development—skills not usually rewarded in our traditional curriculum. "Exceptional students benefit from the use of intuition, divergent thinking, imagination, and spontaneity found in the study of the arts" (Wilson 1989).

In 1989, Professor Richard Rancourt of the University of Ottawa used his Knowledge Accessing Modes Inventory (KAMI) to test some of the students in this high school. He found that most of the arts students tended to view things holistically rather than analytically, were intuitive, preferred visual (spatial) tasks, thought randomly, and were spontaneous, expressive, extroverted, and sometimes impulsive. Rancourt called this pattern the *noetic mode.*

Rancourt's work and and the current study have increased staff and parent awareness of the importance of understanding the learning styles of these adolescents. Both school personnel and parents actively supported the proposal to participate in the Milgram, Dunn, and Price international study of the learning styles of gifted youth. They believed that the Learning Style Inventory (Dunn, Dunn, Price 1984) would provide valuable and practical insights concerning this unusual study body. They hoped the results would provide information about students whose talents are often difficult to identify and whose needs are often not met in the standard Canadian curriculum.

Support from staff and parents was crucial to the success of this research. It was the deciding factor in the board of education's decision to approve this study and contributed to the positive responses from students.

RESEARCH METHODOLOGY

Subjects

All 840 students enrolled in the school were sent a letter describing the research and asking for their participation. Parents of students below eighteen years of age were asked to send in permission forms. Of the 166 students who responded positively, 138 were in the arts program, 28 were in the regular program. Among the arts program participants, 46 were in drama, 25 in dance, 33 in music, and 34 in the visual arts. The subjects were all English-speaking (Anglophones), and did not represent a random sample of the wide variety of cultures represented in modern Canada. The distribution of subjects by grade and sex was presented in Chapter 2, Table 2.1.

Materials

Two instruments were administered, the Learning Styles Inventory (Dunn, Dunn, & Price 1989) and the Tel Aviv Activities Inventory (Milgram 1987). Both instruments were described in detail in Chapter 2. The reliabilities for the twenty-two Learning Style Inventory scores as administered in Canada were all above .60, with nine out of the twenty-two reliabilities .80 or higher and sixteen out of the twenty-two .70 or higher.

Procedures

The Learning Style inventory and the Tel Aviv Activities Inventory were group-administered during a sixty-minute class period. The examiner and both vice-principals were present during the testing session. The only time limit was the end of the period; all students finished. Student names were kept for their learning style profiles only. Coded identity numbers were used in all data analyses to ensure confidentiality.

Although the need for the repetition of items on the Learning Style Inventory had been explained before administering the questionnaires, many students found the repetition frustrating. They expressed their opinions with creative designs on the margins of their question sheets—a delight for human eyes, a disaster for the computers. However, the participants' humor, enthusiasm, and comments indicated their enjoyment of the process. Many commented on the confidence that an understanding of their style of learning had given them, indicating that the problem of repetition did not result in lack of motivation to take the test that would invalidate the scores.

RESEARCH RESULTS

Comparison of Canadian and U.S. Students

We first compared the 166 Canadian students to an equal number of students in the United States who were randomly selected from the data bank provided by Price Systems, Inc. The means and stepwise order of the eleven learning style elements that significantly discriminated between learners in the United States and Canada are presented in Table 12.1.

The Canadian students preferred to learn through their tactile sense more than the Americans. When it came to learning visually, the Americans expressed the stronger preference. The Canadians also reported a stronger preference to learn

Table 12.1
Learning Style Elements that Discriminate between Adolescents in Canada and in the United States: Stepwise Order and Mean Scores

Stepwise Order	LSI Variables	United States (N=166)	Canada (N=166)
1	Temperature	12.80	18.50
2	Teacher Motivated	19.96	17.09
3	Learning Alone/Peer Oriented	21.69	20.39
4	Responsible	13.49	12.25
5	Evening-Morning	17.10	15.20
6	Late Morning	11.66	11.38
7	Tactile	16.56	17.46
8	Afternoon	16.52	15.95
9	Structure	12.42	12.02
10	Visual	9.00	8.19
11	Noise Level	14.40	14.48

in a warmer environment than the Americans. Canadians expressed more of a preference to learn in the evening than the American youngsters, who reported late morning and afternoon as times that they learn best. Adolescents in the U.S. random sample were more teacher motivated and peer oriented than the Canadian students. They were more responsible (or conforming) and preferred more structure than their Canadian counterparts. Finally, the U.S. random sample preferred a more quiet environment when they learned than did the Canadian students. It is important to remember that the Canadian sample was not a random selection of students; 84 percent were in the arts program.

Learning Styles of Artistically Gifted Canadian Adolescents

We next compared learners who received high versus low scores indicating creative performance in each of the eight specific domains.

Table 12.2 summarizes the Canadian student responses to the Learning Style Inventory according to their areas of creative performance (column 1). The second column indicates the number of positive responses on the Activities Inventory needed for a student to be considered gifted in each area of creativity.

Column 3 lists the ratio of gifted students to nongifted students. The final column lists the stepwise order of the Learning Style Inventory elements that significantly discriminated between the groups.

Science. There were eighty-two in the gifted group and seventy-six in the nongifted group. The first variable to enter the discriminant equation was tactile. The gifted students, who usually have multiple perceptual strengths, preferred to learn more through their tactile sense than the nongifted. The gifted were more parent oriented than the nongifted. The nongifted students preferred more structure when receiving assignments than the gifted students. They preferred more variety while learning than the gifted students, who preferred extensive time working with the activities they most enjoyed. The gifted students were more motivated than the nongifted. The nongifted indicated that they were more responsible (or conforming) than the gifted students. The gifted preferred a warmer environment than the nongifted students. The gifted preferred to learn kinesthetically more than the nongifted students.

Social. There were 49 in the gifted group and 112 in the nongifted group. The first variable to enter the discriminant equation was kinesthetic. The gifted were more kinesthetic than the nongifted and preferred to learn in late morning more than the nongifted. The gifted preferred to learn tactically and needed more variety than the nongifted. The nongifted preferred to learn in the afternoon more than the gifted students. The gifted students were more motivated than the nongifted students. The nongifted students preferred a warmer environment when compared to the gifted students.

Dance. There were thirty-eight in the gifted group and fifty-nine in the non-gifted group. The first variable to enter the discriminant equation was persistent. The nongifted indicated that they were more persistent than the gifted. This variable was later removed at step 11. The reason a variable was removed from the discriminant equation was that, at that point in the analysis, it no longer contributed information after the previous variables entered the equation, although by itself or in combination it did uniquely discriminate.

The second variable to enter the discriminant equation was noise level. The gifted preferred a quieter environment than the nongifted. This variable was removed at step 13. The third variable to enter the discriminant equation was kinesthetic. Overall, the gifted were more kinesthetic than the nongifted. The fourth variable was tactile. The nongifted preferred to learn through their tactile preference more than the gifted students. The fifth variable, requires intake, indicated that the gifted preferred more intake than the nongifted. The sixth variable was late morning. The gifted preferred to learn in late morning more than the nongifted. The seventh variable was temperature. The nongifted preferred a warmer environment when compared to the gifted. The eighth variable was needs mobility. The gifted preferred more mobility than the nongifted. The ninth variable showed that the nongifted were more peer oriented than the gifted. The tenth variable was visual. The nongifted preferred to learn through their visual preference more than the gifted. At step 11, persistence was removed. At

Table 12.2
Learning Style Elements that Discriminate between Creative and Noncreative Canadian Learners by Specific Domain

Domain of Creative Performance	Item Ratio Needed to Show Creative Engagement	Ratio of Creative to Noncreative Canadian Students	Stepwise Order of Discriminant Analysis For LSI Elements; (P) Indicates Preference For Creative Group
Science	4/8	82/76	Tactile (P) Parent Figure Motivated (P) Structure Learn in Several Ways Motivation (P) Responsible Temperature (P) Kinesthetic (P)
Social Leadership	8/11	49/112	Kinesthetic (P) Late Morning (P) Tactile (P) Learn in Several Ways (P) Afternoon Motivation (P) Temperature
Dance	2/2	38/59	Persistent (Removed 11) Noise Level (Removed 13) Kinesthetic (P) Tactile Requires Intake (P) Late Morning (P) Temperature Needs Mobility (P) Learning Alone Visual Authority Figures Present (P)
Music	4/9	104/58	Parent Figure Motivated (P) Afternoon Temperature (P) Structure Light (P) Auditory (P)
Art	4/8	74/81	Teacher Motivated (P) Needs Mobility Visual (P) Tactile (P) Requires Intake Afternoon Authority Figures Present (P)

Table 12.2 (continued)

Domain of Creative Performance	Item Ratio Needed to Show Creative Engagement	Ratio of Creative to Noncreative Canadian Students	Stepwise Order of Discriminant Analysis For LSI Elements; (P) Indicates Preference For Creative Group
Literature	4/6	31/126	Parent Figure Motivated (P)
			Noise Level (P)
			Requires Intake
			Persistent
			Motivation (P)
			Kinesthetic
			Design
			Responsible (P)
Drama	2/4	51/54	Afternoon
			Parent Figure Motivated (P)
			Auditory (P)
			Learning Alone
			Needs Mobility (P)
			Responsible (P)
			Tactile (P)
			Persistent
Sports	4/6	99/61	Design
			Kinesthetic (P)
			Noise Level
			Structure (P)
			Requires Intake (P)
			Morning (P)
			Tactile (P)

step 12, authority figures came into the equation. The gifted preferred feedback from an authority figure in their lives more than the nongifted. At step 13, noise level was removed.

Music. There were 104 in the gifted group and 58 in the nongifted group. The gifted were more parent motivated than the nongifted. The nongifted preferred to learn in the afternoon more than the gifted students. The gifted preferred a warmer environment compared to the nongifted. The nongifted wanted more structure than the gifted. The gifted preferred brighter light compared to the nongifted. The gifted preferred to learn through their auditory preference more than the nongifted.

Art. There were seventy-four in the gifted group and eighty-one in the nongifted group. The gifted were more teacher motivated than the nongifted. The nongifted preferred more mobility than the gifted. The gifted were more visual than the nongifted and preferred to learn tactually more than the nongifted. The nongifted needed intake more than the gifted students. The nongifted preferred to learn in the afternoon more than the gifted students. The gifted preferred authority figures present more than the nongifted.

Literature. There were 31 in the gifted group and 126 in the nongifted group. The gifted were motivated more by a parent figure than the nongifted students and they preferred sound to be present more than the nongifted. The nongifted needed intake more than the gifted and indicated that they were more persistent. The gifted were more self-motivated than the nongifted. The nongifted preferred to learn kinesthetically more than the gifted. The gifted preferred an informal design and were more responsible (or conforming) than the nongifted.

Drama. There were fifty-one in the gifted group and fifty-four in the nongifted group. The nongifted preferred to learn in the afternoon more than the gifted. The gifted were more parent figure motivated than the nongifted. The gifted were more auditory than the nongifted. The nongifted were more peer oriented than the gifted. The gifted needed more mobility than the nongifted. The gifted were more responsible (or conforming) than the nongifted and preferred to learn tactually more than the nongifted. The nongifted were more persistent than the gifted students.

Sports. There were ninety-nine in the gifted group and sixty-one in the nongifted group. The nongifted preferred a more formal design while the gifted preferred to learn kinesthetically. The gifted preferred a quiet environment compared to the nongifted. The gifted wanted more structure and needed more intake than the nongifted. The gifted preferred to learn in the morning and were more tactile than the nongifted.

Comparison of Learning Styles Between Arts and Regular Program Students

We next compared the learning styles of students in the arts program (N = 22) with those in the regular program (N = 139).

The first variable to enter the discriminant equation was parent figure motivated. The arts students were more parent figure motivated than the nonarts students. The second variable to enter the discriminant equation was responsible (or conforming). The nonarts students indicated that they were more conforming than the arts students. The third variable was motivation. Overall, the arts students were more motivated than the nonarts students. The fourth variable was temperature. The arts students preferred a warm environment more than the nonarts students. The fifth variable was late morning. The arts students preferred to learn in the late morning more than the nonarts students. The sixth variable was learn in several ways. The nonarts students needed to learn in a variety of ways. The seventh variable was kinesthetic. The arts students preferred to learn kinesthetically more than the nonarts students. The eighth variable was auditory. The nonarts students preferred auditory learning more than the arts students. The ninth variable was tactile. The nonarts students preferred to learn tactually more than the arts students. The tenth variable was teacher motivated. The arts students were more teacher motivated than the nonarts students. The eleventh variable was noise level. The nonarts students preferred more sound than the arts students.

The findings from the comparison of the learning styles of the students in the arts program and the regular program conformed to many of the perceptions the students have of themselves, as well as those the staff and parents have of the students. The arts students were highly motivated in their respective fields and this motivation tended to spill over into other subject areas. They were less conforming than the nonarts students but, at the same time, they tended to respect their arts teachers for their expertise and knowledge. It was not surprising that the arts students reported a preference to learn more kinesthetically, whereas the nonarts students preferred to learn through their auditory and tactile senses. Arts students are performers who create experiences that use their tactile and kinesthetic strengths, and derive a great deal of personal satisfaction from doing so! The learning style that the arts students reported is understandable in terms of the emphasis on creative output reflecting a kinesthetic orientation, rather than passive input more characteristic of an auditory preference.

CONCLUSION

The learning styles of these gifted Canadian students were compared to those of similarly gifted students in other nations. This comparison showed that not only did the students in the various gifted categories at this high school have different learning style profiles, but that these profiles were essentially similar to those of students within the same category from other countries. These similarities will be explored in more detail in Chapter 16.

NOTE

The subjects were all English-speaking—and do not represent a random sample of the wide variety of cultures represented in modern Canada.

Chapter 13

The Learning Styles of Creative Adolescents in Brazil

Solange Wechsler

Brazil is a large country, occupying nearly half of South America with 3,286,470 square miles. It was first visited by Pedro Alvarez Cabral in 1500, and remained a Portuguese colony until 1822.

Brazil is a multiracial society derived from the intermarriage of Indians with whites, blacks, and other immigrant races. The population now is 54 percent white, 38.45 percent mulatto, 5.89 percent black, 0.63 percent Asian, and a few others. The main immigrants to Brazil were from Portugal (31%), Italy (29%), Spain (12%), Germany (15%), and Japan (4%). A small number of native Indians (3%) still live in northern Brazil in the Amazon region (April 1990).

The Brazilian education system is divided into three levels: a primary level consisting of the first eight grades (ages 7 to 15), a secondary level of three grades, and the tertiary level (16 and above) for postsecondary education. Eighty-six percent of the primary students, 42 percent of the secondary students, and 40 percent of the higher education students attend public schools. The quality of primary and secondary education typically differs considerably between public and private schools; the former is generally inferior.

Brazilian public education is facing a serious crisis because of the high dropout rate and academic failure. Nationally, of 1,000 pupils who enter the first grade, 38 percent reach the fourth grade, 12 percent finish the ninth grade, 5 percent finish high school, and less than 2 percent go to college. The dropout rates are even higher in the northern and poorer Brazilian states, where only 23 percent of the students finish the fourth grade and 10 percent reach the ninth grade (Iplan/Ipea, UNICEF, SUDENE 1986).

The most difficult grades to pass are the first to the second elementary grade and the fifth to the sixth elementary grade (junior-high school). Dropout and grade repetition between the first and second elementary grade can reach as high as 56 percent at the national level, and almost 75 percent in the northern Brazilian states.

Wechsler and Oakland (1990) investigated the causes of school dropout. Their results have indicated the existence of complex problems, stemming from the family, school, and teacher. Families low on the socioeconomic scale do not value education. Their children are considered more important when working to contribute to the family income than when attending school. Brazilian public schools, particularly in the northern regions, do not offer adequate physical conditions for learning. For example, they often lack a sufficient number of desks, ventilation, potable water, and necessary teaching materials. The regular four-hour daily class schedule is sometimes shortened to three hours, owing to the high number of school-age children in some areas. The high student-teacher ratio, plus the irrelevance of the school curriculum for these children's lives, increases the difficulty of sustaining motivation. Teachers are poorly trained; poor teaching methods are common problems among almost all teachers in Brazil. Pencil-and-paper exercises are the preferred teaching strategy. Teaching designed to develop creativity, curiosity, and internal motivation for learning is a rare phenomenon.

A country can be fully developed only if there is a great investment in its human potential. The educational crisis in Brazil calls for urgent and creative solutions. The goal of our research is to understand the problems in education and offer solutions.

We have to look for the best strategies to motivate our students to stay in school and to succeed in their studies in order to become productive citizens. Interest in learning style as a tool for solving the pressing educational problems in Brazil directed attention to the various theoretical models purporting to explain this important dimension of the learning process. The model developed by Dunn and Dunn (1978) was chosen because it provides a broad and systematized framework within which to study learning style.

The results of a very large number of studies conducted by Dunn and Dunn (1978) indicated that learning style is of critical importance. When students are taught in ways that complement their learning styles, they achieve higher levels and demonstrate more positive attitudes and behaviors. In addition to these positive effects, negative effects have been noted, particularly with intellectually gifted learners, when learning style is ignored (Dunn, Dunn, & Price, 1985; Gadwa & Griggs 1985; Griggs and Dunn 1988).

Based on this model, Dunn, Dunn, & Price (1985) built the Learning Style Inventory (LSI) to assess learning factors. Numerous investigators reported high psychometric standards of LSI reliability and validity for the North American population (Dunn & Klavas 1988). Dunn, Dunn, and Price (1985) cite twenty-two learning style factors or elements. The Dunn and Dunn learning style model (Dunn & Dunn 1978) and the Learning Style Inventory (Dunn, Dunn, & Price 1985) are described in detail in Chapters 1 and 2.

Many able learners become dropouts in adolescence when they are required to learn in programs antithetical to their learning styles (Gadwa & Griggs 1985; Griggs & Dunn 1988). Even intellectually gifted learners remain unidentified because teachers misinterpret and misunderstand their individual learning styles, particularly when it is in sharp contrast to conventional perceptions of requisite school behavior (Dunn, Dunn, & Price 1985).

Apparently the dropout problem is very great not only in Brazil but also in more developed countries such as the United States. The major difference between the two countries is the grade level at which dropout occurs. In the United States, the education laws are strongly enforced for primary education; accordingly, the dropout problem appears at the high school level among adolescents. In Brazil, the education laws are not adequately enforced, so the dropout appears at the first-grade level among very young students.

The causes of school dropout in the United States and in Brazil are probably very similar (Griggs & Dunn 1988). Research dealing with learning styles of dropouts in the United States can indicate some possible ways of working with dropouts in Brazil. Griggs and Dunn (1988) reported the following learning style pattern for dropout students in the United States: high mobility, learn in several ways (self, pairs, peers, and teachers), evening preferences, informal design, high motivation, auditory, tactual and kinesthetic preferences, low illumination, and high motivation. In another study with dropouts in the United States, Gadwa and Griggs (1985) found additional elements that differentiate between students who drop out of school and those who do not. The dropouts preferred to learn in groups, were teacher motivated, preferred to learn with authority figures present, did not require intake while learning, and needed a low degree of structure.

The results of these studies are relevant to at-risk populations in Brazil. Teachers' lack of knowledge on how to develop talent is leading the younger generation to a very frustrating future. Educators can help to solve this problem by directing their efforts to acquiring an understanding of student learning styles, and to applying this knowledge to their daily classroom activities. Research using the Learning Style Inventory (Dunn, Dunn & Price 1985) indicated its utility not only for identifying learning style preferences but also for using this information to more effectively plan individualized instruction.

Cultural characteristics have a major impact on the ways people handle or process information. Accordingly, one of our main concerns in the present study was to investigate the distinctive learning styles of Brazilian adolescents.

LEARNING STYLES OF CREATIVE ADOLESCENTS

The major goal of education in Brazil is to help students become fully developed persons, not only intellectually, but also emotionally and socially. In this sense, creativity plays a major role since it enables individuals to expand their cognitive abilities, to grow in the direction of emotional health and to establish adequate interpersonal relationships. Looking at learners in Brazil will help to establish directions.

Unfortunately, creative students do not have many chances to actualize their potential in regular classrooms. Traditionally, in Brazil as well as other countries, education has been more aimed at conformity than at originality. Therefore, the product of our education has tended to be more a repressed individual than a fully developed person.

In order to enable creative thinking and behaviors to flourish in the Brazilian classroom, it is necessary, in the first place, to understand the multiple ways that creativity can be manifested. Students can present different types of creative characteristics and our educators need to recognize them and to know how to make better use of them when planning their teaching strategies.

Creativity has been defined in many ways, thus indicating the existence of a multifaceted phenomenon. Indeed, we can refer to a creativity complex, since this concept involves not only personal factors (cognitive, metacognitive, motivational, attitudinal and affective) but also social and environmental factors (Runco, 1990). Many studies related to the creativity concept have investigated these factors in an isolated way. Data is needed in order to help both teachers and students make progress in Brazil. However, research dealing with the interaction among these factors or the combinations of them is rare.

A major contribution to the area of creativity was the work of Torrance (1974) who demonstrated the possibility of assessing both cognitive and personal components related to creativity through valid and reliable procedures using his test, the Torrance Test of Creative Thinking, or TTCT (Torrance, 1974). The test included Thinking Creatively with Pictures and Thinking Creatively with Words.

The studies conducted by Torrance and Ball (1978) and Torrance and Wu (1981) indicated there were various creative characteristics, presented in the drawings, which were valid predictors of adult creative achievements. Work with American samples (Wechsler, 1981) demonstrated the possibility of predicting adult creative achievements not only through drawings but also through words, by assessing creative characteristics expressed in the subjects responses to the verbal TTCT.

There seem to be universal elements or characteristics which can identify creative individuals independently of their culture which is important for our work in Brazil. Our research with Brazilian samples (Wechsler, 1985) pointed to the high relationships among creative characteristics in the TTCT and the subjects' quality and quantity of creative achievements in their real lives.

The huge amount of research using the TTCT, as indicated in the last cumulative bibliography on these instruments (Torrance & Goff, 1990), suggests that these tests are the preferred measure of creativity in the United States. This same tendency is also observed in Brazil by Wechsler (1990), when reviewing the last two decades of studies in creativity and education in this country.

ASSESSING CREATIVITY

Although many studies on creativity carried on in different parts of the world have focused on cognitive measures of creativity (fluency, flexibility, originality, elaboration), our studies in Brazil verified the importance of personality components of creativity (Wechsler 1990, 1991) as a more complex approach for understanding the creative person, his or her creative behavior, and the creative production.

The creative characteristics presented in drawings, which can be assessed by the TTCT (Torrance, 1974) are:

Fluency: quantity of ideas

Flexibility: modifications in the types of ideas

Originality: unusual or new ideas

Elaboration: enrichment of ideas by adding details

Expression of emotions: indications of feelings

Fantasy: indications of imaginary entities

Unusual perspective: drawings from uncommon angles or nonconforming responses

Movement: indications of actions in the pictures

Internal perspective: figures drawn as seen from their insides

Extension of boundaries: drawing beyond the stimulus limit

Context: environments or surroundings to the idea drawn

Expressiveness of titles: going beyond the sample description of the drawing

Combinations: joining two or more stimuli to form a unique drawing

Despite the cultural similarity indicated by the results reported (Torrance & Ball 1978; Torrance & Wu 1981), there seem to be cultural differences in ways of expressing creativity. We observed this by comparing Brazilian and U.S. children's drawings (Wechsler & Richmond 1982). The results obtained from this study called attention to the diversity of ways in expressing creativity through drawings. While Brazilian children demonstrated their creativity more through the expression of emotions, unusual perspective, and extending the boundaries of their drawings, U.S. children had a higher frequency of humor and richness of imagery in their figures. These findings indicate the existence of creative styles in each culture, which have to be taken into consideration when comparing each country in creative productivity. The styles should be recognized by educators and be used in their teaching plans. Teaching strategies that respect the diversity of creative style within each culture provide more opportunities for developing hidden talents in the classrooms.

In the current study we focused on the learning style characteristics of creative adolescents in Brazil. Intelligence was not investigated. Our previous research with Brazilian samples (Wechsler & Richmond 1984) confirmed the Torrance findings (Torrance 1963) with North American samples regarding the very small correlation between creativity and intelligence. The same conclusion was drawn from MacKinnon (1978) in his research with creative individuals, indicating that the level of intelligence required for creativity is, sometimes, surprisingly low. Although some investigators believe that a certain required minimum level of intelligence, which varies from field to field, is required for creative performance, almost all agree that being more intelligent does not guarantee a corresponding increase in creativity.

In addition to drawings, another way to identify creative students during their childhood is to examine their leisure time or out-of-school activities. In her model of giftedness, Milgram (1989, 1990a, 1991a) affirmed that fully developed creative talents, which are a major component of giftedness, are usually observed during adulthood. However, a pre-assessment of creative abilities can be made if we investigate the ways that children and adolescents use their leisure time. This gives us a measure of their main interests and the amount of energy devoted to them.

An inventory to evaluate student creative performance in leisure activities was developed by Milgram (1987, 1990b). This inventory has been used with samples ranging from pre-school to young adults. The creative performance items in the inventory were designed to tap nonacademic talent accomplishment in science, music, fine arts, social leadership, writing, community services, drama, sports, and dance. The leisure activities items evaluate the quantity and quality of out-of-school activities that children and adolescents participate in for their own enjoyment. A detailed explanation of this inventory was presented in Chapter 2.

Just as culture has an impact on divergent thinking, cultural variables can impact on the way students use their leisure time. If in a specific country there are social rewards for some types of activities, such as sports, dance, or music, then one can expect that more creative behaviors will appear in these areas. Therefore, creative activities as related to giftedness tend to vary from country to country.

The purpose of this study was to identify the learning style of Brazilian adolescents in general, and of those with high creative abilities in particular. This effort was based on the conviction that assessment of these variables can be a key component in reducing the serious dropout problem in Brazil.

RESEARCH METHODOLOGY

Subjects

Our sample consisted of 605 subjects attending the regular public and private schools of the city of Brasilia, the capital of Brazil. All socioeconomic levels were represented in this sample. The description of the sample was presented in Chapter 2, Table 2.1.

Instruments

Three instruments were administered to all subjects. Details about the Learning Style Inventory (Dunn, Dunn & Price 1984) and the Tel Aviv Activities Inventory (Milgram 1987) were presented in Chapter 2. The measure used to assess creativity was the Torrance Test of Creative Thinking, Figural A (Torrance 1974). This test is composed of three tasks in which shapes, scribbles, and parallel lines are the stimuli. Subjects are asked to complete the stimuli with different or unusual ideas. The creative characteristics assessed by this test were explained before.

The scoring for originality for the figural creativity test was based on Brazilian norms according to the weight recommended by the test author (Torrance 1974).

Procedure

The two instruments used for the first time in Brazil (the LSI and the Tel Aviv Activities Inventory), were translated into Portuguese and translated back by an American. Some items in the Tel Aviv Activities Inventory had to be adapted to the Brazilian culture, such as receiving silver or gold medals, which is not common in regular Brazilian school competitions.

The three instruments were group-administered in two separate sessions. In the first session, the Learning Style Inventory and the Torrance Test of Creative Thinking were given, and in the second session the Tel Aviv Activities Inventory was administered.

RESEARCH RESULTS

The construct validity of the Portuguese LSI to the Brazilian culture was investigated through factor analysis. A score was created for each subject on each LSI factor derived from this analysis. The relationship among the learning style factors with the figural creativity indicators and the leisure activities was investigated through Pearson correlations.

The factor analysis of the Learning Style Inventory in Portuguese, using Varimax as a rotation method, indicated fourteen main factors that explained 0.68 of the variance. The criterion for the factor selection was the eigenvalue > 1. The item load for each factor was greater than ± .30.

The items composing each factor are described in Table 13.1. Each factor was named after the items that composed it. The fourteen LSI factors derived from this analysis were:

1. Absence of motivation;
2. Group preferences;
3. Family/teacher motivated;

Table 13.1
Factor Analysis of Learning Style Inventory in Portuguese

FACTOR 1		ABSENCE OF MOTIVATION
Item	T	DESCRIPTION
14	.64	I have to be reminded often to do something
49	.63	I have to be reminded to do something
82	.59	I keep forgetting to do things I have been told to do
71	.58	I often forget to do or finish my homework
28	.54	I hardly ever finish all my work
13	.51	I often have troubles finishing things I ought to do
38	.50	It's hard for me to do my school work
59	.42	I cannot get interested in my school work
50	.39	It's hard for me to do things done in the late morning
30	.32	I really don't care much for school
42	-.27	I remember to do what I am told
47	-.30	I usually finish my homework

Eingvalue: 7.03   Variance: .15

FACTOR 2		GROUP PREFERENCES
Item	T	DESCRIPTION
84	.77	When I really have a lot of studing to do like to work with two friends
102	.75	Work with two friends
67	.69	I like working with a group of friends
94	.67	I enjoy being with friends when I study
8	.58	I like to study with one or two friends
17	-.58	I like to work alone
56	-.61	Work alone

Eingvalue: 6.16   Variance: .13

FACTOR 3		FAMILY/TEACHER MOTIVATED
Item	T	DESCRIPTION
53	.55	My parents are interested on how I do in school
37	.52	When I do well in schools,grown-ups in my family are Proud of me
2	.48	I like to make my parents happy by getting good grades
78	.47	My family wants me to get good grades
45	.44	I am happy when I get good grades
97	.44	I think my teacher wants me to get good grades
41	.43	I think my teacher feels good when I get good grades
9	.41	I like to do well in schools
15	.38	I like making my teacher proud of me
63	-.46	No one really cares if I do well in school

Eingvalue: 3.20   Variance: .06

FACTOR 4		TACTILE/FEELING EXPERIENCES
Item	T	DESCRIPTION
99	.57	I really like to build things
80	.57	I like to learn most by building, baking or doing things
35	.52	I really like to do experiences
85	.49	I like to learn through real exPeriences
46	.49	I like to learn by building, baking,doing things
64	.46	I like to shape things with my hands
60	.38	I like to draw, color or trace things
55	.36	I enjoy learning by going places

Eingvalue: 3.07   Variance: .06

204

FACTOR 5   AFTERNOON PREFERENCES
Item T   DESCRIPTION
100 .69   I can study best in the afternoon
96   .66   I remember things best when I study them in the evening
62   .54   I remember best in the afternoon
29   .51   I usually start my homework in the afternoon
103 .50   I do my homework in the afternoon
69 -.39   I remember best in the morning
26 -.36   I remember best early in the morning

Eingvalue: 2.74   Variance: .05

FACTOR 6   LOW MOBILITY
Item T   DESCRIPTION
58   .83   I can sit in one place for a long time
70   .82   I can sit in one place for a long time
95 -.58   It's hard for me to sit for a long time
25 -.65   It's hard to sit for a long time

Eingvalue: 2.02   Variance: .04   Cumulative variance: .49

FACTOR 7   REQUIRES INTAKE
Item T   DESCRIPTION
93   .70   I often eat something when I study
66   .69   I like to drink, eat, chew while studying
24   .57   I often nibble at something as I study
22   .46   I think better when I eat while studying
18 -.56   I do not eat, drink, or chew while studying

Eingvalue: 1.78   Variance: .03

FACTOR 8   LATE MORNING
Item T   DESCRIPTION
75   .67   I think best in late morning
79   .65   Late morning is the best times for me to study
98   .54   I study best around 10:00 in the morning
69   .40   I think best early in the morning
26   .36   I remember things best when I study them early in the morning
12   .36   I am able to study best in the morning

Eingvalue: 1.65   Variance: .03

Table 13.1 (continued)

FACTOR 9	ADULTS' PRESENCE
	DESCRIPTION

Item T

87 .70 I like to have an adult nearby when I doing school work
77 .74 I like adults nearby while I study
98 .47 I like to do things with adults
57 .37 Sometimes I like to learn alone, sometimes with friends or with adults

Eingvalue: 1.55   Variance: .03

FACTOR 10	QUIET ENVIRONMENT
	DESCRIPTION

Item T

32 .61   Sounds keeps me from concentrating
101 .61 Sounds bothers me when studying
1 .45   I study best when it is quiet
44 -.39 I can block out sound when I work
88 -.57 I can ignore most sound when I work

Eingvalue: 1.37   Variance: .02

FACTOR 11	COOL TEMPERATURE
	DESCRIPTION

Item T

36 .78   I feel more comfortable in cool weather
39 .52   I concentrate best when I feel cool
68 -.46 When it is warm I like to go out
10 -.79 I feel more comfortable in warm weather

Eingvalue: 1.31   Variance: .02

FACTOR 12	INFORMAL DESIGN
	DESCRIPTION

Item T

40 .67   I like to relax on rugs, carpets, a couch, a soft chair or a bed when I study
7 .64   I like to sit on a soft chair or couch
6 -.35   I study best at a table
19 -.48 I like to sit in a straight chair

Eingvalue: 1.10   variance: .02

FACTOR 13	NEEDS STRUCTURE
	DESCRIPTION

Item T

4 .72   I like to be told exactly what to do
52 .68   I like to be told what to do

Eingvalue: 1.03   Variance .02

Factor 14	BRIGHT LIGHT
	DESCRIPTION

Item T

65 .60   When I study I put on many lights
3 .47   I like studying with lots of light
16 -.61 I study best when the lights are dim
34 -.34 I study under a shaded lamp

Eingvalue: 1.02   Variance: .02

Cumulative Variance: .68

4. Tactile/feeling preferences;

5. Afternoon preferences;

6. Low mobility;

7. Requires intake;

8. Late morning;

9. Adult's presence;

10. Quiet environment;

11. Cool temperature;

12. Needs structure;

13. Informal room design; and

14. Bright light.

The first six factors accounted for .49 of the variance with eigenvalues > 2.

We examined the relationships among the fourteen learning style factors and the figural creativity indicators. There are few learning styles that are significantly related to figural creativity indicators. Positive associations were observed for tactile and feeling preferences with fluency and elaboration, and for requires intake with the expression of emotions in drawings. Negative associations were observed for quiet environment with the creativity variables of fluency and flexibility. Absence of motivation as well as needs structure were both negatively related to the creativity indicator use of contexts in drawings.

We next examined the correlations among the learning style factors and the creative leisure activities. The total score for creative leisure activities was significantly associated with the following learning styles: tactile/feeling preferences, adult/teacher motivated, late morning preferences, and adult presence. Negative association was verified between the total of the creative leisure activities and absence of motivation.

Tactile/feeling preferences presented the greatest number of significant positive relationships with creative activity. It was related to the following creative leisure activities: sciences, social activities, music, arts, literature, and drama. Adult/teacher motivated was significantly associated with social activities, music, and drama. On the other hand, adult presence was positively related to social activities and drama.

Significant negative associations were observed for absence of motivation with the following creative leisure activities: science, social activities, and arts. Negative association was also verified between late morning preferences and leisure activities in the area of science.

CONCLUSIONS

Interesting conclusions can be drawn about the learning styles, creative thinking, and creative leisure activities of Brazilian adolescents. Six LSI factors explained the largest part of the variance. It is very clear that Brazilian adolescents are not highly motivated to go to school. They prefer to learn in groups and to be valued by important adults such as their parents or their teachers. There is also a need for more tactile-kinesthetic experiences—that is, those emphasizing concrete involvement and feelings instead of traditional school lectures, which provide no affective interaction. Although all high school classes in Brazil are offered in the mornings, these adolescents indicated that they would rather study in the afternoon. They also indicated they can sit for a long time, so there is no need to provide mobility while learning.

If we consider the absence of motivation as a result of several components, we could probably change the direction of the first factor by changing other variables. The need for meaningful and affective relationships is very clear in this study, so perhaps this is the first situation to work on. Brazilian teachers should be advised to develop affective bonds in their classrooms before teaching any cognitive component. The effects of teacher attitude on student academic achievement has been well researched; this is an important variable for the Brazilian classroom.

Some of the Brazilian adolescents' learning preferences are similar to these observed in studies of North American dropouts (Griggs & Dunn 1988; Gadwa & Griggs 1985). These are informal room design, tactual and kinesthetic preferences, learning in groups, and being teacher motivated. Although the Brazilian students in the sample are not dropouts, the existence of the same learning patterns may imply that they are at risk.

Developing emotional bonds when teaching adolescents may not be a high priority for other countries. However, in Brazil, owing to the influence of Latin colonization, the need to be in groups, to feel loved and appreciated by a teacher, and to have emotional experiences in the classroom may be very important. Unfortunately, Brazilian teachers are not aware of this dimension. Their emphasis on developing students' cognitive abilities has resulted in a decrease in motivation rather than an increase. The question of whether we can solve Brazil's dropout problem by developing a more positive affective climate in the classroom is worthy of investigation.

Observing the relationships among learning style and leisure creative activities, we can verify the importance of tactile and feeling experiences for Brazilians' creative achievements, as well as the factors adult presence and adult motivation. As expected, the lack of motivation was negatively related to seven out of the eight creative leisure activities.

Our results indicate that student motivation is more external, dependent on significant adults such as the parents and their teachers. Therefore, in order to increase internal motivation for learning, we should start on external reinforcement for these students by explaining to their parents and teachers the importance of encouraging and rewarding effort in school.

Our results demonstrate that the key to increasing creative production among Brazilian adolescents, and to solve our dropout problem, is to increase motivation in the classroom. We can conclude that the more these adolescents need structure from significant adults, the less they will be able to be creative achievers. Therefore, our path seems to lead toward working with external motivation (peers, family, teacher), changing it, little by little, to internal motivation.

This research investigated student learning styles and creative leisure activities as a way to end school dropout. Our results indicate that the lack of motivation to learn is probably caused by an absence of affective bonds and experiences in the traditional classroom.

Teachers of Latin American students should consider the importance of emotional interactions for people of these cultures and develop a positive affective climate in the classroom.

Research on learning styles should be conducted in different countries in order to know which is the best means to increase educational achievement in different parts of the world, and which are the highest priorities for people in different cultures. The importance of these factors may vary from one culture to the other, depending on their respective values or social rewards for specific behaviors and achievements.

In our research, total figural creativity was the best predictor of total creative leisure activities ($r = .16$, $p < .001$). This finding indicates that it is possible to predict creative achievements through scores on figural creativity tests such as the TTCT. The only area that could not be predicted by any of the creativity indicators was the social. The relationship between divergent thinking and creative leadership has to be more thoroughly investigated in order to be accurately assessed.

The fully developed creative person uses an internal evaluation procedure (Wechsler 1991), as many creative products and behaviors cannot be understood by current society. The concept of learning styles can help us start making learning effective. Nevertheless, we have to bear in mind that the ultimate goal of education is to help students grow up as complete persons in the sense of cognitive, emotional, and social development. Thus, if we want to help Brazilian students actualize their full creative potential, we have to find as many ways as possible to help them acquire an internal frame of reference.

Studies on learning styles are crucial for reaching creative students through their preferred way of thinking and reacting. Just as creative achievements are closely related to high motivation, creative students have to be understood within a cultural perspective, and be helped to develop their full potential.

NOTE

This research was funded by the Brazilian National Agency for Scientific and Technological Advancement (CNPq). The author acknowledges the contribution of Dr. Gary Price, who provided the test material, and the statistical help of Dr. Luiz and Dr. Francisco Stefano Wechsler. A valuable contribution was also made by research assistants Patricia Lima Torres, Ana da Costa Polnia, Smia Jabor Pinheiro, Rita Laura Trestini, Ana Claudia Nunes Fialho, and Monica Lucia Fonseca.

Chapter 14

The Learning Styles of Adolescents in Egypt

Atef Shaftik Soliman

Egypt, one of the most famous civilizations developed before Christ, historically was an active proponent of education. Indeed, in Acts 7:22, the Bible tells us that Moses was taught all the wisdom of the Egyptians and became a great man, in both words and deeds. Alexandria was one of the foremost centers of knowledge in early history; old Alexandria University and the Alexandria Library are famous for the educational leadership they exerted in times past.

In the present, however, Egypt is experiencing many social, economic, and cultural problems. In the past seventy years, Egypt has been involved in four different wars and has suffered various forms of colonization. Today it is experiencing inflation, heavy foreign debts incurred from the wars, poverty, a high birth rate, and, as a result, overpopulation. The Egyptian government cannot provide adequate health and educational services for most of its citizens. Indeed, the Egyptian ministry calculated that, in January 1982, 53 percent of the population was illiterate; the main sufferers are Egypt's women and rural populace (McDermott 1988).

Only children of relatively wealthy families are able to attend school in Egypt; those who do are fortunate and often recognize and appreciate their special status. For some, education is the only way to maintain a comfortable and politically secure life. Relationships between students and their teachers in Egypt are construed as being very different from those experienced by their counterparts in the Western world. Student involvement is in depth, personal, all-consuming, and continually interactive, as exemplified by the following poem written by an unknown Egyptian teacher. Translated, it reads:

> I am my student's Bible.
> He reads *me* most of all.

Today he reads me in my class,
    Tomorrow in the hall.
He may be prodigy or slow,
    Or only "average" be,
He may not read the book of books,
    But he is reading me.

Egyptian schools vary in their architecture, financial support, and clientele, but their ambiance is identical. Students attend school to learn from master instructors; instructors focus solely on imparting as much quality knowledge as possible to their pupils. Learning is serious; the opportunity to learn is treasured. It is rare for teachers to experience student disobedience; poor conduct would be tantamount to broadcasting the student's wish to withdraw from education.

Thus, when we first learned of the research plan to identify the learning styles of gifted and talented adolescents in many nations throughout the world, my colleague Greg Vanderheiden and I became curious about whether Egyptian students' styles would differ from each other's or from those of young people in other parts of the world. Our personal experiences suggested that human beings are unique, but considering the sobriety with which our young people attend school and the degree to which they value the opportunity, our initial thoughts were that only students with a single learning style would—could—survive in our academically oriented, demanding educational system. In Egypt, we do *not* educate everyone.

We had learned about the Dunn and Dunn Learning Style model at a one-week conference in Buffalo, New York, during the summer of 1990. We purchased a computer program to permit us to process individual Learning Style Inventories in our country without necessitating the back-and-forth problems inherent in the international mail system. We decided to include a relatively small group of high school students so that numbers would not preclude completion of this project. It is neither easy to solicit and gain the support of adolescents for extracurricular projects when they have hours of daily assignments to complete nor easy to obtain the secretarial or financial support for a large-scale research investigation.

RESEARCH METHODOLOGY

Participants

Our sample consisted of thirty-six boys and girls in grades 10, 11, and 12 selected from the larger group of registrants enrolled in scout camp in Alexandria during the early fall of 1990. That camp's attendees included participants from the main high schools in Alexandria. Many younger students in grades 6 to 9 also attended, but those were not included in the study. The high schools they attended were noted and the young people were subsequently assigned to one of three groups, each representing the population of one of the three schools. A random sampling of the students from each of those three high schools in Alexandria then was conducted. The selected students thus came from and represented the three kinds of high schools existing in Alexandria: public schools with a typically Egyptian curriculum; private schools with the same typically Egyptian curriculum; and private schools with a more-or-less American curriculum. For initial analysis, the students were grouped in accordance with the type of high school they attended, but later, upon close scrutiny, we found that the learning styles of the students who attended the three different types of educational institutions did not differ significantly from each other. Accordingly, the data of the three types of schools were combined in all subsequent analyses.

That student learning styles ultimately were essentially similar was not surprising. Regardless of the type of curriculum emphasized, the schools basically functioned in the same way—traditionally, conservatively, and teacher directed. The curricula varied only in their degree of intensity; all students studied one or more foreign languages, science, mathematics, philosophy, and psychology. What differentiated the Egyptian from the Americanized curriculum was the number of subjects in each area that had to be completed and the occasional elective that permitted some student choice. The private school with the Egyptian curriculum stressed the acquisition of foreign languages such as English and French in addition to the regular required courses mandated in the public schools.

The Schutz School, the private "American" school included, followed instructional practices similar to some degree to those of many affluent private schools in the United States; it permitted some options and elective courses including physical education, an unusual course for traditional Egyptian high schools. Choice among courses is not normally permitted in other high schools in Alexandria; a standard curriculum is mandated, no options are available, and crowded classrooms are the rule in comparison with high schools in the United States. However, the Schutz classrooms were less crowded than those of other high schools in Alexandria.

The participants who constituted the population for this study were essentially similar culturally and socioeconomically. The major different among the three groups was their proficiency with foreign language. In the Schutz School, English was used on a daily basis for instruction and communication, thus heightening student awareness and ability with this language. The two other schools—and all other high schools in Alexandria—used English as the language of instruction and Arabic, the native language, as the primary means of communication. Thus, the many similarities of this population—culturally, socioeconomically, and educationally—may have contributed to the finding that the learning styles of the three groups of students representing each of the three different participating high schools did not vary much. These findings do not support the view of both Restak (1979) and Thies (1979) that learning style is at least three-fifths biological.

Fewer schools are available in Egypt for similarly sized populations than in the United States, and all families who can afford to do so encourage their children to study hard and perform well. Competition is high; students who attend classes exert their best efforts and are supervised, to a great extent, by their family. It becomes a family embarrassment when a youngster does not perform well. However, one major difference between these students and young adults in Western countries is that parents who work in oil-rich Third World nations with a high percentage of only informally educated and uneducated citizens tend to send their offspring to private schools to obtain what they perceive as a "better education." Interestingly, as an observer of and participant in the culture, I have noted that those parents do not appear to rear their children differently from the way native Egyptians do, nor do they personally deal with their children differently.

In conventional Egyptian schools all students complete the identical curriculum; choice is not available. The study of religion and all basic core disciplines are required by all. In conventional Egyptian homes, all children behave with deference and are subservient to their parents, the older members of their family, and all adults of equal or higher socioeconomic status.

Materials

Learning Style Inventory. The Learning Style Inventory (Dunn, Dunn, & Price 1989) assesses twenty-two elements of an individual's learning style preferences. Each subject rates 104 items on a five-point scale from high disagreement to high agreement. The twenty-two scores yielded by this instrument and a brief description of each are summarized in Chapter 1.

The students were provided with a brief introduction to the concept of learning style and then were administered the Learning Style Inventory (Dunn, Dunn, & Price 1989). Subjects recorded their responses on answer sheets designed for optical reading. The raw scores were processed on the computer disk produced by Price Systems in Lawrence, Kansas, the United States.

Curry (1987) compared the Learning Style Inventory with other measures of learning style and reported very high psychometric standards for this instrument. The test reliability of the Arabic translation of the Learning Style Inventory was estimated by means of analysis of variance (Hoyt 1941). The reliability coefficient range of nineteen elements was .65–.86; the range of three other elements was .56–.58. On the basis of these findings, we concluded that the reliability of the translation was acceptable.

Neither the camp nor the schools these students attended either tested for or maintained records of intellectual giftedness (IQ) or exceptional talents. All students were required to earn good grades and were asked to leave if they did not live up to the school's standards or their teachers' expectations. The schools had never tested for intellectual giftedness (IQ) and the administration was not willing to begin. It was assumed that those adolescents who attended school were motivated to succeed and were from families that required their maintenance of high achievement. Some of the students were less than enthusiastic about taking the Learning Style Inventory, and did not return it; others did so out of a sense of compliance. Only a minority of students seemed inquisitive about their own learning style. That individuals learn differently is a new concept in Alexandria and appeared not to be taken seriously by some of the young people who participated. Despite my previous account, some students were extremely enthusiastic learning about their personal traits and also wanted to know how to "improve" their style. On the other hand, some students were careless and indifferent to the results.

RESEARCH RESULTS

According to both the Learning Style Inventory results and my observations, little difference existed among the learning styles of the three groups of high school students in this sample (see Table 14.1). In fact, equal percentages in the extreme categories of 0–20 and 70–80 were evidenced for the twenty-two criteria. However, almost half the students were very responsible (conforming) and that was particularly true of those who attended the Schutz School (where some options and elective were available), in contrast to the lower responsibility (nonconformity) scores of students in the other schools where no options existed. Of those who did not attend the high school where some options were permitted, three were highly nonconforming and most of the others responded that whether or not they did what was required depended on their interest and motivation in the task.

There are several possible explanations for this finding. Perhaps, when permitted some choice, teenagers become more conforming, for they then have little need to challenge authority; when restricted, nonconformity may develop or flourish. Another interpretation of these data may be that some of the Schutz School students' parents were out of the country and the youngsters were living (boarding) in the school. Does the responsibility for one's self when parents are not readily available cause the emergence of responsibility or conformity?

Another interesting finding of this study was that less than 3 percent of the population preferred learning with peers, whereas more than 47 percent strongly preferred learning alone and the remaining adolescents had no strong inclination in either of those two directions. In the United States some educators believe that students learn best in groups; that may be accurate for some, but it does not seem to be accurate for this population, most of whom did not wish to learn with peers. Twenty percent of the students were highly motivated, ranging in the 60–80 sections of the LSI, but others merely studied because it was required or expected of them. Three of the thirty-six students reported very low motivation, and I intend to follow up on those to learn whether they remain in school.

In addition, few students were auditory; most were not and 25 percent were extremely low-auditory preferents. Although some students were low visual, low tactual, or low kinesthetic, in contrast with the 8 percent highly auditory students,

Table 14.1
Learning Style of Egyptian Adolescents: Means, Standard Deviations, Percent of Scores Indicating High and Low Preferences

Learning Style Element	Mean Scores	Standard Deviation	Percentage of Standard Scores Equal to or Less Than 40	Percentage of Standard Scores Equal to or Greater Than 60
Noise	44.58	9.25	38.89	5.56
Light	53.67	11.51	11.11	38.89
Temperature	43.50	9.84	27.78	0.00
Design	56.56	10.73	8.33	33.33
Motivation	52.31	9.52	8.33	19.44
Persistence	48.94	10.48	25.00	19.44
Responsible	55.08	10.93	8.33	44.44
Structure	50.89	12.41	30.56	27.78
Learn Alone	41.50	8.04	47.22	2.78
Authority-Figure Present	44.14	9.65	38.89	13.89
Several Ways	41.33	10.83	41.67	0.00
Auditory	48.08	8.29	25.00	8.33
Visual	52.42	15.13	8.33	38.39
Tactual	48.44	10.10	22.22	5.56
Kinesthetic	54.94	10.78	8.33	38.89
Intake	44.78	9.61	33.33	5.56
Morning	58.97	10.35	11.11	52.70
Late Morning	49.56	8.78	16.67	11.11
Afternoon	49.75	9.76	13.89	11.11
Mobility	47.53	14.40	27.78	13.89
Parent Motivated	48.00	2.68	19.44	8.33
Teacher Motivated	50.36	10.18	13.89	16.67

39 percent were highly visual, and 39 percent were highly kinesthetic in schools in which all of direct instruction was lecture or discussion. There is, however, an emphasis on extensive required reading. To the best of my knowledge, virtually no instruction occurs through kinesthetic learning. Perhaps, despite the high grades these students earn, they might achieve better if instruction responded to their combined visual and kinesthetic preferences. We have read that in the United States, research supports the premise that students be taught through their perceptual strengths. With the revelation that most of these students preferred learning in ways other than lecture and taking notes, apparently the schools in Egypt should experiment with instructional alternatives.

In this nation, in which our schools tend to be authoritarian, only 14 percent of the respondents preferred an authoritative teacher in contrast with the 39 percent who preferred a collegial teacher. With the exception of the consistent need among these students for bright light and a formal design and their high responsibility or conformity trait, this population of adolescents divided itself into essentially four groups:

1. Those who required quiet (6 percent) versus those who preferred sound (39 percent) and those for whom noise level was unimportant while learning (the majority);

2. Those who were highly persistent (19 percent) versus those who were not (25 percent) and the majority for whom persistence levels varied dependent upon interest and motivation;

3. Those who wanted intake while learning (6 percent) versus those who completed their assignments before eating, snacking, or using beverages (33 percent) and the majority; and

4. Those who preferred learning in the morning (53 percent) versus those who were evening preferents (11 percent) and approximately 35 percent of those for whom time of day was relatively unimportant.

Interestingly, none of the youngsters in this study preferred instructional variety or instructional change. Although 42 percent strongly preferred routines and patterns, many reported that whether or not they wanted to learn in several, rather than in a single, method depended on exactly what the change would be.

After examining individual rather than group clustering, we found that 11 percent of our students were strongly global; another 5 percent were somewhat global. Fully one-third of our students were highly analytic. The majority of these students had many analytic traits: needing bright light, quiet, a formal design, no intake, and being persistent while learning (Dunn, Cavanaugh, Eberle, & Zenhausern 1982). These data paralleled previously reported findings of high-IQ students in the United States (Dunn & Price 1980). Apparently, a similar pattern exists in Alexandria.

CONCLUSIONS

This investigation was undertaken as an initial effort to determine whether students in the high schools in Alexandria varied in learning style. It was assumed that, if clear and definitive learning style characteristics were evidenced, alternative—and perhaps more cost-efficient—ways of providing instruction might be possible for more students than merely for those from affluent families.

Differences in learning style were evidenced, although in some ways many of our students appear to conform to traditional patterns of education. In other ways, they certainly do *not*. Because our population clearly was not auditory preferenced, it is not necessary for these high schoolers to be in daily contact with teachers who lecture. The strongly visual students might profit from printed matter and, because so many were learn-alone preferents who accepted or required imposed structure, they could learn in other than school locations with highly structured instructional materials such as Programmed Learning Sequences (Dunn & Dunn 1978, 1992, 1993).

Differences also were evidenced between global and analytic students. Both groups might profit from use of Programmed Learning Sequences, which are designed with a global introduction—to attract the interest of holistic processors—and which teach the material in small sequential steps. If it were possible to mass-produce such paper materials, it might be feasible to distribute them among motivated young people who want to become educated, but who currently cannot afford to attend our already overcrowded schools.

Too, motivated young people in rural populations could utilize such materials to learn either independently or with others without having to incur the costs of transportation to and living expenses in urban centers. For those who are capable of functioning independently and who prefer decision-making options rather than the structure of Programmed Learning Sequences, Contract Activity Packages (Dunn & Dunn 1978, 1992, 1993) also might provide effective alternative means of obtaining an education.

One obvious limitation is that we did not identify the learning styles of those young people who currently do *not* attend school. It is possible that the styles of such adolescents differ substantially from those who do. However, this investigation was a preliminary attempt to begin to use learning style instrumentation to determine whether the knowledge gained from such an inquiry might yield insights into a small population of Egyptian students, and whether that information might be valuable for planning possible improvements in our educational system. In the humble perception of this researcher, both objectives were met.

Chapter 15

The Learning Styles of Adolescents in Greece

John Spiridakis

Greece is on the threshold of dramatic change as the unprecedented alliance of thirteen European countries begins to take form. Education in Greece, an enduring institution whose structure and goals have been vigorously debated by social philosophers and politicians from the political left, right, and center, is confronting both new and ongoing challenges. The critical role of Greek education as the molder of a productive society and an enlightened citizenry has been articulated in the past. However, in the symbiotic relationship between education and society, Greek education maintains a great deal of autonomy and seems, not unlike bureaucratized institutions in other nations, to resist or ignore evolving social forces altering the complexion of the society it ostensibly serves.

At this critical juncture in the history of Greece, Greek educators and leaders are grasping for innovative ideas, approaches, and methodologies that will be responsive to individual student characteristics and needs. Policymakers and educators face challenges such as providing high school students with greater access to higher education and a revamped primary and secondary education system that prepares ''Euro-citizens'' able to compete and function creatively and effectively in the technological world of the twenty-first century.

The promise of important educational innovations was manifest in the new national law of September 1985 governing primary and secondary education in Greece. The new law held the promise of revolutionizing a school system that has embraced authoritarian principles in the past, even while extolling principles of democracy and equal educational opportunity. The sweeping scope of the new law provided for wider participation of parents, teachers, students, and community members in various aspects of educational planning and management. It also altered the goals of schooling, underscoring the role of education as a vital socializer of good citizens and of values of decency and responsibility. The new law's key aims for primary and secondary education included, in part, the following as reported by the "Council of Europe Newsletter" (1986)

- Students must be helped to ascribe equal social value to manual and intellectual work.
- Students must be helped to understand the significance of art, science and technology, to respect human values, and to care about and promote our civilization.
- Students must be helped to develop a spirit of friendship and cooperation with all nations with a view to making the world a better, just and peaceful place. (p. 4)

Elementary and secondary school teachers are challenged to seek new ways to implement these ambitious objectives. Educational researchers and teacher trainers in Greece need to consider, and indeed are considering, educational research conducted in the United States and other countries on innovative practices such as learning styles. This writer, for example, was invited to participate in a worldwide conference in Greece to present information on the role of learning styles in the classroom (Spiridakis 1988). During the past ten years, American studies and Greek-American cross-cultural research on topics such as self-concept, special education, mathematics and science achievement, and political socialization have been utilized by Greek educators in the training of Greek elementary and secondary school teachers (Flouris, Coulopoulos & Spiridakis 1981; Psomiades, Orfanos, & Spiridakis 1988).

THE GREEK EDUCATIONAL SYSTEM

It has been said about the Greeks that they

were the first real educators of our western world . . . for they were the first western people to think seriously and profoundly about educating the young, the first to ask what education is, what it is for, and how children and men should be educated. (Castle 1961, p. 10)

In Greece today, education plays a central role as a socializing agent, preparing its young to become productive members of society. Greek parents, regardless of their socioeconomic status, value a good education for their children, including acceptance into the highly selective Greek universities. All students ostensibly have a chance to achieve this goal, since education is free in Greece even at the tertiary level (Kazamias 1990).

With the return of civilian government after seven years of military dictatorship, a new constitution and a series of laws were adopted in 1976–77 that brought fundamental changes to the educational system. Highlights of Oliver's (1982) summary of the changes initiated by the laws include the following:

1. Extension of compulsory education from six to nine years;
2. Provisions of free education at all levels;

3. Establishment of the common languages *demotike*, (as opposed to *Katharevousa*) as the official language through the university;

4. Abolition of lower vocational schools (grades 7–9);

5. Division of the secondary school into two cycles—a three-year compulsory gymnasium (grades 7–9) and three-year noncompulsory selective lyceum (grades 10–12);

6. Abolition of entrance examinations for the gymnasium;

7. Abolition of end-of-year examinations in the three grades of the gymnasium;

8. Revision of primary and secondary curricula, with more emphasis on physical science and mathematics;

9. Utilization of modern Greek translations of ancient Greek texts in the gymnasium;

10. Organization of three types of technical-vocational schools;

11. Revision of the selection system for higher education; and

12. Establishment of Center for Educational Research and Teacher in-service training (KEME) to conduct research, advise the Ministry of National Education and Religion, prepare curricula, provide further training for teachers, and supervise the writing and publication of textbooks. (p. 20)

In spite of the many changes Greece has undergone in its political system— alternating among constitutional monarchies, military dictatorships, and parliamentary democracy—its educational system has remained fairly stable. This stability is attributable to several factors, among them strong centralized control and supervision of the schools, lack of funds to support experimentation and change, the conservative influence of the church, and the more than 100 years' imposition of an "official" or pure form of the Greek language, *Katharevousa* as the language of instruction (Massialas, Flouris, & Cassotakis 1988; Kazamias 1988).

The Greek educational system comprises five levels. First is the pre-primary level (ages 3.5–5.5), which is called *nepiagogeion*. Second is the primary level (grades 1–6), which is called *dimotiko*. The third level is the lower secondary (grades 7–9), called the gymnasium. The fourth level is the upper secondary or lyceum (grades 10–12). The fifth is the tertiary level, which consists of universities and technological educational institutes (Massialas et al. 1988).

The upper-secondary level of education is divided into three types of lyceums: the general lyceum, the technical lyceum, and the multilateral lyceum. There are also general vocational-technical schools at this level, with a three-year program of general studies and vocational-technical education.

Ten years ago, examinations were abolished and all successful gymnasium graduates can now enter the lyceum. In comparison to those of the gymnasium, the educational goals of the lyceum employ educational enrichment and in-depth study. As Massialas and his colleagues (1988) further observed, the lyceum is viewed as an important training ground for youth seeking positions of leadership in Greek society.

Since 1981, the first two years of the lyceum involve common subjects. In the third and final year, in addition to the core subjects there are five elective concentration cycles offered. These concentrations are referred to as Desme A, stressing mathematics and science; Desme B, stressing medical sciences; Desme C, emphasizing philological and legal sciences; Desme D, emphasizing the social sciences; and Desme E, for students who do not wish to pursue higher education. However, Desme E has been the least popular alternative since the majority of Greek high school students aspire to admission to Greek higher education (Massialas et al. 1988). Also available, but not favored, are the vocational-technical schools—one- or two-year programs to train technicians and other specialized personnel for immediate employment.

Greek secondary schools remain basically autocratic in nature in spite of the movement and regulations to make the schools more democratic. Teachers also continue to display authoritarian teaching and classroom management styles, and school policies continue to stress student obligations and responsibilities rather than student rights (Massialas et al. 1988).

LEARNING STYLES

The literature abounds with evidence of the efficacy of learning styles–oriented teaching in elementary and secondary-level classrooms (Dunn & Dunn 1992, 1993). An excellent synthesis of that research was reported by Dunn, Beaudry, and Klavas (1989).

Relationships between culture and learning style have also been reported in the literature in recent years. Studies have illustrated similarities as well as differences between the learning style characteristics of Anglo-Americans and members of other ethnic or racial groups (Ramirez & Castaneda 1974; Dunn, Gemake, Jalali, Zenhausern, Quinn, & Spiridakis 1990). Instructional similarities and differences among members of the same culture have been identified (Dunn & Griggs 1990). Various modes of assessing learning styles of different cultural and linguistic groups were suggested by American educators (Spiridakis 1983; Dunn & Griggs 1990). The learning styles of Greek learners had not been previously investigated.

For purposes of this initial study of the learning styles of high school students in Greece, the focus was on highlighting points of convergence or divergence in certain learning styles of Greek as compared to American high school students. The Learning Style Inventory (LSI) (Dunn, Dunn, & Price 1989) was utilized to diagnose student styles for a variety of reasons. Most important, it offers a comprehensive view of learning style characteristics. It is also a practical instrument that teachers, administrators, and researchers can use to identify the learning styles of different cultural groups. The LSI is also an important tool in prescribing particular instructional teaching approaches, methods, and materials that match the identified learning styles of students (Spiridakis 1983). Moreover, it has been the most widely used instrument to assess learning styles in the United States (Keefe 1982).

RESEARCH METHODOLOGY

Participants

The sample consisted of 113 boys and girls age 16 to 17, enrolled in the lyceum (tenth or eleventh grade of high school). The students were from high schools in urban and semiurban areas. The full spectrum of occupational status in Greece constituted the subject's background. Athens and Thessalonika were the large urban areas involved, whereas Thrace, Pelopponesos, and Crete were the semiurban locations.

The curriculum adhered to by the groups tested, and the textbooks used by the students, were essentially similar. As Kostakis (1988) noted:

In contrast to North American school systems, the Greek school system is centralized and standardized; for specific grade levels, curricula and even textbooks are uniform for all students throughout the country. (p. 236)

The Greek participants were all enrolled in tenth and eleventh grades of college-preparatory cycles of study, and each had to complete rigorous coursework to remain in school.

Materials

For purposes of this study, the Learning Style Inventory (Dunn, Dunn, & Price 1989), which consists of 104 dichotomous items, was initially translated from English to Greek and, afterward, translated back from Greek to English. It then was reviewed by a panel of experts to increase its validity. Reliability of the translation was determined by the test-retest correlation method (Spiridakis 1991).

RESEARCH RESULTS

Comparison of Greek and U.S. Students

A discriminant analysis was performed in order to compare the learning styles of the 113 students from Greece with a comparable random sample of 113 students in grades 10 and 11 from the United States.

The thirteen LSI variables that discriminated between learners in Greece and in the United States are presented in Table 15.1. The overall estimated effectiveness of the thirteen variables in discriminating between Greek and American students was 84.07 percent.

The learning style variable that accounted for the most significant difference between the two groups, and which entered the discriminant equation first, was parent-figure motivated, with the U.S. sample significantly more parent-figure

Table 15.1
Learning Style Elements that Discriminate Between Adolescents in Greece and in the United States: Stepwise Order and Mean Scores

Stepwise Order	LSI Variables	United States (N=113)	Greece (N=113)
1	Parent Figure Motivated	17.21	13.12
2	Tactile	16.31	15.72
3	Noise Level	14.55	14.22
4	Temperature	15.52	14.12
5	Design	12.0	10.96
6	Evening-Morning	17.62	17.49
7	Motivation	31.69	26.88
8	Learn in Several Ways	13.00	11.00
9	Afternoon	16.48	15.00
10	Requires Intake	15.19	14.24
11	Authority Figures Present	11.52	11.04
12	Responsible	13.40	12.46
13	Needs Mobility	13.50	12.79

motivated than the Greek sample. The second variable to enter the discriminant equation was tactile. The United States sample preferred to learn through its tactile preference significantly more than did the Greek sample.

The third variable to enter the discriminant equation was noise level. Overall, the U.S. adolescents preferred sound present significantly more than did the Greek sample. Preferring sound present while learning tends to be a global, rather than an analytic, characteristic (Dunn, Bruno, Sklar, & Beaudry 1990; Dunn, Cavanaugh, Eberle, & Zenhausern 1982). The fourth variable was temperature. The U.S. sample preferred a warmer environment compared with the Greek sample. Greek students, of course, enjoy a year-round warm climate, which may make this item less meaningful for them.

The fifth variable was design. Overall, the U.S. sample preferred a more formal design than did the Greek sample. Needing a formal setting design when studying new and difficult academic information tends to be an analytic characteristic; requiring informal or less formal seating tends to be a global trait (Dunn, Bruno, Sklar, & Beaudry 1990: Dunn, Cavanaugh, Eberle, & Zenhausern 1982). Needing sound and a less formal seating design while learning suggest that the Greek students tended to be more global than the U.S. students. This finding was unexpected. The current study was the first comparing the learning styles of Greek and U.S. adolescents. The sample was small and efforts should be made to replicate these findings before drawing conclusions.

The sixth variable was evening and morning. Overall, the U.S. students preferred learning in the morning more than the Greek sample, which preferred learning in the evening. Many Greek families enjoy restful afternoons, which may be catalytic to a nocturnal preference on their part in this category. The seventh variable was motivation. Overall, the U.S. sample was significantly more self-motivated than the Greek sample. The eighth variable was learning in several ways. Overall, the U.S. sample preferred more variety and alternatives than the Greek sample, suggesting that American youngsters required a diversity whereas, in contrast, the Greeks tended to prefer fixed patterns and routines.

The ninth variable was afternoon. Overall, the U.S. sample preferred to learn more in the afternoon than did the Greek sample. Greeks often sleep in the afternoon and, as indicated, often prefer heavy concentration in the evening. The tenth variable was requires intake. Overall, the U.S. sample preferred more intake than the Greek sample. The eleventh variable was authority figures present. Overall, the U.S. sample preferred authority figures present more than did the Greek sample. Greek adolescents tend to rebel against authority in the school setting, perhaps reflecting the historically democratic, participative mode of operation nationally, which has achieved prominence in recent years.

The twelfth variable was responsible, which tends to indicate degrees of conformity versus nonconformity. Overall, the U.S. sample was more conforming than the Greek sample. Individuality and a questioning, nonconforming attitude are extremely popular among Greek adolescents today, especially in the wake of promised continuing liberal reforms in education at the high school level. The thirteenth variable was needs mobility. Overall, the U.S. sample needed more mobility than the Greek sample. Greek youngsters are socialized from a very young age to sit quietly and attend throughout their schooling; not surprisingly they may have internalized such behavior, not having been exposed to other patterns of mobility in an educational setting.

CONCLUSIONS

The findings indicated differences between learning styles of Greek adolescents and their age peers in the United States. On certain variables there well may be cultural or environmental reasons for these differences. For example, this study was temporarily impeded by a general strike of secondary school students throughout Greece. Greek high schools were effectively shut down for several weeks as students protested delays in promised reforms in areas such as the selection of Greek high school students for entrance into Greek universities, where admission was offered to approximately one-third of Greek high school graduates. Such political efficacy and attitudes may help to explain the resistance of Greek high school students to conformity and authority figures; for example, the traditional Greek educational setting of rigid classroom instruction and atmosphere may explain the lesser need for intake and mobility.

Greek students also are conditioned to the lecture approach, and are motivated usually by the need to earn good grades and pass the national entrance examination for university admission, more than anything else. Their preference for following routines and patterns rather than a variety of instructional methods also may contribute to their tolerance of such traditional instructional styles.

Since Greek students are still encouraged to take a "siesta" in the afternoons, the U.S. preference for afternoon learning over the Greeks also is not surprising.

The Greek student is not exposed to a variety of innovative teaching styles and curricula. Thus, Greek students find it ignominious to respond positively to "learning in several ways." Moreover, students are not exposed to divergent teaching styles or activities that might respond to their preferred modes of learning, such as auditory vs. visual, global vs. analytic. In addition, high school teachers usually are not given specific skills for innovative classroom instructional designs. As Kostakis (1988) has stated:

There is little leeway for specialized classroom technologies or differences among technologies to develop. . . . Few secondary-school teachers receive pedagogical training. Even at the primary school level—where teachers have taken pedagogy courses—the modes of student-teacher interaction are homogeneous across subjects. (p. 237)

There is a movement in Greece to decentralize the school system and to invite more experimentation and divergence from the national curriculum. New technologies and educational reform, such as the incorporation of learning styles into the curriculum, are on the horizon. The initial findings stated herein point to the need to assess and examine more closely the learning styles of Greek students so that teachers and administrators can utilize each student's characteristics to individualize the curriculum and instructional process. Indeed, as Greece looks forward to full participation in the European economic community, Greek students will be called upon to respond to more divergent styles of thinking and behaving in interacting with their new European family members.

The disparity between the rhetoric of reform in Greek education and reality may have to decrease to achieve truly democratic education that provides what Kazamias (1990), quoting Panoutsos, refers to as "equality of opportunity for access and continuation into the various levels of the educational system" (p. 29). While accommodation of learning styles may not in and of itself be the precursor for achieving pluralism and meritocratic selection in Greek education, it may yet prove to be a concomitant, attendant force for unimpeded education and equal educational opportunity in Greece.

Psacharopoulos's (1990) perception regarding the goal of a new unified dynamic European community and citizenry in 1992 is relevant and revealing in regard to the future of Greek education and society:

The key to the changes and new developments would be less state involvement in education and the professions, and increased competitiveness and accountability of the *system to the users themselves* (i.e., students and professionals), rather than having to rely for everything on a benevolent government. (p. 73)

Chapter 16

The Learning Styles of Gifted Adolescents Around the World: Differences and Similarities

Gary E. Price and Roberta M. Milgram

In the preceding chapters the learning styles of gifted and talented adolescents in seven countries—Brazil, Canada, Guatemala, Israel, Korea, the Philippines, and the United States—were presented and discussed. Both the Learning Style Inventory (Dunn, Dunn, Price 1975, 1979, 1981, 1984, 1989) and the Tel Aviv Activities Inventory (Milgram 1987, 1990) were administered to all individuals in these countries. The theoretical background and detailed instructions for the administration and scoring of the two instruments were presented in Chapters 1 and 2. (Adolescents in Egypt and Greece completed the Learning Style Inventory only. Accordingly, no data were available for gifted-nongifted comparisons, and these countries are not included in this integrative chapter.)

Our goal is to examine the findings from the seven countries collectively, to integrate them and to draw overall conclusions about the learning styles of adolescents in general, and of gifted learners in particular, throughout the world. This chapter is divided into three sections. The first and second sections are concerned with cross-cultural differences and similarities in learning style and in creativity among adolescents representing a wide range of intelligence and creative abilities. In the third section we summarize the data on learning styles of gifted youngsters in the seven countries. We compare and contrast the cross-cultural findings and examine the learning style characteristics that seem to be found in gifted youngsters across cultures. Our inquiry was guided by the broad theoretical views of giftedness and learning style presented in Chapter 1 that included learners whose abilities were reflected in overall academic ability and/ or in eight specific domains of creativity—science, social leadership, dance, music, art, literature, drama, and sports.

LEARNING STYLE: CROSS-CULTURAL DIFFERENCES AND SIMILARITIES

In Chapters 7 through 13, the various learning style components of each cultural group were compared with a comparable random sample of adolescents in the United States. In this section we expand our investigation to include in-depth comparisons of cross-cultural differences and similarities among all eight cultures. We first highlight the cross-cultural differences by examining the learning style elements that most characterize learners within each of the eight cultural groups. We next compare the elements that characterize the learning styles of adolescents across a number of cultures.

The twenty-two learning style scores were subjected to separate one-way analyses of variance by eight cultural groups. Brazil, Canada, Israel, Korea, the Philippines, and the United States were each represented as one cultural group and Guatemala as two—that is, Guatemalan and Mayan. The F ratios for the twenty-two learning style scores ranged from 7.53 to 142.71 and were all highly significant (p < .00001). The means, standard deviations (in parentheses), and F ratios that resulted from the analyses are presented in Table 16.1.

Cross-Cultural Differences

There were cross-cultural differences in the rank order of the twenty-two learning style elements in the eight cultures. For example, learners in Canada and the United States expressed the highest preference for learning with sound present, whereas many adolescents from Israel and the Mayans preferred silence. These complex differences are presented graphically in Figure 16.1. The relative preference of each of the eight cultures for each of the twenty-two learning style elements is designated by the placement of a symbol representing each group on a vertical axis in a position ranging from 1 to 8, indicating high to low scores, respectively. In other words, the ranks of 1 or 2 that appear high on Figure 16.1 were interpreted as indicating a high preference for that learning style by that cultural group and ranks 7 or 8 that appear low on the figure as indicating a low preference. The learning style preferences of each cultural group are discussed below.

The twenty-two learning style elements were designed by two-letter abbreviations as follows:

NO	Noise
LT	Light
TE	Temperature
DE	Design
MT	Motivation
PR	Persistence

Table 16.1
Learning Style Variables by Country: Means, Standard Deviations, and F Ratios

LSI Area	ISR	PHI	KOR	USA	CAN	GUA	BRA	MAY	F=
N=	985	379	92	1058	166	615	605	49	
Personality									
Self Motivation	28.80	32.84	32.08	30.34	30.14	30.90	30.20	32.41	34.77*
	(4.46)	(3.47)	(3.44)	(5.08)	(4.36)	(5.00)	(6.01)	(5.43)	
Parent Motivat	15.43	27.50	17.51	16.84	15.83	17.12	14.51	18.20	61.37*
	(2.52)	(2.03)	(1.94)	(2.75)	(2.67)	(2.85)	(3.83)	(2.61)	
Teacher Motivat	17.28	19.53	19.55	18.70	17.09	19.88	18.52	20.59	45.90*
	(3.27)	(2.80)	(2.38)	(3.42)	(3.15)	(3.71)	(3.70)	(3.88)	
Persistance	15.28	16.94	15.86	16.47	15.65	16.41	15.89	15.84	21.58*
	(2.21)	(2.51)	(2.98)	(3.03)	(2.88)	(2.83)	(3.39)	(3.40)	
Responsible	14.01	13.31	12.77	12.64	12.25	13.71	12.95	13.35	16.54*
	(3.18)	(3.19)	(3.37)	(3.58)	(3.56)	(3.50)	(3.44)	(3.13)	
Structure	11.95	13.13	12.71	11.75	12.02	13.20	12.92	14.57	20.19*
	(3.30)	(3.15)	(3.00)	(3.73)	(3.85)	(3.25)	(3.42)	(3.24)	
Intake	15.70	15.47	10.57	18.24	17.96	13.67	14.93	10.12	106.57*
	(4.40)	(4.71)	(3.99)	(4.25)	(4.51)	(4.86)	(4.56)	(3.52)	
Mobility	13.19	13.73	10.88	14.54	14.30	12.97	11.82	12.24	33.94*
	(4.21)	(4.01)	(4.12)	(4.07)	(4.40)	(3.69)	(3.93)	(2.89)	
Social									
Alone/Peer	19.96	21.16	21.46	21.25	20.39	20.83	22.08	20.16	7.53*
	(5.65)	(5.48)	(6.04)	(6.35)	(6.41)	(6.30)	(6.44)	(5.85)	
Authority	11.08	11.72	9.48	11.14	11.04	10.71	13.52	12.36	51.66*
	(2.86)	(2.77)	(2.60)	(3.07)	(2.79)	(3.50)	(3.74)	(3.28)	
Several Ways	12.80	13.25	12.58	12.99	12.48	11.97	12.44	12.57	7.66*
	(3.38)	(2.98)	(3.38)	(3.23)	(3.36)	(3.45)	(3.42)	(3.32)	

*P$\leq$.00001

Table 16.1 (continued)

LSI Area	ISR	PHI	KOR	USA	CAN	GUA	BRA	MAY	F=
N=	985	379	92	1058	166	615	605	49	
Environmental									
Noise	11.43 (4.10)	12.69 (3.73)	12.59 (3.44)	14.43 (4.65)	14.48 (4.79)	12.97 (3.52)	12.35 (4.54)	11.82 (3.03)	42.41*
Light	13.49 (2.96)	14.81 (3.07)	12.18 (3.53)	12.93 (3.60)	13.20 (3.54)	12.93 (3.34)	13.41 (3.44)	11.39 (3.48)	18.38*
Temperature	16.45 (3.65)	10.79 (3.36)	13.51 (3.42)	16.03 (4.03)	18.50 (3.72)	13.66 (3.18)	15.02 (3.56)	14.22 (2.79)	142.71*
Design	12.29 (3.67)	10.77 (3.13)	16.58 (3.35)	9.29 (3.52)	9.43 (3.68)	11.88 (3.07)	11.09 (3.60)	13.59 (2.66)	106.15*
Perceptual									
Auditory	13.02 (3.24)	12.91 (2.77)	11.74 (3.13)	13.67 (3.27)	14.43 (3.09)	14.62 (2.94)	14.06 (3.19)	15.39 (3.01)	26.85*
Visual	9.09 (2.57)	9.76 (2.17)	10.01 (2.38)	8.59 (2.65)	8.19 (2.54)	10.17 (2.38)	10.20 (2.57)	9.71 (2.28)	41.74*
Tactile	15.66 (3.89)	16.59 (3.88)	16.35 (4.10)	15.69 (4.29)	17.46 (4.12)	17.28 (3.79)	14.71 (4.56)	19.02 (3.99)	26.88*
Kinesthetic	23.07 (5.08)	26.77 (3.58)	26.22 (4.05)	24.17 (4.28)	26.34 (3.63)	25.58 (4.56)	22.76 (4.98)	25.96 (5.44)	50.57*
Time									
Evening/Morning	16.58 (4.86)	17.10 (4.37)	20.22 (4.29)	15.20 (4.95)	15.22 (5.22)	20.57 (4.33)	20.76 (4.73)	22.45 (5.03)	135.58*
Late Morning	12.53 (2.86)	11.33 (2.60)	12.30 (3.14)	11.27 (2.87)	11.38 (2.88)	10.69 (2.88)	12.55 (3.63)	12.19 (2.28)	33.17*
Afternoon	16.00 (3.33)	17.41 (3.41)	15.26 (3.46)	15.89 (3.68)	15.95 (3.02)	16.57 (3.79)	14.40 (4.12)	16.57 (3.63)	27.84*

*P$\leq$.00001

Figure 16.1
Learning Style Inventory: Rank Order of Scores by Culture

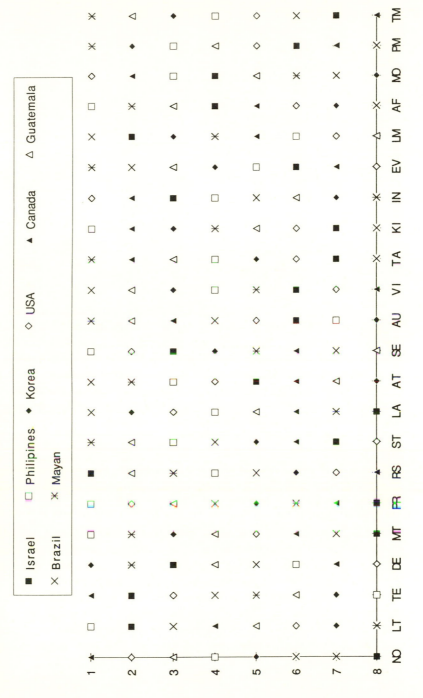

RS   Responsibility
ST   Structure
LA   Alone/Peer
AT   Authority Figures
SE   Several Ways
AU   Auditory
VI   Visual
TA   Tactile
KI   Kinesthetic
IN   Intake
EV   Evening—Morning
LM   Late Morning
AF   Afternoon
MO   Mobility
PM   Parent Motivated
TM   Teacher Motivated

The Israeli students preferred bright light and a warm environment. They were responsible (conforming) and preferred to learn in the late morning. In addition, the Israeli group preferred a quiet environment, were low on self-motivation, did not want structure, preferred to learn alone, did not want to learn through their tactile or kinesthetic senses, and were not teacher motivated.

The Filipino students preferred bright light, a cool environment, were self-motivated and persistent, liked to learn in a variety of ways in the afternoon, were kinesthetic, but did not want to learn auditorially.

The Korean students wanted low light, a cool environment, a formal design, were peer oriented, and did not want authority figures present. They also did not want to learn auditorially but, rather, preferred visual and kinesthetic instructional resources. They did not want intake, wanted to learn more in the late morning than in the afternoon, did not want mobility, and were parent and teacher motivated.

The U.S. students preferred sound present, an informal design, and learning in varied ways. They were persistent, nonconforming, preferred little structure, did not want to learn primarily visually, wanted intake while studying, and preferred evening but not the late morning. They also needed mobility.

The Canadian students wanted sound present, a warm environment, intake, and an informal design. They were neither persistent nor responsible, did not want to learn visually, preferred learning through their tactile and kinesthetic preferences, preferred evening, needed mobility, and were neither parent nor teacher motivated.

The Guatemalan group was persistent, responsible, wanted structure, did not want authority figures present, did not want to learn in several ways, wanted to learn through their auditory and visual preferences, did not want to learn in late morning, and were teacher motivated.

The Mayan students wanted to learn alone, in a quiet environment with dim light and a formal design. They were self-motivated, preferred structure and an authority figure present, and reported auditory and tactile preferences. They wanted to learn in the early morning or afternoon, were parent and teacher motivated, and did not require intake.

The Brazilian students were not self-motivated, were peer oriented, wanted authority figures present, did not want to learn in several ways, were visual but neither tactile nor kinesthetic, wanted to learn in either early or late morning but not in the afternoon, needed little mobility, and were not parent-figure motivated.[1]

Cross-Cultural Similarities

To ascertain if there were similarities among the learning styles of the various cultural groups we investigated, we again used the data presented in Figure 16.1 to compare the learning style preferences reported by the eight cultural groups. It should be recalled that preference for a particular learning style in a given cultural group was defined by the rank order of the mean score for that element within the culture. The ranks of 1 or 2 that appear high on Figure 16.1 are interpreted as a high preference for that learning style by that cultural group and ranks 7 or 8 that appear low on the figure are interpreted as a low preference. Cultural similarities in learning style preferences are discussed below.

Personality. Cultural similarities were found in this area which include the following learning style elements: self-motivation, parent motivation, teacher motivation, persistence, responsible (conforming), structure, intake, and mobility.

The individuals who were most self-motivated were the Filipinos, Mayans, and Koreans. The individuals who were least self-motivated were the Canadians, Brazilians, and Israelis. Those individuals who were most parent-figure motivated were the Mayan, Korean, and Filipino students. Those who were least parent-figure motivated were the Israeli, Canadian, and Brazilian students. The most teacher motivated were the Mayan, Guatemalan, Filipino, and Korean students; the least teacher motivated were the Brazilian, Israeli, and Canadian students.

Filipino, U.S., and Guatemalan students were the most persistent; the least persistent were the Mayan, Canadian, Brazilian, Israeli, and Korean students. The most responsible or conforming individuals were the Israeli, Guatemalan, and Mayan; the least responsible or conforming were Korean, U.S., and Canadian students. Individuals preferring the most structure were the Mayan, Guatemalan, and Filipino; individuals preferring the least amount of structure were from Canada, Israel, and the United States. Individuals preferring the most intake were from the United States, Canada, and Israel. Individuals preferring the least intake were from Guatemala, Korea, and the Mayan students. Those youngsters who preferred the most mobility were from the United States, Canada, and the Philippines. The least need for mobility was reported by Mayan, Brazilian, and Korean students.

Social. The social area includes: preferring to learn alone, with peers, with authority figures present, and in several ways—which means sometimes alone or with peers and at other times with authority figures present.

Individuals who most preferred to learn with peers were the Brazilian, Korean, and U.S. students. Individuals who most preferred to learn alone were the Canadian, Mayan, and Israeli students. Individuals who wanted authority figures present were the Brazilian, Mayan, and Filipino students, and the individuals who least wanted authority figures present were the Canadian, Guatemalan, and Korean students. Individuals who needed the most variety were the Filipino, U.S., and Israeli students. Individuals least preferring variety were the Canadian, Brazilian, and Guatemalan students.

Environmental. The environmental elements include sound present or quiet, bright or dim light, warm or cool temperature, and a formal versus informal design.

In the area of sound, the Canadian and U.S. students preferred sound present, and the Mayan and Israeli students preferred the most quiet environment. The Filipino, Israeli, and Brazilian students preferred the brightest light and the Korean, U.S., and Mayan students preferred the least amount of light. The Canadian, Israeli, and U.S. students preferred the warmest environment, and the Guatemalan, Korean, and Filipino students preferred the coolest environment. The Korean, Mayan, and Israeli students preferred the most formal design, and the Canadian, U.S., and Filipino students preferred the most informal design.

Perceptual. The perceptual area indicates whether individuals prefer to receive information through their auditory, visual, tactile, and/or kinesthetic perceptual senses.

The individuals most preferring to learn through their auditory sense were the Mayan, Guatemalan, and Canadian students, whereas the individuals least preferring to learn through their auditory sense were the Israeli, Filipino, and Korean students. The individuals having the strongest visual preference were the Brazilian, Guatemalan, and Korean students. Conversely, individuals least preferring to learn through their visual sense were the Israeli, U.S., and Canadian students. The most tactile students were the Brazilian, Mayan, Canadian, and Guatemalan students. The individuals preferring to learn least through their tactile preference were the U.S., Israeli, and Brazilian students. The individuals preferring to learn most through their kinesthetic sense were the Filipino, Canadian, and Korean students. The individuals least preferring to learn through their kinesthetic senses were the U.S., Israeli, and Brazilian students.

Time. The learning style preference of time includes the time of day in which an individual is most productive. Time periods include early morning, late morning, afternoon, and evening. Those individuals most preferring to learn in the early morning were the Mayan, Brazilian, and Guatemalan students; those least preferring to learn in the evening were the Israeli, Canadian, and U.S. students. Those individuals most preferring to learn in late morning were the Brazilian, Israeli, and Korean students; those individuals least preferring to learn in the late morning were from the Philippines, the United States, and Guatemala. The individuals most preferring to learn in the afternoon were Filipinos, Mayans, and Guatemalans. The individuals preferring to learn least in the afternoon were from the United States, Korea, and Brazil.

There were some learning style preferences reported by adolescents to a greater or lesser degree in all the cultures that we investigated. These cross-cultural similarities in learning style among learners in the eight cultures are graphically presented in Figure 16.2. Notice, for example, that although the means are not identical, high scores on overall self-motivation and a preference for kinesthetic-oriented learning and a low preference for visual-type learning activities were reported by youngsters in widely dispersed parts of the world.

To summarize, the findings demonstrate extensive cross-cultural differences in learning style among the eight cultures. In addition, however, some learning style preferences were shared by youngsters in a number of cultures. One especially remarkable finding was that some highly important learning style preferences were shared by learners in all countries we studied.

The data indicated that cultural background is an important individual difference that dramatically influences learning style. As such, cultural influences on the learner at any given time merit attention for matching teaching strategies to learning style. If we consider the multicultural backgrounds of many learners in schools in the United States today, this finding takes on additional significance.

The finding of learning style preferences across culture is particularly interesting and, to the best of our knowledge, has not been reported elsewhere. Youngsters in countries throughout the world described themselves as highly self-motivated and with a strong preference for kinesthetic versus visual learning. This finding should be regarded by teachers and administrators as evidence that individualized learning style–oriented instruction merits serious attention as an alternative to current whole-class, group-oriented practices.

CREATIVE ACTIVITY: CROSS-CULTURAL DIFFERENCES AND SIMILARITIES

In Chapters 7 through 13 we examined and compared students' creative activities within each culture. In this chapter we broaden the cross-cultural comparisons to include the seven cultural groups for which complete data on creative activities is available. Canada, Israel, Korea, the Philippines, and the United States were each represented as one cultural group and Guatemala as two—that is, Guatemalan and Mayan. We first examined the types of creative endeavors reported as high versus low frequency within each of the seven

Figure 16.2
Learning Style Inventory: Raw Scores by Culture

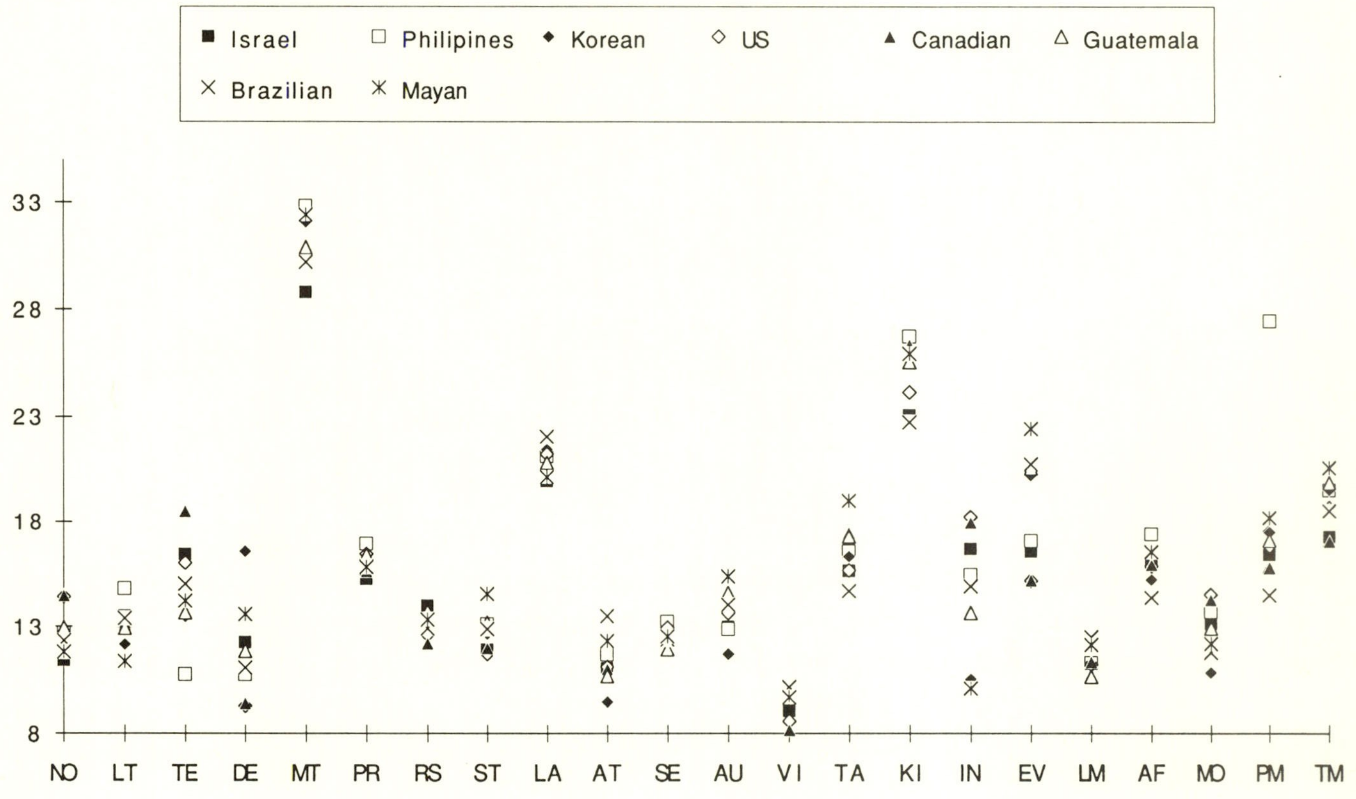

cultural groups, and next inspected the similarity in creative activity among the cultures by comparing the seven cultural patterns of high and low frequency of creative activities in the eight domains.

The eight domain scores for creative activity were subjected to separate one-way analyses or variance by seven cultural groups. The F ratios for the eight creativity domains ranged from 4.61 to 254.99 and were all highly significant (p < .00001).

Cross-Cultural Differences

There were cross-cultural differences in the rank order of the eight domain scores of creative activity *within* the seven cultures. The relative degree of creative activity in each domain within each culture is depicted in Figure 16.3 by a vertical bar with a different design representing each culture. The bars are placed on a vertical axis in a position ranging from one to eight indicating high to low rank *within* that culture, respectively.

The Israeli students ranked highest in terms of drama and literature and ranked lowest in terms of music and art. The Filipino students ranked highest in literature and ranked lowest in social leadership, dance, and drama. The Korean students ranked highest in science and literature and ranked lowest in the areas of sports, drama, and dance. The U.S. students ranked highest in sports, science, dance, and music and ranked lowest in the area of literature. The Canadian students ranked highest in science, social leadership, music, art, literature, drama, and sports and ranked lowest, but not very low, in dance. The Guatemalan students ranked highest in the areas of social leadership, art, drama, and sports and ranked lowest in the area of music. The Mayans ranked highest in dance and ranked lowest in science, art, and literature.

Cross-Cultural Similarities

In addition to the differences presented above, we investigated whether there might be similarities in creative activity that cut across cultures just as there had been in learning style preferences. Accordingly, we again used the data reported in Figure 16.3 to compare the seven cultures on the degree of activity in each domain. It should be recalled that a great deal of activity in a particular domain of creative activity for a given cultural group was defined by the rank order of the mean score for that element within the culture. The ranks of 1 or 2 that appear high on Figure 16.3 are interpreted as indicating a large amount of activity in that domain for the cultural group, and ranks 7 and 8 that appear low on Figure 16.3 as indicating a small amount of activity.

Canadian, United States, and Korean students reported a large amount of activity in science. Israeli and the Mayan students, by contrast, reported a small

Figure 16.3
Rank Order of Creative Activity Domain Scores Within Culture

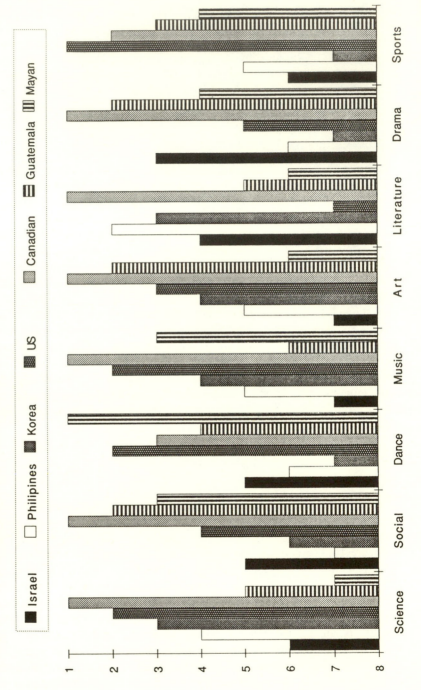

amount. Social leadership was a domain of high activity for the Canadians and the Guatemalans and low activity for Korean and Filipino students. In dance, the Mayan and the U.S. students reported a large amount of activity whereas Filipino and Korean students specified a small amount. In the area of music, the Canadian and U.S. students were the highest and the Guatemalan and Israeli students were the lowest. In the area of art, the Canadian and Guatemalan students were the highest and the Mayan and the Israeli learners described their activity in art as low. Literature was the domain of high activity for Canadian and Filipino students and low activity for the Mayans and those from the United States. In the area of drama, the Canadian and Guatemalan students reported a large amount of activity and the Filipino and Korean students a small amount. In the area of sports, the U.S. and Canadian students reported much activity and the Israeli and Korean students reported little activity.

In summary, the findings demonstrated that, despite some similarities among cultures, there were clear cross-cultural differences in creative activity among the seven cultures. These findings provide impressive support for the postulation in the Milgram 4 × 4 model of giftedness that culture influences the individual's creative activity in each specific domain of giftedness. In addition, however, in creative activity as in learning-style preferences, there are some foci of activity that are shared by more than one culture.

We reported in an earlier section of this chapter that adolescents in countries throughout the world have different learning-style preferences and that higher achievement and more positive attitudes would be likely to result if teaching strategies were matched to these preferences. These findings may be very helpful to educators in each country striving to match learning style and teaching strategies. For example, by examining individual learning styles we may find a youngster to be independent and activity oriented. The findings reported in this section may be used to specifically identify creative kinesthetic activities when differentiating curricula and individualizing structure in a given country. However, when prescribing instructional strategies or resources, it is crucial to respond to individual, rather than group, preferences, for within every cultural group there are many differences.

LEARNING STYLES OF GIFTED ADOLESCENTS: CROSS-CULTURAL DIFFERENCES AND SIMILARITIES

Cross-Cultural Differences

The data on the differences in learning style between gifted and nongifted learners in the different 4 × 4 domains within each culture were reported in the chapters on each country. The findings from six countries, where complete comparable data were available—Canada, Guatemala, Israel, Korea, the Philippines, and the United States—are summarized in Table 16.2. The summary is designed to facilitate comparison of the cross-cultural patterns of learning-style elements that discriminated between students within each cultural group who were gifted and nongifted in the eight domains of creative activity and/or in academic achievement based upon grade point average (GPA). We first computed the learning-style variables that discriminated between the gifted and nongifted students five or more times out of the nine domain comparisons within each cultural group.

For the Israeli group, the variables that discriminated most were kinesthetic, tactile, teacher motivated, sound, light, authority figures present, and temperature. For the Filipino students, the variables that discriminated most were kinesthetic, auditory, persistence, and intake. For the Korean culture, the variables that discriminated most were structure, temperature, kinesthetic, and parent motivated. For the U.S. culture, the variables that discriminated most were kinesthetic, afternoon, authority figures present, structure, responsible, and motivation. For the Canadians, the variables that discriminated most were tactile, kinesthetic, and temperature. For the Guatemalan students, the variables that discriminated most were mobility, structure, and persistence.

These learning-style profiles for each culture provide strong evidence for the existence of cross-cultural differences in learning style for the different categories of gifted versus nongifted learners.

Cross-Cultural Similarities

We found a certain degree of similarity among gifted learners in the six cultures in learning-style preferences when giftedness was defined in terms of academic ability (grade point average) or in terms of outstanding activity in each of the eight domains of creative activity. On the basis of the data presented in Table 16.2, one can ascertain which learning-style variables significantly discriminated between gifted and nongifted students in each of the nine creative activity domains. Unfortunately, space limitations do not allow a detailed analysis of the learning-style similarities of gifted versus nongifted learners among different cultures. The following discussion is designed to provide the reader with a model of how the data presented in Table 16.2 may be interpreted.

The data presented in the first column of Table 16.2 depict the learning-style elements that significantly discriminated between science-gifted and science-nongifted learners in each of the six countries. Persistence discriminated between science-gifted and nongifted for five of the six cultural groups—Israel, the Philippines, Korea, the United States, and Guatemala. In all five cultures, science-gifted students were more persistent than were their nonscience-gifted peers.

Tactile preferences discriminated between gifted versus nongifted students in science in five of the six cultural groups—Israel, the Philippines, Korea, Canada, and Guatemala. The science-gifted students in all five cultures indicated a stronger preference to learn through their tactile sense than did nongifted students. Science-gifted students also reported a stronger preference for learning kinesth-

Table 16.2
Learning-Style Elements that Discriminated Between Creative and Noncreative Students by Domain and Culture

Domain	Science						Social Leadership						Dance						Music						Art					
Country / LSI Elements	IS	PH	KO	US	CA	GU	IS	PH	KO	US	CA	GU	IS	PH	KO	US	CA	GU	IS	PH	KO	US	CA	GU	IS	PH	KO	US	CA	GU
Noise	5*		9*				4*	2*		8*			5	5*		2		6*	7*						2*					5*
Light			6	5			10*		4		9	7		1		4		7		2	5*		5*	7	10*	4	8*	1		
Temperature	9	4*	3	2	7*		10*		4	9		7											3*		3			1		
Design				1*		5		4	3*	2*	6*	5	6						4					5*		6*		10		
Motivation			7*	5*		7*	10*	1*		2*	6*	2	3	6*							5						5*	5*		
Persistance	6*	7*	1*	5*		7*	2*			7*		1*	2*	4*				5		6	4*			8*	3		7			6*
Responsible	10*		8	6	2*				6*	7*		4	4*					2*	2*	2*	3		4				7	5*	6	3
Structure			5	4*	3							10	4						3*		7	7			5		2			
Alone/Peer	11*		4					9*										9					6*		4*	9*	3	7*		4
Authority	7		10										1*		2*	5*	12*			5*					2*	3*	1*	4*		1*
Several Ways	12	3				4	5*	5*	2		4*			8*	3				1*	1*	1*		1*		6*	1*			5	2*
Auditory	2	2					6	3*				6	7					10	10*					3*						
Visual							7						11*	4*		1*		8	12	4*	3				4*		3*			
Tactile	1*	1*	2*		1*	1*	1*	3*	1*	3*	1*	3*	9*	3*		4		8	9*	8*	6*			1*	3*	6*		6	3*	
Kinesthetic	3*				8*	10*	3*			1*		9*	10	5*	9*	3*	7*		8	2	1*	2			9*	7*		2	6*	
Intake			3*		3*				1	4*		9*	11*	1	1*	5*			6				1*		4*			5	2*	
Evening/Mom		5				8*	7			2*			8		4*	6*		4*	12	4*	4	3								
Late Morning																				3	6*	6*								
Afternoon					6*			8		5		11	2*	6*					9*	8*	8*		2			3*			6	
Mobility					9*			6		5		8		10*	8*		1		8	2			6					2		
Parent Mot	4				2*		8		7					11*					6				1*		7	6*			6	
Teacher Mot	8*	6					9*						12*			3			5*						9*	7*				7*

*Gifted higher than nongifted

#The Canadian students were from a school that did not give grades.

The number is the rank for the importance of the variable with 1 as high.

Table 16.2 (continued)

Domain	Literature						Drama						Sports						GPA					
Country	IS	PH	KO	US	CA	GU	IS	PH	KO	US	CA	GU	IS	PH	KO	US	CA	GU	IS	PH	KO	US	CA#	GU
LSI Elements																								
Noise	1	1*			2*			3*	4*						8	3			1*		7*			
Light	8	4	3				6						4*	4						10*	2*			
Temperature			7						1				2*					1	6*		5*		4*	
Design			5*	5*			5		3*				5*					3*	8	1*	7	3		9
Motivation		2		4	1*				7			8								9*	1*			8*
Persistance	3*			8*					6*										7		6	12*		1*
Responsible			3			2		3*	1*			1		2	3*	4*				3	2*	10		6
Structure	10	6						5*		4				1*	2				13		6			
Alone/Peer	3		4									3*		6	6				4		4			
Authority	7*		2	7*			3*						5*	3*			4		3*		2	11		3
Several Ways	9*	4		8		3	2*		3*						7*				11	5*	3*			
Auditory	10*						1*	1*		7*			6		2*	10*			12*	11*	9*		5*	
Visual	6						4*		7	5*					3*	2*			14*	8				
Tactile		5*	1*			5			4					4		6*					1*			
Kinesthetic	5	5*							5					1						7*	4			
Intake	7*									2	1		3	9*			2		2	4*	10		2*	
Evening/Mom	4		5*	1*		6*				5*			1*						5		5			
Late Morning		1	6	1*				6	2*		2*				1*		1*		10	6*	8	8*		7
Afternoon		8	10					2	6	4*				7*					9					

etically than the nonscience-gifted in Israel, Canada, and Guatemala. Science-gifted students preferred to learn in a cooler area when they were from Korea or the United States but in a warmer environment when they were Canadians. Individuals who were science-gifted preferred a formal design when from the Philippines and the United States; those from Israel or Guatemala preferred an informal design. Science-gifted students in Israel and Guatemala indicated that they were responsible (conforming). Those from the United States and Canada, by contrast, neither wanted to be conforming nor follow through on what they were directed to do by others. Science-gifted learners from Korea and Canada indicated that they did not want structure, but those from the United States did.

Science-gifted Korean, United States, and Guatemalan students preferred to learn alone more than their nonscience-gifted peers. By contrast, science-gifted learners in Israel preferred to learn with their peers. Science-gifted individuals from Israel, the Philippines, and Canada preferred to learn in several ways rather than routinely in one way—that is, alone, or with peers, or with an authority figure present.

Across-Culture and Across-Domain Similarities

In the final analysis, we investigated whether certain learning style preferences characterized gifted learners regardless of the domain in which their exceptional abilities were focused. We ascertained which learning style elements discriminated best between gifted and nongifted learners within and across cultures when the nine domains of giftedness were combined. We calculated the number of times the learning style variables entered the discriminant equation to significantly discriminate between the gifted and nongifted for the six cultural groups.

The variable to discriminate most between gifted and nongifted learners for each of the six cultural groups was kinesthetic. The next variable to discriminate most was tactile. These interesting findings confirmed and extended those reported consistently in the research literature on giftedness in the United States. The perceptual areas of kinesthetic and tactile consistently discriminated most between gifted and nongifted learners in the United States. The data of the current study indicated that even across cultural groups, gifted students preferred to learn more through tactile and kinesthetic preferences than nongifted students. Unfortunately, in all cultures, much of teaching for gifted students occurs through auditory methods. Accordingly, the practical implications of the current findings are of considerable importance.

The next learning style variables to most discriminate between gifted and nongifted learners across culture were structure, parent motivated, temperature, afternoon, motivation, and authority figures present. The variables that discriminated least were several ways, needing variety, evening or morning and late morning.

In summary, the findings of this international study provide considerable empirical support for the theoretical models of learning style and of giftedness proposed by Dunn, Dunn, and Price and by Milgram, respectively. On the basis of these theoretical formulations, distinct learning style patterns for gifted students appear to reflect both the domain in which their abilities are focused and the culture in which they develop.

CONCLUSIONS

This chapter analyzed the international data from three perspectives. The first perspective compared students' scores on the learning style elements by culture. The second perspective examined creative activities by culture. The third perspective synthesized the three areas of learning style, creativity, and culture. Despite some similarities among cultures and even several strong style preferences reported by youngsters in all cultures, there were clear cross-cultural differences in learning style preferences and in creativity. There were, however, as many differences among individuals within each cultural group as between groups.

Gifted and nongifted students within each culture reported significantly different learning style characteristics. Thus, instruction provided for one group is unlikely to be beneficial, and actually may be detrimental, for the other group. Therefore, gifted and nongifted students should not be grouped heterogeneously. Rather, homogeneous grouping is likely to permit maximum achievement for each group—if the grouping takes into account the specific domain of talent and if the instruction provided complements the learning styles of the students to whom it is delivered.

Gifted adolescents who comprised the population for this nine culture investigation described themselves as highly motivated and with strong preferences for kinesthetic and/or tactual, as opposed to visual and auditory, instruction. Most conventional schooling occurs through lecture, discussion, and/or reading. These approaches place heavy emphasis on auditory and visual abilities. One conclusion based upon our findings is that, in traditional schools, gifted students are not being taught through their modality strengths.

Another conclusion focuses on the gifted students' preferences for learning alone rather than in groups. Cooperative learning and small-group instructional strategies have been recommended for secondary students in many countries. Our findings indicate that very few gifted students prefer to work with other students. Their preferences are to work independently or, if faced with difficulty, to receive direction from an authoritative adult. Previous research revealed that students achieved significantly higher achievement and attitude scores when permitted to learn in the social groupings they preferred (DeBello 1985; Giannitti 1988; Griggs 1989; Miles 1987; Perrin 1990).

It is important to note the wide distribution of energy levels among gifted students. Although some learn well in the morning, many more prefer late morning, afternoon, and evening, in ascending order as their best time for concentration. Previous research documents the influence of time-of-day energy patterns on achievement (Andrews 1990; Freeley 1984; Gardiner 1986; Lemmon 1986; Lynch 1981; Virostko 1983). Again, conventional schooling appears to be unresponsive to the majority of gifted adolescents whose preferred time of day is often not in the early morning.

The cross-cultural differences reflect, to some extent, the dissimilarity in opportunity for creative activity in the diverse cultures. This disparity in opportunity apparently influenced individuals' ability to develop in specific talent areas. Thus, if access to creative activities, information, or role models is not available, adolescents may never develop their potential giftedness in that domain—which clearly supports Milgram's 4 × 4 model and Dunn, Dunn, and Treffinger's thesis (1992).

Despite different cultural background, our findings provide some support for the idea that students gifted in a particular domain have learning style traits that are essentially similar. Gifted students in each domain—overall intellectual ability, science, art, dance, drama, mathematics, literature, music, or sports—reported learning styles that were similar to each other's but significantly different from the styles of other creative groups and from the styles of the nongifted.

The findings of this international study provide considerable empirical support for the theoretical models of learning style and of giftedness proposed by Dunn, Dunn, and Price and by Milgram, respectively. On the basis of these theoretical formulations one would expect distinct learning style patterns for gifted students that reflect both the domain upon which their abilities are focused and the culture in which they develop.

The benefits of teaching nongifted students for learning style have been clearly established. Our findings indicate that similar advantages would probably accrue to gifted learners as well if teaching strategies were matched with their learning styles. These data highlight the need to determine the learning style strengths of gifted and nongifted students from each culture and to provide an instructional environment rich in opportunity for creative activity and responsive to each learner's characteristics. This is a formidable professional challenge for educators but children everywhere deserve nothing less.

NOTE

1. The results reported in this chapter are based on comparison of the twenty-two Learning Style Inventory scores derived by G. Price from the data reported in seven cultures. The results reported in Chapter 13 on Brazil compared the learning style of youngsters in only one culture. Any discrepancies between the data reported here and in Chapter 13 reflect the different method of LSI scoring that was used in Brazil only.

References

Albert, R. S. (1975). Toward a behavioral definition of genius. *American Psychologist*, *30*, 140–51.

Albert, R. S., & Runco, M. A. (1986). The achievement of eminence: A model of exceptionally gifted boys and their families. In R. J. Sternberg and J. E. Davidson (Eds.), *Conceptions of giftedness*, 32–57. New York: Cambridge University Press.

———. (1987). The possible dispositions of scientists and non-scientists. In D. N. Jackson and J. P.Rushton (Eds.), *Scientific excellence: Origins and assessment*. Beverly Hills: Sage.

———. (1989). Independence and cognitive ability in gifted and exceptionally gifted boys. *Journal of Youth and Adolescence*, *18*, 221–30.

———. (in press). A longitudinal study of exceptionally gifted boys and their families: Rationale, procedures, and midterm findings. In R. Subotnik and K. Arnold (Eds.), *Beyond Terman: Longitudinal studies of giftedness*. Norwood, NJ: Ablex.

Al-Sabaty, I., & Davis, G. A. (1989). Relationship between creativity and right, left, and intergrated thinking styles. *Creative Research Journal*, *2*, 111–17.

Amabile, T. M. (1989). *Growing up creative*. New York: Crown.

Amabile, T. M., Goldfarb, P., & Brackfield, S. C. (1990). Social influences on creativity: Evaluation, coaction, and surveillance. *Creativity Research Journal*, *3*, 6–21.

Andrews, R. H. (1990, July-September). The development of a learning styles program in a low socioeconomic, underachieving North Carolina elementary school. *Journal of Reading, Writing, and Learning Disabilities: International*, *6*(3), 307–14.

———. (1991). Insights into education: An elementary principal's perspective. In *Hands-on approaches to learning style: A practical guide to successful schooling*, 50–53. New Wilmington, PA.: Association for the Advancement of International Education.

Annotated bibliography. (1993). New York: Center for the Study of Learning and Teaching Styles. St. John's University.

April, E. (1990). *Almanaque abril: Uma enciclopedia em um volume* (April almanac: The encyclopedia in one volume). Sao Paulo: Editora Abril.

Austin, A. B., & Draper, D. C. (1981). Peer relationships of the academically gifted: A review. *Gifted Child Quarterly*, *25*, 129–33.

Aviram, A., & Milgram, R. M. (1977). Dogmatism, locus of control, and creativity in children educated in the Soviet Union, the United States, and Israel. *Psychological Reports*, *40*, 27–34.

Ayman-Nolley, S. (in press). Vygotsky's perspective on the development of imagination and creativity. *Creativity Research Journal*.

Bailin, S. (in press). *Achieving extraordinary ends: An essay on creativity*. Norwood, NJ: Ablex.

Balazs, E. (1982). Movement therapy in the classroom. In E. T. Nickerson and K. S. O'Laughlin (Eds.), *Helping through action: Action-oriented therapies*. Amherst, MA: Human Resource Development Press.

Bandler, R., & Grinder, J. (1979). *Frogs into princes*. Moab, UT: Real People Press.

Barbe, W., & Milone, M. (1982). Modality characteristics of gifted children. *G.C./T*, 21 (January–February), 2–5.

Barron, F., & Harrington, D. M. (1981). Creativity, intelligence, and personality. *Annual Review of Psychology*, *32*, 439–76.

Bauer, M. (1991). The relationships between and among learning styles perceptual preferences, instructional strategies, mathematics achievement, and attitude toward mathematics of learning disabled and emotionally handicapped students in a suburban junior high school. Doctoral dissertation, St. John's University.

Beaty, S. A. (1986). The effect of inservice training on the ability of teachers to observe learning styles of students. *Dissertation Abstracts International*, *47*, 1998A.

Blackburn, A. C., & Erickson, D. B. (1986). Predictable crises of the gifted student. *Journal of Counseling and Development*, *64*, 552–555.

Block, L. (1988) *Spider, spin me a web*. Cincinnati, OH: Writer's Digest Books.

Bloom, B. S. (1985). *Developing talent in young people*. New York: Ballantine Books.

Bogen, J. E. (1975). Some educational aspects of hemispheric specialization. *UCLA Educator*, *17*, 24–32.

Boyer, E. L. (1987). Early schooling and the nation's future. *Educational Leadership*, *44*, 4–8.

Branton, P. (1966). *The comfort of easy chairs*. FIRA Technical Report No. 22A. Herfordshire, England: Furniture Industry Research Association.

Brennan, P. K. (1982). Teaching to the whole brain. In James W. Keefe (Ed.), *Student learning styles and brain behavior*, 212–14. Reston, VA: National Association of Secondary School Principals.

———. (1984). An analysis of the relationships among hemispheric preference and analytic/global cognitive style, method of instruction, gender, and mathematics achievement of tenth-grade geometry students. *Dissertation Abstracts International*, *45*, 3271A.

Broberg, G. E., & Moran, J. D. (1988). Creative potential and conceptual tempo in preschool children. *Creativity Research Journal*, *1*, 115–21.

Brophy, J. (1986). Teacher influences on student achievement. *American Psychologist*, *41*, 1069–77.

Brunner, R., & Hill, D. (1992, April). Using learning styles research in coaching. *Journal of Physical Education, Recreation, and Dance*, *63*(4), 61.

Brunner, C. E., & Majewski, W. S. (1990, October). Mildly handicapped students can succeed with learning styles. *Educational Leadership*, *48*(02), 21–23.

Bruno, J. (1988). An experimental investigation of the relationships between and among hemispheric processing, learning style preferences, instructional strategies, academic achievement, and attitudes of developmental mathematics minority students in an urban technical college. *Dissertation Abstracts International*, *48*(5), 1066A.

Burke, B. C., Chrisler, J. C., & Devlin, A. S. (1989). The creative thinking, environmental frustration, and self-concept of left-and right-handers. *Creativity Research Journal*, *2*, 279–85.

Canfield, A. A., & Lafferty, J. C. (1976). *Learning style inventory*. Detroit: Humanics Media.

Carbo, M. (1980). An analysis of the relationship between the modality preferences of kindergarteners and selected reading treatments as they affect the learning of a basic sight-word vocabulary. *Dissertation Abstracts International*, *41*, 1389A.

Carbo, M., Dunn, R., & Dunn, K. (1986). *Teaching students to read through their individual learning styles*. Englewood Cliffs, NJ: Prentice-Hall.

Carnegie Council on Adolescent Development. (1989). *Turning points: Preparing youth for the 21st century*. New York: Carnegie Corporation of New York. (ED 312 322).

Carruthers, S., & Young, A. (1982). Preference of condition concerning time in learning environments of rural versus city eighth grade students. *Learning Styles Network Newsletter*, *1*(2).

Castle, E. B. (1961). *Ancient education and today*. Athens, GA: Penguin Books.

Chambers, J. (1973). College teachers: Their effects on creativity of students. *Journal of Educational Psychology*, *65*, 326–34.

Chand, I., & Runco, M. A. *Problem finding skills as components in the creative process*. Manuscript submitted for publication.

Clark-Thayer, S. (1987). The relationship of the knowledge of student-perceived learning style preferences and study habits and attitudes to achievement of college freshmen in a small urban university. *Dissertation Abstracts International*, *47*, 4046A.

———. (1988). Designing study skills programs based on individual learning styles. *Learning Styles Network Newsletter*, *9*(3), 1, 4.

Claxton, C., & Murrell, P. (1987). *Learning styles: Implications for improving educational practices*. Washington, DC: ERIC Clearinghouse on Higher Education.

Cody, C. (1983). Learning styles, including hemispheric dominance: A comparative study of average, gifted, and highly gifted students in grades five through twelve. *Dissertation Abstracts International*, *44*, 1631A.

Coleman, S. J. (1988). An investigation of the relationships among physical and emotional learning style preferences and perceptual modality strengths of gifted first-grade students. *Dissertation Abstracts International*, *50*(04), 874A.

College-level remedial education in the fall of 1989. (1991). U.S. Department of Educational Research and Improvement, NCES91–191a, Stick No. 065–000–00456. Washington, DC: Government Printing Office.

Conti, G., & Welborn, R. (1986). Teaching learning styles and the adult learner. *Lifelong Learning*, *9*(8), 20–24.

Council of Europe Newsletter, (1986, February). Genera: UNESCO.

Cox, C. (1926). *Genetic studies of genius. Vol. 2: The early mental traits of three geniuses*. Stanford, CA: Stanford University Press.

Cox, J., Daniel, N., & Boston, B. O. (1985). *Educating able learners. Programs and promising practices*. Austin, TX: University of Texas Press.

Crino, E. M. (1984). An analysis of the preferred learning styles of kindergarten children and the relationship of these preferred learning styles to curriculum planning for kindergarten children. *Dissertation Abstracts International, 45,* 1282A.

Crites, J. O. (1978). *Manual: Career maturity inventory.* Monterey, CA: CTB/McGraw-Hill.

Cropley, A. J. (in press). *More ways than one: Fostering creativity.* Norwood, NJ: Ablex.

Cross, J. A. (1982). Prevalence of internal locus of control in artistically talented students. Unpublished research project, University of Alabama.

Csikszentmihalyi, M. (1990). The domain of creativity. In M. A. Runco & R. S. Albert (Eds.), *Theories of creativity,* 190–212. Newbury Park, CA: Sage.

Curry, L. (1987). *Integrating concepts of cognitive or learning styles: A review with attention to psychometric standards.* Ottawa, Ontario: Canadian College of Health Services Executives.

Cutshall, A. (1964). *The Philippines: Nation of islands.* Princeton, NJ: D. Van Nostrand.

Davis, D., & Schwimmer, P. C. (1981). Style—a manner of thinking. *Educational Leadership, 38,* 376–77.

Dean, W. L. (1982). A comparison of the learning styles of educable mentally retarded students and learning disabled students. *Dissertation Abstracts International, 43,* 1923A.

DeBello, T. (1985). A critical analysis of the achievement and attitude effects of administrative assignments to social studies writing instruction based on identified, eighth grade students' learning style preferences for learning alone, with peers, or with teachers. *Dissertation Abstracts International, 47,* 68A.

———. (1990). Comparisons of eleven major learning styles models: Variables, appropriate populations, validity of instrumentation, and the research behind them. *Journal of Reading, Writing, and Learning Disabilities International, 6*(3) 203–22.

DeGregoris, C. N. (1986). Reading comprehension and the interaction of individual sound preferences and varied auditory distractions. *Dissertation Abstracts International, 47,* 3380A.

Delisle, J. R. (1982) Striking out: Suicide and the gifted adolescent. *Gifted/Creative/Talented, 13,* 16–19.

Della Valle, J. (1984). An experimental investigation of the word recognition scores of seventh-grade students to provide supervisory and administrative guidelines for the organization of effective instructional environments. *Dissertation Abstracts International, 45,* 359A.

———. (1990, July-September). The development of a learning styles program in an affluent, suburban New York elementary school. *Journal of Reading, Writing, Learning Disabilities: International, 6*(3), 315–22.

Dembo, M. (1988). *Applying educational psychology in the classroom.* Third ed. New York: Longman.

Denny, D., & Wolf, R. (1984). Comparison of two personality tests as measures of left-right brain cerebral hemisphere preference and creativity correlates. *Journal of Creative Behavior, 8,* 142–46.

Douglas, C. (1979). Making biology easier to understand. *American Biology Teacher, 41*(5), 277–99.

Drew, M. (1992). An experimental investigation of the relationships between and among ethnicity, story content, learning style instructional strategies, and their effects on the story-recall of fourth- fifth-, and sixth-grade Cajun and Louisiana Indian underachievers. Doctoral dissertation.

Dudek, S. Z., & Hall, W. (in press). Consistency and change: IPAR architects 25 years later. *Creativity Research Journal, 4*.

Dunn, R. (1984). How should students do their homework? *Early Years, 15*(4), 43–45.

———. (1987). Research on instructional environments: Implications for student achievement and attitudes. *Professional School Psychology, 2*, 43–52.

———. (1989a). Individualizing instruction for mainstreamed gifted children. In R. Milgram (Ed.), *Teaching gifted and talented learners in regular classrooms*, 63–111. Springfield, IL: Charles C. Thomas.

———. (1989b, Fall). Teaching gifted students through their learning style strengths. *International Education, 16*(51), 6–8.

———. (1989c, Summer). Do students from different cultures have different learning styles? *International Education, 16*(50), 40–42.

———. (Spring, 1990a). When you really have to lecture, teach students through their perceptual strengths, part one. *International Education, 17*(53), 1, 6–7.

———. (1990b). Teaching young children to read: Matching methods to learning styles perceptual processing strengths, part two. *International Education, 17*(55), 5–7.

———. (1990c). Rita Dunn answers questions people ask about learning styles. *Educational Leadership, 48*(2), 15–19.

———. (1990d). Understanding the Dunn and Dunn learning styles model and the need for individual diagnosis and prescription. *Journal of Reading Writing, and Learning Disabilities: International, 6*(3) 223–47.

Dunn, R., Beaudry, J. A. & Klavas, A. (1989). Survey of research on learning styles. *Educational Leadership, 48*(6) 50–58.

Dunn, R., Bruno, A., & Gardiner, B. (1984). Put a cap on your gifted program. *Gifted Child Quarterly, 28*, 70–72.

Dunn, R., Bruno, J., Sklar, R., & Beaudry, J. (1990). Effects of matching and mismatching minority developmental college students' hemispheric preferences on mathematics scores. *Journal of Educational Research, 83*(5), 283–88.

Dunn, R., Cavanaugh, D., Eberle, B., & Zenhausern, R. (1982). Hemispheric preference: The newest element of learning style. *American Biology Teacher, 44*(5), 291–94.

Dunn, R., DeBello, T., Brennan, P., Krimsky, Jr., & Murrain, P. (1981). Learning style researchers define differences differently. *Educational Leadership, 38*, 372–75.

Dunn, R., Deckinger, E. L., Withers, P., & Katzenstein, H. (1990, Winter). Should college students be taught how to do homework? The effects of studying marketing through individual perceptual strengths. *Illinois School Research and Development Journal, 26*(3), 96–113.

Dunn, R., Della Valle, J., Dunn, K., Geisert, G., Sinatra, R., & Zenhausern, R. (1986). The effects of matching and mismatching students' mobility preferences on recognition and memory tasks. *Journal of Educational Research, 79*(5), 267–72.

Dunn, R., & Dunn, K. (1972). *Practical approaches to individualizing instruction: Contracts and other effective teaching strategies*. Nyack, NY: Parker Publishing.

———. (1974). Learning style questionnaire. In *Educator's self-teaching guide to individualizing instructional programs*. Englewood Cliffs, NJ: Prentice-Hall.

———. (1975). Educator's self-teaching guide to individualizing instructional programs. Englewood Cliffs, NJ: Prentice-Hall.

————. (1978). *Teaching students through their individual learning styles: A practical approach*. Reston, VA: Reston Publishing.

————. (1992). *Teaching elementary students through their individual learning styles*. Boston: Allyn & Bacon.

————. (1993). *Teaching secondary students through their individual learning styles*. Boston: Allyn & Bacon.

Dunn, R., Dunn, K., and Price, G. E. (1975, 1979, 1981, 1984, 1989). *Learning style inventory*. Lawrence, KS: Price Systems.

————. (1977). Diagnosing learning styles: Avoiding malpractice suits against school systems. *Phi Delta Kappan, 58*, 418–20.

————. (1980). The learning style characteristics of gifted children. *Gifted Child Quarterly, 24*(1), 33–36.

————. (1985). *Manual: Learning style inventory*. Lawrence, KS: Price Systems.

————. (1982, 1990). *Productivity environmental preference survey*. Lawrence, KS: Price Systems.

Dunn, R., Dunn, K., Primavera, L., Sinatra, R., & Virostko, J. (1987). A timely solution: A review of research on the effects of chronobiology on children's achievement and behavior. *Clearing House, 61*(1), 5–8.

Dunn, R., Dunn, K., & Treffinger, D. J. (1992). *Bringing out the giftedness in your child*. New York: John Wiley & Sons.

Dunn, R., Gemake, J., Jalali, F., Zenhausern, R., Quinn, P., & Spiridakis, J. (1990, April). Cross-cultural differences in learning styles of elementary-age students from four ethnic backgrounds. *Journal of Multicultural Counseling and Development, 18*(2), 68–93.

Dunn, R., Giannitti, M., Murray J., Geisert, G., Rossi, I., & Quinn, P. (1990). Grouping students for instruction: Effects of individual vs. group learning style on achievement and attitudes. *Journal of Social Psychology, 130*(4), 485–94.

Dunn, R., & Griggs, S. A. (1988a). High school dropouts: Do they learn differently from those who remain in school? *The Principal, 34*(1), 1–8.

————. (1988b). *Learning style: Quiet revolution in American secondary schools*. Reston, VA: NASSP.

————. (1989). Learning styles: Quiet revolution in American secondary schools. *Momentum, 63*(1), 40–42.

————. (1990). Research on the learning style characteristics of selected racial and ethnic groups. *Journal of Reading, Writing, and Learning Disabilities: International, 6*(3). 261–80.

Dunn, R., & Klavas, A. (1988). *A Review of articles and books*. Jamaica, NY: Learning Styles Network, School of Education and Human Service, St. John's University.

Dunn, R., Krimsky, J., Murray, J., & Quinn, P. (1985). Light up their lives: A review of research on the effects of lighting on children's achievement. *Reading Teacher, 38*(9), 863–69.

Dunn, R., & Price, G. E. (1980). Identifying the learning style characteristics of gifted students. *Gifted Child Quarterly, 24*, 33–36.

Dunn, R., Griggs, S. A. and Price, G. E. (in press). Comparison of the learning styles of fourth-, fifth-, and sixth-grade male and female Mexican American students in southern Texas and same-grade students in the general population of the United States. *Journal of Multicultural Development and Counseling*.

Dunn, R., Price, G. E., Dunn, K., & Griggs, S. A. (1981). Studies in students' learning styles. *Roeper Review*, *4*(2), 38–40.

Dunn, R., Bruno, J., Sklar, R., & Beaudry, J. (1990). Effects of matching and mismatching minority developmental college students' hemispheric preferences on mathematics scores. *Educational Research*, *83*(5), 283–88.

Dunn, R., White, R. M., & Zenhausern, R. (1982). An investigation of responsible versus less responsible students. *Illinois School Research and Development*, *19*(1), 19–24.

Edelman, M. W. (1987). *The children's time*. Washington, DC: Children's Defense Fund.

Eisenstadt, S. N. (1951). Youth, culture, and social structure in Israel. *British Journal of Sociology*, *2*, 104–14.

————— (1967), *Israeli society*. New York: Basic Books.

Erikson, E. H. (1950). *Childhood and society*. New York: Norton.

Fadley, J. L., & Hosler, V. N. (1979). *Understanding the alpha child at home and at school*. Springfield, IL: Charles C. Thomas.

Feist, G. J. (1991). Synthetic analytic thought: Similarities and differences among art and science students. *Creativity Research Journal*, *4*, 145–56.

Feldhusen, J. F., Bahlke, S. J., & Treffinger, D. J. (1969). Teaching creative thinking. *Elementary School Journal*, *70*, 48–53.

Fitt, S. (1975). The individual and his environment. In T. G. David and B. D. Wright (Eds.), *Learning environments*. Chicago: University of Chicago Press.

Fleming, V. J. (1989, August). Vocational classrooms with style. *Vocational Education Journal*, *10*(1), 36–39.

Flouris, G., Coulopoulos, D., & Spiridakis, J. (1981). *Self-concept of the child*. Athens, GA: Orosimo Press.

Forman, S. G., & McKinney, J. D. (1978). Creativity and achievement of second graders in open and traditional classrooms. *Journal of Educational Psychology*, *70*, 101–07.

Fox, L. H., & Washington, J. (1985). Programs for the gifted and talented: Past, present, and future. In F. D. Horowitz and M. O'Brien (Eds.), *The gifted and talented: Developmental perspectives*, 197–221. Washington, DC: American Psychological Association.

Freeley, M. E., (1984). An experimental investigation of the relationships among teachers' individual time preferences, inservice workshop schedules, instructional techniques and the subsequent implementation of learning style strategies in participants' classrooms. *Dissertation Abstracts International*, *46*, 403A.

Gadwa, K., & Griggs, S. A. (1985). The school dropout: Implications for counselors. *School Counselor*, *33*, 9–17.

Galbraith, J. (1983). *The gifted kids' survival guide*. Minneapolis, MN: Free Spirit.

Gardiner, B. (1986). An experimental analysis of selected teaching strategies implemented at specific times of the day and their effects on the social studies achievement test scores and attitudes of fourth-grade, low achievers in an urban school setting. *Dissertation Abstracts International*, *47*, 3307A.

Gardner, H. (1982). What we know (and do not know) about the two halves of the brain. In. H. Gardner (Ed.), *Art, mind, and brain*, 278–85. New York: Basic Books.

—————. (1983). *Frames of mind*. New York: Basic Books.

Garrett, S. L. (1991). The effects of perceptual preference and motivation on vocabulary and attitude test scores among high school students. Doctoral dissertation, University of La Verne, CA.

Geisert, G. (1991, March). Teacher union involvement in year-round schooling. Reprinted from *Government Union Review: A Quarterly Journal on Public Sector Labor Relations*, *11*(2), 6, 14.

Getzels, J. W., & Jackson, P. W. (1962). *Creativity and intelligence: Explorations with gifted students*. New York: John Wiley & Sons.

Giannitti, M. C. (1988). An experimental investigation of the relationships among the learning style sociological preferences of middle-school students (grades 6, 7, 8), their attitudes and achievement in social studies, and selected instructional strategies. *Dissertation Abstracts International*, *49*, 2911A.

Glover, J. A., Ronning, R. R., & Reynolds, C. (1989). *Handbook of creativity*. New York: Plenum.

Gochenour, T. (1990). *Considering Filipinos*. Yarmouth, ME: Intercultural Press.

Goertzel, V., & Goertzel, M. G. (1962). *Grades of eminence*. London: Constable.

Gorsky, H. (1990). *Creative thinking as a predictor of creative performance in elementary school students*. Unpublished master's thesis, Tel-Aviv University. (In Hebrew. Available from author, c/o R. M. Milgram, Tel-Aviv University School of Education, Ramat-Aviv, Israel 69978.)

Gough, H. G. (1979). A creative personality scale for the adjective check-list. *Journal of Personality and Social Psychology*, *37*, 1398–405.

Graham, B. C., Sawyers, J. K., & DeBord, K. B. (1989). Teacher's creativity, playfulness, and style of interaction with children. *Creativity Research Journal*, *2*, 41–49.

Gregorc, A. F. (1979). Learning/teaching styles: Potent forces behind them. *Educational Leadership*, *36*(4), 234–36.

Gregorc, A. F. (1985). *Inside styles: Beyond the basics*. Columbia, CT: Gregorc Associates.

Griggs, S. A. (1984). Counseling the gifted and talented based on learning styles. *Exceptional Children*, *50*, 429–32.

———. (1985). *Counseling students through their individual learning styles*. Ann Arbor, MI: Educational Resource Information Center for Counseling and Personnel Services. (Available from Center for the Study of Learning and Teaching Style, St. John's University, Jamaica, New York 11439.)

———. (1989, November). Students' sociological grouping preferences of learning styles. *The Clearing House*. Washington, DC: Heldref Publications, *63*(3), 135–39.

———. (1991). *Learning style counseling*. Ann Arbor, MI: Educational Resource Information Center for Counseling and Personal Services. (Available from Center for the Study of Learning and Teaching Style, St. John's University, New York 11439.)

Griggs, S. A., & Dunn, R. (1984). Selected case studies. *Gifted Child Quarterly*, *28* 115–19.

———. (1988). High school dropouts: Do they learn differently from those students who remain in school? *The Principal*, *34*(1), 1–7.

Griggs, S. A., & Price, G. (1980a). Learning styles of gifted versus average junior high school students. *Phi Delta Kappan*, *61*, 361.

————. (1980b). Comparison between the learning styles of gifted versus average suburban junior high school students. *Roeper Review*, *3*, 7–9.

————. (1982). A comparison between the learning styles of gifted versus average junior high school students. *Creative and Gifted Child Quarterly*, *7*, 39.

Griggs, S. A., Price, G. E., Kopel, S., & Swaine, W. (1984). The effects of group counseling with sixth-grade students using approaches that are compatible versus incompatible with selected learning style elements. *California Association for Counseling and Development Journal*, *5*, 28–35.

Gruber, H. (1985). Giftedness and moral responsibility: Creative thinking and human survival. In F. D. Horowitz and M. O'Brien (Eds.), *The gifted and talented*, 301–30. Washington, DC: American Psychological Association.

————. (1988). The evolving systems approach to creative work. *Creativity Research Journal*, *1*, 27–51.

————. (1956). The structure of intellect. *Psychological Bulletin*, *53*, 267–93.

Guilford, J. P. (1967). *The nature of human intelligence*. NY: McGraw-Hill.

————. (1968). *Creativity, intelligence, and their educational implications*. San Diego, CA: Knapp/EDITS.

Guzzo, R. S. (1987). Dificuldades de apprenddizagem: Modalidade de attencao e analise de tarefas em materials didaticos. Doctoral dissertation, University of Saint Paulo, Institute of Psychology, Brazil.

Hale-Benson, J. E. (1982). *Black children: Their roots, culture, and learning styles*. Baltimore, MD: Johns Hopkins University Press.

Hanson, J., Silver, H., & Strong, R. (1984). Research on the roles of intuition and feeling. *Roeper Review*, *6*, 167–70.

Harp, T. Y., & Orsak, L. (1990, July-September). One administrator's challenge: Implementing a learning style program at the secondary level. *Journal of Reading, Writing, and Learning Disabilities International*, *6*(3), 335–42.

Hedges, L. V., Giaconia, R. M., & Gage, N. L. (1981). *Meta-analysis of the effects of open and traditional education*. Stanford, CA: Stanford University Program on Teaching Effectiveness.

Helson, R. (1987). Which of those women with creative potential became creative: In R. Hogan & W. H. Jones (Eds.), *Perspectives in personality*, Vol. 2, 51–92. Greenwich, CT: JAI.

Hennessey, B. (1990). The effect of extrinsic constraint on children's creativity while using a computer. *Creativity Research Journal*, *2*, 151–68.

Hill, J. E. (1964). *Cognitive style interest inventory* (Available from Oakland Community College, 2480 Opdyke Road, Bloomfield Hills, Michigan).

Hoceavar, D. (1979). Ideational fluency as a confounding factor in the measurement of originality. *Journal of Educational Psychology*, *71*, 191–96.

Hodges, H. (1985). An analysis of the relationships among preferences for a formal/informal design, one element of learning style, academic achievement, and attitudes of seventh- and eighth-grade students in remedial mathematics classes in a New York City junior high school. *Dissertation Abstracts International*, *45*, 2791A.

Holland, J. L. (1961). Creative and academic performance among talented adolescents. *Journal of Educational Psychology*, *52*, 136–47.

Holland, J. L., & Austin, A. W. (1962). The prediction of the academic, artistic, scientific, and social achievement of undergraduates of superior scholastic aptitude. *Journal of Educational Psychology*, *53*, 132–43.

Holland, J. L., & Nichols, R. C. (1964). Prediction of academic and extracurricular achievement in college. *Journal of Educational Psychology*, *55*, 55–65.

Holland, J. L., & Richards, J. M., Jr. (1965). Academic and nonacademic accomplishment: Correlated or uncorrelated? *Journal of Educational Psychology*, *56*, 165–74.

Hong, E., Whiston, S. C., & Milgram, R. M. (in press). Leisure activities in career guidance for gifted and talented adolescents: A validation study of the Tel Aviv Activities Inventory, *Gifted Child Quarterly*.

Hong, E., Milgram, R. M., & Whiston, S. C. (in press). Leisure activities in adolescents as a predictor of occupational choice in young adults, *Journal of Career Development*.

Hoppe, K. D., & Kyle, N. (1990). Dual brain, creativity, and health. *Creativity Research Journal*, *3*, 150–57.

Houtz, J. C., Jambor, S. O., Cifone, A., & Lewis, C. D. (1989). Locus of evaluation control, task directions, and type of problem effects on creativity. *Creativity Research Journal*, *2*, 118–25.

Hoyt, C. F. (1941). Test reliability estimated by analysis of variance. *Psychometrics*, *6*, 153–60.

Hunt, D. E. (1979). Learning style and student needs: An introduction to conceptual level. In J. W. Keefe (Ed.), *Student learning style: Diagnosing and prescribing programs*, 27–38. Reston, VA: National Association of Secondary School Principals.

Ignelzi-Ferraro, D. M. (1989). Identification of the preferred conditions for learning among three groups of mildly-handicapped high school students using the learning style inventory. *Dissertation Abstracts International*, *51*(3), 796A.

Ingham, J. (1989). An experimental investigation of the relationships among learning style, perceptual preference, instructional strategies, training achievement, and attitudes of corporate employees. *Dissertation Abstracts International*, *51*, 02A.

———. (1991). Matching instruction with employee perceptual preferences significantly increases training effectiveness. *Human Resource Development Quarterly.* 2(1), 53–64.

Iplan/Ipea, UNICEF, SUDENE, (1986). *O menor e apobrez* (The young and the poor). Serie instrumentos para a acao, n.5, Brasilia: UNICEF.

Isaksen, S. G., Ed. (1987). *Frontiers of creativity research: Beyond the basics*. Buffalo, NY: Bearly Ltd.

Isaksen, S. G., & Treffinger, D. (1985). *Creative problem solving: The basic course*. Buffalo, NY: Bearly Ltd.

Jacobs, R. L. (1987). An investigation of the learning style differences among Afro-American and Euro-American high, average, and low achievers. *Dissertation Abstracts International*, *49*(01), 39–A.

Jalali, F. (1988). A cross cultural comparative analysis of the learning styles and field dependence/independence characteristics of selected fourth-, fifth-, and sixth-grade students of Afro, Chinese, Greek, and Mexican heritage. *Dissertation Abstracts International*, *50*(62), 344A.

Janos, P. M., & Robinson, N. M. (1985). Psychosocial development in intellectually-gifted children. In F. D. Horowitz & M. O'Brien (Eds.), *The gifted and talented:*

Developmental perspectives, 149–95. Washington, DC: American Psychological Association.

Jarsonbeck, S. (1984). The effects of a right-brain and mathematics curriculum on low achieving, fourth grade students. *Dissertation Abstracts International, 45* 2791A.

Johnson, C. D. (1984). Identifying potential school dropouts. *Dissertation Abstracts International, 45*, 2397A.

Kazamias, Andreas, (1988). The curse of Sisyphus in Greek educational reform: A socio-political and cultural interpretation. *Modern Greek Studies Yearbook, 6*, 33–53.

Keefe, J. W. (1982). Assessing student learning styles: An overview. In *Student learning styles and brain behavior*, 43–53. Reston, VA: National Association of Secondary School Principals.

Keefe, J. W., Monk, J. S., Languis, M., Letteri, C. A., & Dunn, R. (1986). *Learning style profile*. Reston, VA: National Association of Secondary School Principals.

Kerr, B. A., & Miller, J. (1986). (Eds.) Introduction: Special issue: Counseling the gifted and talented. *Journal of Counseling and Development, 64*, 547.

Kfir, B. (1989). Creative thinking and creative performance as predictors of creative achievements in architecture. Unpublished master's thesis, Tel-Aviv University. (In Hebrew. Available from author, c/o R. M. Milgram, Tel-Aviv University, School of Education, Ramat-Aviv, Israel 69978.)

Kirby, J. R., & Das, J. P. (1977). Reading achievement, I.Q., and simultaneous-successive processing. *Journal of Educational Psychology, 69*(5), 64–70.

Kirby, P. (1979). *Cognitive style, learning style, and transfer skill acquisition*. Information Series 195, National Center for Research in Vocational Education. Columbus, OH: Ohio State University.

Kirton, M. J. (1976). Adaptors and innovators: A description and measure. *Journal of Applied Psychology, 61*, 622–29.

———. (1987). Adaptors and innovators: Cognitive style and personality. In S. G. Isaksen (Ed.), *Frontiers of creativity research: Beyond the basics*, 282–304. Buffalo, NY: Bearly Ltd.

———. (1988). Adaptors and innovators: Problem solvers in organizations. In K. Gronhaug & G. Kaufman (Eds.), *Innovation: A cross-disciplinary perspective*, 65–85. Oslo: Norwegian University Press.

Kivlighan, J. R., Hageseth, J. A., Tipton, R. M., & McGovern, T. V. (1981). Effects of matching treatment approaches and personality types in group vocational counseling. *Journal of Counseling Psychology, 28*, 315–20.

Klavas, A. (1990). Resources for teachers and trainers getting started with learning styles. *Journal of Reading, Writing, and Learning Disabilities: International, 6*(3), 369–77.

———. (1991). Implementation of the Dunn and Dunn learning styles model in United States elementary schools: Principals' and teachers' perceptions of factors that facilitated or impeded the process. Doctoral dissertation, St. John's University.

Koester, L. S., Farley, F. H. (1977). Arousal and hyperactivity in open and traditional education. Paper presented at the annual convention of the American Psychological Association, San Francisco. ERIC Document Reproduction Service No. ED 155 543.

Kohlberg, L. (1987). The development of moral judgment and moral action. In L. Kohlberg (Ed.), *Child psychology and childhood education: A cognitive developmental view*. New York: Longman.

Kostakis, A. (1987, October). Differences among school outputs and educational production functions. *Sociology of Education, 60*, 232–41.

Kreitner, K. R. (1981). Modality strengths and learning styles of musically talented high school students. Unpublished master's dissertation, Ohio State University.

Krimsky, J. (1982). A comparative analysis of the effects of matching and mismatching fourth-grade students with their learning style preferences for the environmental element of light and their subsequent reading speed and accuracy scores. *Dissertation Abstracts International, 43*, 66A.

Kroon, D. (1985). An experimental investigation of the effects on academic achievement and the resultant administrative implications of instruction congruent and incongruent with secondary, industrial arts students' learning style perceptual preferences. *Dissertation Abstracts International, 46*, 3247A.

Lan Yong, F. (1989). Ethnic, gender, and grade differences in the learning style preferences of gifted minority students. Doctoral dissertation, Southern Illinois University at Carbondale.

Learning Styles Network Newsletter, Winter, 1993. New York: St. John's University's Center for the Study of Learning and Teaching Styles.

Learning style profiles of underachieving elementary students. *Learning Styles Network Newsletter* (1991, Winter). NY: St. John's University's Center for the Study of Learning and Teaching Styles, *11*(3), 1, 8.

LeClair, T. J. (1986). The preferred perceptual modality of kindergarten-aged children. *Master's Abstracts, 24*, 324.

Lemmon, P. (1985). A school where learning styles make a difference. The *Principal, 64*(4), 26–29.

Lengal, O. (1983). Analysis of the preferred learning styles of former adolescent psychiatric patients. *Dissertation Abstracts International, 44* 2344A.

Letteri, C. A. (1980). Cognitive profile: Basic determinant of academic achievement. *Journal of Educational Research, 73*, 195–99.

Levy, J. (1979, September). Human cognition and lateralization of cerebral functions. *Trends in Neuroscience, 2*, 222–225.

―――. (1982, Autumn). What do brain scientists know about education? *Learning Styles Network Newsletter, 3*(3), 4–5, 8.

Lindauer, M. S. (in press). Creativity in aging artists: Contributions from the humanities. *Creativity Research Journal*.

Luria, A. R. (1973). *The working brain*. London: Penguin.

Lynch, P. K. (1981). An analysis of the relationships among academic achievement, attendance, and the learning style time preferences of eleventh- and twelfth-grade students identified as initial or chronic truants in a suburban New York school district. *Dissertation Abstracts International, 42*, 1880A.

Lyne, N. A. (1979). The relationship between adult students' level of cognitive development and their preference for learning format. Doctoral dissertation, University of Maryland.

MacKinnon, D. W. (1978). *In search of human effectiveness*. New York: Creative Education Foundation.

MacMurren, H. (1985). A comparative study of the effects of matching and mismatching sixth-grade students with their learning style preferences for the physical element of intake and their subsequent reading speed and accuracy scores and attitudes. *Dissertation Abstracts International, 46* 3247A.

Madison, M. B. (1984). A study of learning style preferences of specific learning disability students. *Dissertation Abstracts International, 46*, 3320A.

Majorikbanks, K. (1983). Families and their learning environment. London: Routledge & Kegan.

Marcus, L. (1977). How teachers view learning styles. *NASSP Bulletin* (61), 408: 112–14.

Marland, S. P., Jr. (1972). *Education of the gifted and talented*. Washington, DC: U.S. Government Printing Office.

Martini, M. (1986). An analysis of the relationships between and among computer-assisted instruction, learning style perceptual preferences, attitudes, and science achievement of seventh-grade students in a suburban, New York school district. *Dissertation Abstracts International, 47*, 877A.

Massialas, B. G., Flouris, G., & Cassotakis, M. (1988). Greece. In *World education encyclopedia*, Vol. 1, 479–95.

Masten, W. G. (1989). Learning style, repeated stimuli, and originality in intellectually gifted adolescents. *Psychological Reports, 65*, 751–54.

McClelland, D. C. (1963). An aspect of scientific performance. In C. W. Taylor & F. Barron (Eds.), In *Scientific creativity: Its recognition and development*, 184–92. New York: Wiley.

———. (1973). Testing for competence rather than "intelligence." *American Psychologist, 28*, 1–14.

McDermott, A. (1988). *Egypt from Nassar to Mubarak: A flawed revolution*. London: Croom Helm Publishing.

McEwen, P. (1985). Learning styles, intelligence, and creativity among elementary school students. Unpublished masters project, Buffalo State College, Center for Studies in Creativity.

McLaughlin, J. (1990). *Building a case for arts education: An annotated bibliography of major research*. Lexington, KY: Kentucky Alliance for Arts Education.

Mednick, S. A. (1962). The associative basis for the creative process. *Psychological Review, 69*, 200–32.

Mein, J. R. (1986). Cognitive and learning style characteristics of high school gifted students. *Dissertation Abstracts International, 48*, 04, 880A.

Middle school reading program produces "phenomenal" results. (1991, Spring). *Learning Styles Network Newsletter* NY: St. John's University's Center for the Study of Learning and Teaching Styles, *12*(1), 1–3.

Mickler, M. L., & Zipert, C. P. (1987). Teaching strategies based on learning styles of adult students. *Community/Junior College Quarterly, 11*, 33–37.

Miles, B. (1987). An investigation of the relationships among the learning style sociological preferences of fifth-and sixth-grade students, selected interactive classroom patterns, and achievement in career awareness and career decision-making concepts. *Dissertation Abstracts International 48* 2527A.

Milgram, R. M. (1980). Creativity as original problem-solving in lower- and middle-class children of different ability levels. Tel Aviv University, Ramat Aviv, Israel. Technical report submitted to the Israel Foundation Trustees; The Ford Foundation in Israel. *Resources in Education*, Educational Resources Information Center (ERIC), November 1981.

———. (1983). A validation of ideational fluency measures of original thinking in children. *Journal of Education Psychology, 75*, 619–24.

————. (Ed.) (1989). *Teaching gifted and talented learners in regular classrooms*. Springfield, IL: Charles C. Thomas.

————. (1990a). Creativity: An idea whose time has come and gone? In M. A. Runco & R. S. Albert (Eds.), *Theories of creativity*. Newbury Park, CA: Sage.

————. (1987, 1990b), *Tel Aviv activities inventory*, Tel Aviv: Tel Aviv University, School of Education.

————. (Ed.). (1991a). *Counseling gifted and talented learners: A guide for counselors, teachers, and parents*. Norwood, NJ: Ablex.

————. (1991b). Career education for gifted and talented learners. In R. Milgram (Ed.), *Counseling gifted and talented children: A guide for teachers, counselors, and parents*. Norwood, NJ: Ablex.

————. (1992). Identifying gifted and talented children and adolescents around the world. In. U. P. Gielen, L. L. Adler, & N. A. Milgram (Eds.), *Psychology in international perspective*, 233–248. International Council of Psychologists, Special Anniversary Volume.

————. (in press). Predicting outcomes of giftedness through intrinsically motivated behavior in adolescence. In S. G. Isaksen, M. M. Murdock, R. L. Firestien, & D. J. Treffinger (Eds.), *Nurturing and developing creativity: The emergence of a discipline*. Norwood, NJ: Ablex.

Milgram, R. M., & Arad, R. (1981). Ideational fluency as a predictor of original problem-solving. *Journal of Educational Psychology*, *73*, 568–72.

Milgram, R., & Goldring, E. B. (1991). Special education options for gifted and talented learners. In R. Milgram (Ed.), *Counseling gifted and talented children: A guide for teachers, counselors, and parents*, 23–26. Norwood, NJ: Ablex.

Milgram, R. M., & Milgram, N. A. (1976a). Group versus individual administration in the measurement of creative thinking in gifted and nongifted children. *Child Development*, *47*, 563–65.

————. (1976b). Creative thinking and creative performance in Israeli children. *Journal of Educational Psychology*, *68*, 255–59.

Milgram, R. M., Milgram, N. A., & Landau, E. (1974). Identification of gifted children in Israel: A theoretical and empirical investigation. Tel Aviv University, Ramat Aviv, Israel. Technical report submitted to the Israel Ministry of Education. *Resources in Education*, Educational Resources Information Center (ERIC), April 1980.

Milgram, R. M., Milgram, N. A., Rosenbloom, G., & Rabkin, L. (1978). Quantity and quality of creative thinking in children and adolescents. *Child Development*, *49*, 385–88.

Milgram, R. M., Moran, J. D., Sawyers, J. K., & Fu, V. (1987). Original thinking in Israeli preschool children. *School Psychology International*, *8*, 54–58.

Milgram, R. M. & Rabkin, L. (1980). A developmental test of Mednick's associative hierarchies of original thinking. *Developmental Psychology*, *16*, 157–58.

Milgram, R. M., Yitzak, V., & Milgram, N. A. (1977). Creative activity and sex-role identity in elementary school children. *Perceptual and Motor Skills*, *45*, 71–376.

Miller, A. (in press). Einstein and Poincare. *Creativity Research Journal*.

Miller, L. M. (1985). Mobility as an element of learning style: The effect its inclusion or exclusion has on student performance in the standardized testing environment. Unpublished master's dissertation, University of North Florida.

Miller, C. D., Alway, M., & McKinley, D. (1987). Effects of learning styles and strategies on academic success. *Journal of College Student Personnel*, *28*(5), 399–404.

Moran, J. D., Milgram, R. M., Sawyers, J. K., & Fu, V. R. (1983). Original thinking in preschool children. *Child Development*, *54*, 921–26.

Mudd, S. A. (1987). Analytic review of the Kirton adaptation innovation inventory. St. Louis: University of Minnesota, Social and Behavioral Sciences Documents, 163pp.

Moreno, Z. T. (1983). Psychodrama. In H. I. Kaplan & B. J. Sadock (Eds.), *Comprehensive group psychotherapy*, 2nd Ed. Baltimore: William & Wilkins.

Murrain, P. G. (1983). Administrative determinations concerning facilities utilization and instructional grouping: An analysis of the relationships between selected thermal environments and preferences for temperature, an element of learning style, as they affect word recognition scores of secondary students. *Dissertation Abstracts International*, *44* 1749A.

Murray, C. A. (1980). The comparison of learning styles between high and low reading achievement subjects in the seventh and eighth grades in public middle school. *Dissertation Abstracts International*, *41*, 1005A.

Myers, I., & McCaulley, M. (1985). *Manual for the Myers-Briggs type indicator*. Palo Alto, CA: Consulting Psychologists Press.

National Commission on Excellence in Education. (1983). *A Nation at risk: The imperative for educational reform*. Washington, DC: U.S. Government Printing Office.

National Commission on Secondary Education for Hispanics: Hispanic policy development project. (1984). *Make something happen: Hispanics and urban high school reform, Vol. 1*. Washington, DC: U.S. Government Printing Office.

Nganwa-Bagumah, Margaret J. (1986). Learning styles: The effects of matching and mismatching pupils' design preferences on reading comprehension tests. Bachelor's dissertation, University of Transkei, South Africa.

Nicholls, J. (1983). Originality in the person who will never produce anything useful or creative. In R. S. Albert, *Genius and eminence: A social psychology of creativity and exceptional achievement*, 265–79. New York: Pergamon.

Ochse, R. (1990). *Before the gates of excellence: The determinants of creative genius*. New York: Cambridge University Press.

Okuda, S. M., Runco, M. A., & Berger, D. E. (1990). Creativity and the finding and solving of real-world problems. *Journal of Psychoeducational Assessment*, *9*, 45–53.

Oliva, P. (1988). Education and community views. In R. A. Gorton, G. T. Schneider, & J. C. Fisher (Eds.), *Encyclopedia of school administration & supervision*, 104–105. Phoenix, NY: Oryx Press.

Oliver, E. E. (1982). Greece: A study of the educational system and a guide to the academic placement of students in educational institutions of the United States. In *World Education Series*, Washington, DC: American Association of Collegiate Registrars and Admissions Office.

Orsak, L. (1990a, July-September). Learning styles and love: A winning combination. *Journal of Reading, Writing, and Learning Disabilities: International*, *6*(3), 343–46.

———. (1990b). Learning styles versus the Rip Van Winkle syndrome. *Educational Leadership*, *48*(2), 19–20.

Ortar, G. (1980). *Milta intelligence scale*. Jerusalem, Israel: Hebrew University School of Education and Israel Ministry of Education.

O'Quin, K., & Besemer, S. P. (1989). The development, reliability, and validity of the Revised Creative Product Semantic Scale. *Creativity Research Journal, 2*, 267–75.

Paskowitz, B. U. (1985). A study of the relationship between learning styles and attitudes toward computer programming of middle-school gifted students. *Dissertation Abstracts International, 47*(03), 697A.

Paulu, N. (1987). *Dealing with dropouts: The urban superintendents' call to action*. Washington, DC: U.S. Government Printing Office.

Pederson, J. K. (1984). The classification and comparison of learning disabled students and gifted students. *Dissertation Abstracts International, 46*, 342A.

Pellegrini, A. (in press). Rough and tumble play. *Creativity Research Journal*.

Perkins, D. N. (1981). *The mind's best work*. Cambridge, MA: Harvard University Press.

Perrin, J. (1993). *Learning style inventory: Primary version*. New York: Learning Styles Network, St. John's University.

———. (1984). An experimental investigation of the relationships among the learning style sociological preferences of gifted and non-gifted primary children, selected instructional strategies, attitudes, and achievement in problem solving and rote memorization. *Dissertation Abstracts International, 46*, 342A.

———. (1990). The learning styles project for potential dropouts. *Educational Leadership, 48*(2), 23–24.

Perrone, P. (1986). Guidance needs of gifted children, adolescents, and adults. *Journal of Counseling and Development, 64*, 6564–66.

Pirozzo, R. (1981). Gifted underachievers. *Roeper Review, 5*, 18–21.

Pizzo, J. 1981). An investigation of the relationships between selected acoustic environments and sound, an element of learning style, as they affect sixth grade students' reading achievement and attitudes. *Dissertation Abstracts International, 42*, 2475A.

Pizzo, J., Dunn, R., and Dunn, K. (1990, July-September). A sound approach to reading: Responding to students' learning styles. *Journal of Reading, Writing, and Learning Disabilities: International, 6*(3), 249–60.

Price, G. E. (1980a). Which learning style elements are stable and which change over time? *Learning Styles Network Newsletter, 1*(3), 1.

———. (1980b). Research using the learning style inventory. Paper presented at the Second Annual Conference on Teaching Students Through Their Individual Learning Styles, New York.

Price, G. E., Dunn, R., Dunn, K., & Griggs, S. A. (1981). Studies in students' learning styles. *Roeper Review, 4*(2), 38–40.

Prichard, B. (1985). Parenting gifted children—the fun, the frustration. *G.C./T, 41*, 10–13.

Psacharopoulos, G. (1990). Education and the professions in Greece in the light of 1992. *European Journal of Education, 25*, 1, 61–74.

Psomiades, H., Orfanos, S., & Spiridakis, J. (1988). *Education and Greek-Americans*. New York: Pella Publishing.

Ramirez, M., & Casteneda, A. (1974). *Cultural democracy: Bicognitive development and education*. New York: Academic Press.

Rancourt, R. (1988). *Knowledge accessing modes inventory*. Ottawa, Ontario: University of Ottawa.

Renzulli, J. (1978). What makes giftedness? Reexamining a definition. *Phi Delta Kappan*, *60*, 180–84.

———. (1980). What we don't know about programming for the gifted and talented. *Phi Delta Kappan*, *61*, 601–602.

———. (Ed.). (1986a). *Systems and models for developing programs for the gifted and talented*. Mansfield Center, CT: Creative Learning Press.

———. (1986b). The three-ring conception of giftedness: A developmental model for creative productivity. In R. Sternberg & J. E. Davidson (Eds.), *Conceptions of giftedness*, 53–92. New York: Cambridge University Press.

Restak, R. (1979). *The brain: The last frontier*. NY: Doubleday.

Review of research on perceptual strengths. (1991). *Learning Styles Network Newsletter*, *12*(1), 4–8.

Rhodes, M. (1961). An analysis of creativity. *Phi Dela Kappan*, *42*, 305–10.

Ricca, J. (1983). Curricular implications of learning style differences between gifted and non-gifted students. Doctoral dissertation. State University of New York at Buffalo.

———. (1984). Learning styles and preferred instructional strategies of gifted students. *Gifted Child Quarterly*, *28*, 121–26.

Richards, J. M., Jr., Holland, J. L., & Lutz, S. W. (1967). Prediction of student accomplishment in college. *Journal of Educational Psychology*, *58* 343–55.

Rodrigo, R. (1989). A comparison of the profiles of the learning styles of first-grade pupils at the Ateneo de Manila grade school for the school year 1988–89. Unpublished master's thesis, Ateneo de Manila University, Quezon City, Philippines.

Rodriquez, F. (1988). Minorities and the school system. In R. A. Gorton, G. T. Schneider, & J. C. Fisher (Eds.), *Encyclopedia of school administration and supervision*, 172–73. New York: Oryx Press.

Roe, A. (1963). Personal problems and science. In C. W. Taylor & F. Barfon (Eds.), *Scientific creativity: Its recognition and development*, 132–38. New York: Wiley.

Rosenblatt, R. & Winner, E. (1988). The art of children's drawing. In H. Gardner & D. Perkins (Eds.), *Art, mind, and education*. Urbana, IL: University of Chicago Press, 3–15.

Rosenthal, N. R. (1977). A prescriptive approach for counselor training. *Journal of Counseling Psychology*, *24*, 231–37.

Rothenberg, A., & Hausman, C. (1976). *The creativity question*. Durham, NC: Duke University Press.

Rubin, Z. (1982). Does personality really change after 20? In K. Gardner (Ed.), *Readings in developmental psychology*, 425–32. Boston, MA: Little, Brown.

Runco, M. A. (1984). Teachers' judgments of creativity and social validation of divergent thinking tests. *Perceptual and Motor Skills*, *59*, 711–17.

———. (1986). Maximal performance on divergent thinking tests by gifted, talented, and nongifted children. *Psychology in the Schools*, *23*, 308–15.

———. (1988). Creativity research: Originality, utility, and integration. *Creative Research Journal*, *1*, 1–7.

———. (1989). Parents' and teachers' ratings of the creativity of children. *Journal of Social Behavior and Personality*, *4*, 73–83.

———. (1993). Cognitive and psychometric issues in creativity research. In S. G.

Isaksen, M. C. Murdock, R. L. Firestien, & D. J. Treffinger (Eds.), *Understanding and recognizing creativity: The emergence of a discipline*. Norwood, NJ: Ablex.

————. (Ed.). (1991). *Divergent thinking*. Norwood, NJ: Ablex.

————. (in press-a). Children's divergent thinking and creative ideation. *Developmental Review*.

————. (in press-b). Cognitive and psychometric issues in creativity research. In S. G. Isaksen, M. C. Murdock, R. L. Firestien, & D. J. Treffinger (Eds.), *Understanding and recognizing creativity: The emergence of a discipline*. Norwood, NJ: Ablex.

————. (in press-c). The evaluation, valuative, and divergent thinking of children. *Journal of Creative Behavior*.

Runco, M. A., & Albert, R. S. (1985a). Exceptional giftedness in early adolescence and intrafamilial divergent thinking. *Journal of Youth and Adolescence, 15*, 333–42.

————. (1985b). The reliability and validity of ideational originality in the divergent thinking of academically gifted and nongifted children. *Educational and Psychological Measurement, 45*, 483–501.

————. (1987). The threshold hypothesis regarding creativity and intelligence: An empirical test with gifted and nongifted children. *Creative Child and Adult Quarterly, 11*, 212–18.

————. (Eds.). (1990). *Theories of creativity*. Newbury Park, CA: Sage.

Runco, M. A., & Chad, I. (in press). Problem finding skills as components in the creative process. *Journal of Personality and Individual Difference*.

Runco, M. A., & Okuda, S. M. (1991). Problem-discovery, divergent thinking, and the creative process. *Journal of Youth and Adolescence, 17*, 211–20.

Runco, M. A., & Vega, L. (1989). Evaluating the creativity of children's ideas. *Journal of Social Behavior and Personality, 5*, 439–52.

Sawyers, J., Moran, J. D., Fu, R., & Milgram, R. (1983). Familiar versus unfamiliar stimulus items in measurement of original thinking in young children. *Perceptual and Motor Skills, 57*, 51–55.

Schmeck, R. R., Ribich, F., & Ramanaiah, N. (1977). Development of self-report inventory for assessing individual differences in learning processes. *Applied Psychological Measurement, 1*, 413–31.

Sewall, T. J. (1986). *The measurement of learning style: A critique of four assessment tools*. Green Bay, WI: University of Wisconsin Assessment Center.

Shea, T. C. (1983). An investigation of the relationship among preferences for the learning style element of design, selected instructional environments, and reading achievement with ninth-grade students to improve administrative determinations concerning effective educational facilities. *Dissertation Abstracts International, 44*, 2004A.

Simonton, D. K. (1983). Formal education, eminence, and dogmatism: The curvilinear relationship. *Journal of Creative Behavior, 17*, 149–62.

————. (1984). *Genius, creativity, and leadership*. Cambridge, MA: Harvard University Press.

————. (1987) Developmental antecedents of achieved eminence. *Developmental Review, 4*, 131–69.

————. (1988). *Scientific genius*. New York: Cambridge University Press.

Sims, J. E. (1988). A comparative analysis of the learning styles of black-American,

Mexican-American, and white-American third-and fourth-grade students in traditional public schools. Doctoral dissertation, University of Santa Barbara.

————. (1989). Learning style: Should it be considered? *Oregon Elementary Principal*, *50*(2), 28.

Sinatra, C. (1990, July-September). Five diverse secondary schools where learning style instruction works. (1990, July-September). *Journal of Reading, Writing, and Learning Disabilities: International*, *6*(3), 323–34.

Smith, G.J.W., & Carlsson, I. (1990). *The creative process*. New York: International Universities Press.

Smolucha, F. (in press). The relevance of Vygotsky's theory of creative imagination for contempory research on play. *Creativity Research Journal*.

Snider, K. P. (1985). A study of learning preferences among educable mentally impaired, emotionally impaired, learning disabled, and general education students in seventh, eighth, and ninth grades as measured by response to the learning styles inventory. *Dissertation Abstracts International*, *46*, (05), SECA, 1251.

Sperry, R. (1964). The great cerebral commissure. *Scientific American*, *210*, 42–52.

Springer, S. P., & Deutsch, G. (1985). *Left brain, right brain*, Rev. (Ed.). New York: W. H. Freeman.

Spiridakis, J. (1983, Summer). Three diagnostic tools for use with the bilingual child. *Bilingual Journal*, *7*, 4.

————. (1988). Learning styles: An overview. *Technology and Education*, Proceedings of Third International Educational Conference, Orthodox Academy of Crete, October 15th–18th, 1987. Crete, Greece: Educational Society of Greece, Athens, 92–108.

————. (1991). Greek version of the learning style inventory. Photocopy. New York: St. John's University.

Steinberg, D. J. (1989). *The Philippines: A singular and plural place*. Boulder, CO: Westview Press.

Sternberg, R. J. (1990). T & T is an explosive combination: Technology and testing. *Educational Psychologist*, *25*(3&4), 201–22.

Sternberg, R. J., (Ed.). (1988). *The nature of creativity*. New York: Cambridge University Press.

Sternberg, R. J., & Davidson, J. E. (Eds.). (1986). *Conceptions of giftedness*. New York: Cambridge University Press.

Stewart, E. D. (1981). Learning styles among gifted/talented students: Instructional technique preferences. *Exceptional Children*, *48*(2), 134–38.

Stigler, J., & Stevenson, H. (1985). How Asian teachers polish each lesson to perfection. *American Education*. Washington, DC: Association of American Educators.

Sutton-Smith, B. (in press). The role of toys in the instigation of playful creativity. *Creativity Research Journal*.

Sykes, S., Jones, B., & Phillips, J. (1990, October). Partners in learning styles at a private schools. *Educational Leadership*, *48*(2), 24–26.

Tanenbaum, R. (1982). An investigation of the relationships between selected instructional techniques and identified field dependent and field independent cognitive styles as evidenced among high school students enrolled in studies of nutrition. *Dissertation Abstracts International*, *43*, 68A.

Tannenbaum, A. J. (1983). *Gifted children: Psychological and educational perspectives*. New York: Macmillan.

Tappenden, V. J. (1983). Analysis of the learning styles of vocational education and nonvocational education students in eleventh and twelfth grades from rural, urban, and suburban locations in Ohio. *Dissertation Abstracts International, 44*, 1326A.

Tegano, D. W., Sawyers, J. K., & Moran, J. D. (1989). Problem finding and solving in play: The teacher's role. *Childhood Education, 66*(2), 92–97.

Terman, L. M. (1935). *Genetic studies of genius: Mental and physical traits of a thousand gifted children.* Stanford, CA: Stanford University Press.

Terman, L. M., & Oden, M. H. (1947). *Genetic studies of genius: Vol. 4: The gifted child grows up: Twenty-five-year follow-up of a superior group.* Stanford, CA: Stanford University Press.

————. (1959). *Genetic studies of genius. Vol. 5: The gifted child at mid-life: Thirty-five-year follow-up of the superior child.* Stanford, CA: Stanford University Press.

Thies, A. (1979). A brain-behavior analysis of learning style. In J. W. Keefe (Ed.), *Students learning styles; Diagnosing and prescribing programs,* 55–61. Reston, VA: National Association of Secondary School Principals.

Tingley-Michaelis, C. (1983). Make room for movement. *Early Years, 13*(6), 26–29.

Thoresen, C. E., & Mahoney, M. J. (1974). *Behavioral self control.* New York: Holt, Rinehart, & Winston.

Thrasher, R. (1984). *A study of the learning style preferences of at-risk sixth- and ninth-grade students.* Pompano Beach, FL: Florida Association of Alternative School Educators.

Tolan, S. S. (1985). The exceptionally gifted child in school. *G/C/T, 41,* 10–13.

Torrance, E. P. (1963). *Education and the creative potential.* Minneapolis: University of Minnesota Press.

————. (1968). A longitudinal examination of the fourth-grade slump in creativity. *Gifted Child Quarterly, 12,* 195–99.

————. (1970). *Encouraging creativity in the classroom.* Dubuque, IA: William C. Brown.

————. (1974). *The Torrance tests of creative thinking—IICI Manual and Scoring Guide: Verbal test A, figural test.* Lexington, KY: Ginn.

————. (1981). Predicting the creativity of elementary school children (1958–1980) and the teacher who made a difference. *Gifted Child Quarterly, 25,* 55–62.

————. (1982). Hemisphericity and creative functioning. *Journal of Research and Development in Education, 15,* 29–37.

————. (1987). *Survey of the uses of the Torrance tests of creative thinking.* Bensenville, IL: Scholastic Testing Service.

Torrance, E. P. & Ball, O. E. (1978). *Streamlined scoring guide and norms manual for figural form A—IICI.* Athens, GA: Georgia Studies of Creative Behavior.

Torrance, E. P., & Goff, K. (1990). *Cumulative bibliography on the Torrance tests of creative thinking.* Athens, GA: Georgia Studies of Creative Behavior.

Torrance, E. P. & Wu, T. H. (1981). A comparative longitudinal study of adult creative achievements of elementary school children identified as highly intelligent and highly creative. *Creative Child and Adult Quarterly, 6,* 71–76.

Trautman, P. (1979). An investigation of the relationship between selected instructional techniques and identified cognitive style. *Dissertation Abstracts International, 40,* 1428A.

Treffinger, D. J. (1986). Gifted education and learning styles: New connections. *Learning Styles Newsletter, 7*(1), 4.

————. (1988). Components of creativity: Another look. *Creative Learning Today*, *2*(5), 1–4.

————. (1989). From potentials to productivity: Designing the journey to 2,000. *Gifted Children Today*, January-February 17–21.

————. (1991a). Future goals and directions. In N. Colangelo & G. Davis (Eds.), *Handbook of gifted education*, 441–49. Boston, MA: Allyn and Bacon.

————. (1991b). School reform and gifted education—opportunities and issues. *Gifted Child Quarterly*, *35*(1), 6–11.

————. (1991c). Creative productivity: Understanding its sources and nurture. *Illinois Council for the Gifted Journal*, *10*, 6–8.

Treffinger, D. J., Tallman, M. C., & Isaksen, S. G. (in press). Creative learning and problem solving: An overview. In M. Runco, (Ed.), *Problem finding, problem solving, and creativity*. Norwood, NJ: Ablex.

UNICEF/IBGE (1987). *Criancas e adolescentes: Indicadores socials*. (Children and adolescents: social indicators). Rio de Janeiro: Fundacao Instituto Brasileriro de Georgrafia e Estatistica.

Urbschat, K. (1977) A study of preferred learning modes and their relationship to the amount of recall of CVC trigrams. *Dissertation Abstracts International*, *38*, 2356–5A.

Vignia, R. A. (1983). An investigation of learning styles of gifted and non-gifted high school students. *Dissertation Abstracts International*, *44*, 3653A.

Virostko, J. (1983). An analysis of the relationships among academic achievement in mathematics and reading, assigned instructional schedules, and the learning style time preferences of third, fourth, fifth, and sixth grade students. *Dissertation Abstracts International*, *44*, 1683A.

Walberg, H. J., & Stariha, W. E. (in press). Enlarging human capital: Learning, creativity, and eminence. *Creativity Research Journal*.

Wallach, M. A. (1985). Creativity testing and giftedness. In F. D. Horowitz & M. O'Brien (Eds.), *The gifted and talented: Developmental perspectives*, 99–123. Washington, DC: American Psychological Association.

————. (1970). Creativity. In P. H. Mussen (Ed.), *Carmichael's manual of child psychology*, Vol. 1, Third Ed., 1211–72. Washington, DC: American Psychological Association.

————. (1971). *The intelligence/creativity distinction*. Morristown, NJ: General Learning Press.

Wallach, M. A., & Kogen, N. (1965). *Modes of thinking in young children*. New York: Holt, Rinehart & Winston.

Wallach, M. A., & Wing, C. W., Jr. (1969). *The talented student: A validation of the creativity-intelligence distinction*. New York: Holt, Rinehart & Winston.

Wasson, F. R. (1980). A comparative analysis of learning styles and personality characteristics of achieving and underachieving gifted elementary students. *Doctoral Dissertations*, 1980–1981. Ann Arbor, MI: University Microfilms International.

Wechsler, S. (1981). Identifying creative strengths in the responses to the verbal forms of the Torrance test of creative thinking. *Dissertation Abstracts International*, *42*, 3521 A, University Microfilms, n–82, 01588.

————. (1985). Assessment of verbal creative strengths in Brazilian adults. *School Psychology International*, *6*, 133–38.

————. (1990). Issues on stimulating creativity in the schools: A South American perspective. Paper presented at the International Research Conference on Creativity, Buffalo, NY.

————. (1991). Identificacao e desenvolvimento da criatividade (Identification and development of creativity).

Wechsler, S. & Richmond, B. (1982). Creative strengths of Brazilian and American children. *Interamerican Journal of Psychology, 16*, 27–32.

————. (1984). Influencias da dotacao intelectual e criativa no adjustamento em sala de aula (Influences of intellectual and creative capabilities on school adjustment). *Arquivos Brasileiros de Psicologia Aplicade, 36*, 138–47.

Wechsler, S., & Oakland, T. (1990). Preventive strategies for promoting the education of low income Brazilian children: Implications for school psychologists from other third-world nations. *School Psychology International, 11*, 83–90.

Weinberg, F. (1983). An experimental investigation of the interaction between sensory modality preference and mode of presentation in the instruction of arithmetic concepts to third grade underachievers. *Dissertation Abstracts International, 44*, 1740A.

Westbrook, B. W. (1972). *Career knowledge test.* Chapel Hill, NC: Center for Occupational Information.

Wheeler, R. (1980). An alternative to failure: Teaching reading to students' perceptual strengths. *Kappa Delta Pi Record, 17*(2), 59–63.

————. (1983). An investigation of the degree of academic achievement evidenced when second-grade, learning disabled students' perceptual preferences are matched and mismatched with complementary sensory approaches to beginning reading instruction. *Dissertation Abstracts International, 44*, 2039A.

White, R. (1981). An investigation of the relationship between selected instructional methods and selected elements of emotional learning style upon student achievement in seventh grade social studies. *Dissertation Abstracts International, 42*, 995–03A.

Wilson, M. (1989). *The arts and special education project.* Ottawa, Ontario: Ottawa Board of Education.

Wing, C. W., Jr., & Wallach, M. A. (1971). *College admissions and the psychology of talent.* New York: Holt, Rinehart & Winston.

Witkin, H. A. (1977). Educational implications of cognitive style. *Review of Educational Research, 47*, 1–64.

Wittig, C. (1985). Learning style preferences among students high or low on divergent thinking and feeling variables. Unpublished master's dissertation, State University College at Buffalo of New York, Center for Studies in Creativity.

Wolf, F. M., & Larson, G. L. (1981). On why adolescent formal operators may not be creative thinkers. *Adolescence, 62*, 345–48.

Zak, F. (1989). Learning style discrimination between vocational and nonvocational students. *Dissertation Abstracts International, 50*, 12A, 3843A.

Zenhausern, R. (1978). *Revised dominance scale.* New York: St. John's University.

————. (1979). *Differential hemispheric activation test.* New York: St. John's University, Department of Psychology.

————. (1980). Hemispheric dominance. *Learning Styles Network Newsletter*, New York: St. John's University and the National Association of Secondary School Principals, *1*, 3.

Zuckerman, H. (1977). *Scientific elite: Nobel laureates in the United States.* New York: Free Press.

Name Index

Subject Index

Achievement tests, problems with using, 37–38
Activities Inventory (1987), 25
Analytic learners, 19–20; characteristics of, 39
Art, learning style preferences in: for American students, 132; for Canadian students, 193–95; for Filipino students, 158; for Korean students, 184
Auditory learning, 17
Authority, learning style and, 16

Brain lateralization theory, 9
Brazil, factors affecting education in, 197–99
Brazil, gifted adolescents in: assessing creativity, 201–2; conclusions of study, 207–9, cross-cultural differences of learning styles compared with other countries, 235; cross-cultural similarities of learning styles compared with other countries, 235–37; learning style preferences, 203, 207; learning style preferences of creatively gifted, 199–200; research methodology used to study, 202–3

Canada, factors affecting education in, 187–88

Canada, gifted adolescents in: art and, 193–94; conclusions of study, 195; cross-cultural differences of creative activity compared with other countries, 237, 239; cross-cultural differences of learning styles compared with other countries, 230, 234; cross-cultural differences of learning styles in gifted adolescents compared with other countries, 241–42; cross-cultural similarities of creative activity compared with other countries, 237, 239, 241; cross-cultural similarities of learning styles compared with other countries, 235–37; cross-cultural similarities of learning styles in gifted adolescents compared with other countries, 242, 245; dance and, 191, 193; drama and, 194; Knowledge Accessing Modes Inventory (KAMI), 188; learning style preferences, 190–91, 193–94; learning style preferences of arts and regular program students compared, 194–95; learning style preferences of Canadian students compared with U.S. students, 189–90; literature and, 194; music and, 193; research methodology used to study,

About the Editors and Contributors

MARY RUE BRODHEAD is an educational consultant in Ottawa, Ontario, Canada, and co-author of *Teaching Learning for a Changing World*, a training package designed for teachers who teach Canadian students about developing countries.

EVA SAZO DE MENDEZ is Professor at Universidad del Valle, Universidad Francisco Marroquin and Universidad Rafael Landivar, in Guatemala City, Guatemala, Central America. She is currently completing an M.A. Program in Social Research at Universidad de Costa Rica. She is coordinating the Fourth National Educational Encounter on Initial Education and edits a bulletin for the World Health Organization.

RITA DUNN is Professor in the Division of Administrative and Instructional Leadership and Director of the Center for the Study of Learning and Teaching Styles at St. John's University, New York. She is co-author of 13 books including: *Learning Styles: Quiet Revolution in American Secondary Schools*; *Bringing Out the Giftedness in Every Child: A Guide for Parents*; *Teaching Elementary Students through their Individual Learning Styles*; and *Teaching Secondary Students through their Individual Learning Styles*.

SHIRLEY A. GRIGGS is Professor of Counselor Education in the Division of Human Services and Counseling at St. John's University, New York City. She has published approximately 45 articles on learning styles, child abuse and neglect, the gifted and talented, value issues in counseling, counselor licensure, and death education. She is the author of *Learning Styles Counseling*.

JOANNE INGHAM is Director of Adult Learning and Corporate Training at the Center for the Study of Learning and Teaching Styles, and Academic Advisor, Office of Academic Attainment at Adelphi University, New York.

ROBERTA M. MILGRAM is Associate Professor in the School of Education at Tel Aviv University, Israel. She has been studying giftedness and creativity in children and adolescents in Israel and in the United States for more than 20 years. She has published over 50 articles on the subject and edited two books: *Teaching Gifted and Talented Learners in Regular Classrooms* and *Counseling Gifted and Talented Children: A Guide for Counselors, Teachers and Parents*.

GARY E. PRICE is Professor and Co-Director of Training, Department of Counseling Psychology at the University of Kansas, Lawrence, Kansas. He has conducted workshops in the area of learning styles, published numerous articles and chapters, and recently has co-authored a monograph entitled *Counseling College Students Through Their Individual Learning Styles*. He is President of Kansas Association for Specialists in Group Work.

MARK A. RUNCO is Professor of Child Development at California State University, Fullerton. Dr. Runco is the founding editor since 1988 of the *Creativity Research Journal* and is senior editor of the *Creativity Monograph Series* (18 volumes). He has published several dozen articles on creativity and giftedness, is editor of *Theories of Creativity* and *Problem Finding, Problem Solving and Creativity*, and co-editor of *Divergent Thinking*.

SHAWN OKUDA SAKAMOTO is a doctoral student in Cognitive Psychology at the Claremont Graduate School and an educational researcher in the Western Regional Office of the Johns Hopkins University Center for Academically Talented Youth. Her research interests include the study of giftedness and creativity, and testing and assessment of creativity and its application.

EDWIN C. SELBY has been a music teacher in public schools since 1969. He is the founder and director of the Sussex Student Theater Project. This project provides middle school students with the opportunity to write and produce original plays. He is Chair of the Board of Directors of the Sussex County, New Jersey Teen Arts Festival.

RICHARD SINATRA is Professor of Reading and Director of the Reading Clinic of the Division of Human Services and Counseling, School of Education and Human services at St. John's University, New York. He has published numerous articles on reading, writing, special education, and visual literacy and a book entitled *Visual Literacy Connections to Thinking, Reading and Writing*. He is co-author of *Using the Right Brain in the Language Arts*.

ATEF SHAFTIK SOLIMAN currently is teaching at Alexandria University, Egypt. He has taught basic and advanced biology, chemistry, physics, and earth sciences. He is a member of the American Institute of Biological Sciences, the Genetics Society of America, Egyptian Society of Genetics, and Sigma Xi.

JOHN SPIRIDAKIS is Associate Professor of Education at St. John's University, New York. He has conducted research and workshops on the role of learning styles in the education of students of various cultural and linguistic backgrounds. He has published numerous articles, chapters, and books on topics relating to the education of students in Greece and in the United States.

BERNADYN SUH is Associate Professor at the School of Education, Dowling College, New York. Dr. Suh has taught at Hofstra University, St. John's University, and Dowling College at the undergraduate and graduate levels. Her areas of interest include gifted education, early childhood education, children's literature, human growth and development, and learning styles.

DONALD J. TREFFINGER is President of the Center for Creative Learning, Inc., in Sarasota, Florida, and Professor of Creative Studies at Buffalo State College in Buffalo, New York. He served as editor of the *Gifted Child Quarterly*. He has published over 150 journal articles, essays, and reviews and co-authored 50 chapters and books, including *Creative Problem Solving: The Basic Course*, *Bringing Out Giftedness in Every Child: A Guide for Parents* and *Creative Thinking and Problem Solving in Gifted Education*.

SOLANGE WECHSLER is Associate Professor at the University of Brasilia, and Visiting Professor at the Pontifical Catholic University of Campinas in Brazil. In 1988 she founded and is the current President of the Brazilian School Psychology Association. She has published articles and book chapters in English and Portuguese on learning styles and culture, the identification and development of creativity, creativity and mental health, educating the creative gifted student, psychological assessment, and the role of the school psychologist.

ISBN 0-275-93640-6

9 780275 936402

HARDCOVER BAR CODE